AMERICA IN THE SEVENTIES

AMERICA IN THE TWENTIETH CENTURY

John Robert Greene, *Series Editor*

AMERICA
IN THE
SEVENTIES

Stephanie A. Slocum-Schaffer

With a Foreword by *John Robert Greene*

SYRACUSE UNIVERSITY PRESS

Library of Congress Cataloging-in-Publication Data

Slocum-Schaffer, Stephanie A.
America in the seventies / Stephanie A. Slocum-Schaffer.— 1st ed.
p. cm.—(America in the twentieth century)
Includes bibliographical references and index.
ISBN 0–8156–2973–7 (alk. paper)—ISBN 0–8156–2998–2 (pb : alk. paper)
1. United States—History—1969– 2. Nineteen seventies. I. Title.
II. Series.
E855.S58 2003
973.924—dc21
2003005728

Manufactured in the United States of America

To Eric

Thank you

Stephanie A. Slocum-Schaffer is assistant professor of political science at Shepherd College, Shepherdstown, West Virginia. Prior to serving on the Shepherd College faculty, Professor Slocum-Schaffer taught at Gettysburg College and the American University and held the post of assistant director of the Center for Congressional and Presidential Studies at the American University and assistant provost and associate provost at Gettysburg College. Her research has focused on a variety of areas, most notably, education policy, presidential decision making, the political psychology of leadership, and American voting behavior.

Contents

Foreword

John Robert Greene

"THERE JUST NEVER SEEMS to be enough time"—"The textbook is so bland; the students won't read it"—"Don't *teachers* ever write?—"If I could only find more than one book that I feel good about assigning."

These are several of the complaints endemic to those of us who teach survey American history courses. The book series America in the Twentieth Century was designed to address these issues in a novel fashion that attempts to meet the needs of both student and instructor alike. Using the decade as its organizing schema (admittedly a debatable choice, but it is our experience that chronology, not theme, makes for a better survey course), each book tackles the main issues of its time in a fashion at once readable and scholarly in nature. Authors are chosen by the editors of this series primarily for their teaching skills—indeed, each book proposal was accompanied by syllabi that showed the prospective author's course pedagogy. In fact, contributors have been urged to write these books from their lecture notes and limit footnote references that can often distract or intimidate the student-reader. In a departure from virtually every textbook series of note, one member of our editorial board is a presently sitting college student, whose comments on the manuscript may well be the most helpful of all. Each volume ends with a Bibliographical List representing the author's "favorite books," as they would recommend them to their students. It is, admittedly, not an exhaustive list, but no list of our favorite work is.

The result is a readable, concise, and scholarly series of books from master teachers who know what works in the college classroom. We offer it to college instructors and their students in hopes that they will, in the works of the Latin maxim, do the one thing that we all hope in the academy that professor and student will do together, *Tolle et Lege*—"Take and Read."

AMERICA IN THE SEVENTIES

1

Nixon

Our Father's Betrayal

LET US BEGIN OUR DISCUSSION of Richard Nixon's presidency by acknowledging that it is nearly impossible to think about his presidency (let alone talk or write about it) without thinking of the Watergate scandal. However, it would be a mistake to see this important presidency as *only* about a president's fall from grace; the Nixon presidency was about more than the break-in of the Watergate complex and the only resignation in United States history of one of its presidents. It was about great personal diplomacy and foreign policy triumphs, about creating new relationships in intergovernmental affairs, and about bringing an end to the first war that America could not win. It was about the creation of a corporate organization of government and about the birth of a new relationship in the United States between the chief executive and the press. Perhaps more than anything else, however, Nixon's time as president was about power. It was about who has it in the American system of government and about how far the limits of that power can be pushed. The legacy of that time was a reordering of the relationships in American government and a backlash against attempts to push the boundaries of power too far.

When Richard Milhouse Nixon was elected president of the United States in 1968, he was no stranger to politics, having lived the political life for more than twenty years. For one of those two decades, Nixon had been working to win the presidency, even after a dreadful and painful defeat (in 1960) to John Kennedy by only 113,000 votes. When Election Day dawned in 1968, the candidate feared yet another loss. He had been stumping for peace in Vietnam on the campaign trail, but as secret talks continued to suggest a settlement in Asia, Nixon felt his lead ebbing away. When the sun rose that morning in 1968, it shone on a candidate who felt insecure, reflecting and already representing a nation that was gripped with its own insecurities and confusion.

Indeed, Nixon won the 1968 election with only 43.4 percent of the national vote, a margin of only 499,704 votes over Hubert Humphrey. The election was something of a rejection of Lyndon Johnson's administration, but in saying "no" to the Democrats, the American people were not sure who to say "yes" to—the moderately conservative Nixon (43.4 percent of the vote) or the radically racist Wallace (13.5 percent). To understand how the Nixon administration unfolded as it did in the 1970s, we must understand the feeling in America in 1968, the sentiment that brought him—barely—to power: America was divided by Vietnam, racked with the hatred of racism, bloodied by violence and riots, and riddled with inflation. It was a time of great transformation and transition at home and abroad, and the great majority of the people of the United States—who were neither far-right hawks nor far-left doves—longed for resolution and for cautious leadership. Into this world came Richard M. Nixon, promising in his acceptance speech that the great objective of his administration would be to bring the American people together.

Nixon: The Man, the Administration

Richard Nixon was not destined to fulfill that promise; instead the many betrayals of his administration tore the nation apart. And perhaps it was because of the high hopes pinned on the Nixon presidency that the betrayals and the losses were so much more painful. We know what the hopes were that brought Nixon to power, but what can explain the betrayals? It is difficult to say with any surety, as many scholars will lament that the Nixon administration is probably the most studied in history but the least understood. Nonetheless, we must try to begin to understand, and to do that we need to get a glance at the inner workings of the man at the center of the storm.

Richard Nixon has been described in many ways, usually negatively. He is often characterized as cold and humorless, awkward and uncomfortable, a man who inspired suspicion rather than trust. But these are the descriptions of the public persona of Richard Nixon, and they carry the tarnish that comes with looking backward through the lens of Watergate. Certainly these descriptions are too flat, too simplistic, to capture the man. Those who knew him personally provide a much more complex picture. Some of them have described Richard Nixon as a sort of Dr. Jekyll and Mr. Hyde because of two distinct sides: a dark, devious, coldly calculating side and a caring, thoughtful, generous side. Indeed, those closest to him (such as longtime friend and speechwriter Raymond Price) often spoke of Nixon's light and dark sides, suggesting that they were at war with each other. Other scholars and Nixon intimates claim that he had "survivor guilt," inspired by the deaths from tuberculosis of his two brothers. This guilt, says Michael Genovese in his book *The Nixon Presidency,* led Nixon to "behave in ways that invited his own demise" throughout his life (1990, 12). Whatever is said of the thirty-seventh president, both the personal friends of Richard Nixon and the scholars who have studied him seem to agree that he was an insecure and paranoid man. America's "first political paranoid with a majority" is what one of his former speechwriters, William Safire, called him (Genovese 1990, 7). David Abrahamsen, author of *Nixon versus Nixon: An Emotional Tragedy,* calls Richard Nixon "an injustice collector" (1978): the kind of man who held long grudges and remembered every affront.

Many scholars believe that Richard Nixon's operating style was deeply rooted in his insecurity and paranoia. According to Michael Genovese, for example, Nixon was unable to differentiate between disagreements and disloyalties, he had a tendency to see political opponents as enemies, and he looked at the political world as extraordinarily hostile and full of people "out to get him" (1990, 15). Indeed, Nixon himself wrote: "I believe in the battle, whether it is the battle of the campaign or the battle of this office, which is a continuing battle" (as cited in Hargrove 1974, 177). If politics was Nixon's battle, then he was prepared to do anything to win. In this respect, he was truly Machiavellian: the goal of winning inevitably justified the means. For example, Nixon won the nickname "Tricky Dick" in his early political contests because of his nastiness and aggressiveness on the campaign trail, as well as his willingness to employ misleading tactics (if not outright lies). Most perplexing is the fact that Nixon would turn to dirty tricks even when he was the clear front-runner in the race! Although Richard Nixon later learned to soften his style and to act more "presidential," the derogatory nickname stuck to him like glue. Later in his career, Nixon's mastery of "realpolitik"—his ability to completely (and pragmatically) reverse long-standing positions in such policy areas as wage and price controls, the welfare state, and Communism—did nothing to dispel the sense that he was shifty. Joan Hoff calls this pragmatism in Nixon his "aprincipled nature" (1994, 3), meaning that Nixon did not lack morals so much as he lacked any awareness of conventional moral standards.

So when Richard Nixon entered the White House in 1969 his personality and "aprincipled nature" came with him. Unfortunately, the resulting style of leadership and management that grew from them came with him too, and it was not long before his paranoid manner began to permeate the entire administration. Given his approach to governing, it is lamentable that the president chose to surround himself with men who were extremely loyal but also painfully ignorant of national issues and political processes. According to Evans and Novak in their 1971 book on the Nixon presidency, the president relied heavily on this personal staff—"his men"—at the expense of the professionals in the cabinet and bureaucracy, and his loyalists quickly built a protective wall around the president that isolated him. Richard Hargreaves (1973) reports that one of the president's ex-aides later wrote: "Nixon's own insecurity caused him to need the protection of men willing to do whatever he wished. In return they wielded unmeasured influence" (240).

Men such as Harry Robbins (H. R.) Haldeman and John D. Ehrlichman ("The Germans," as they came to be known) served Nixon daily and closely, becoming his true confidants and advisers. In fact Haldeman, Nixon's chief of staff, quickly became known as the administration's "gatekeeper": he organized the president's time, protected and isolated him, and was willing to do the president's dirty work. Nixon was so isolated and protected as president, in fact, that he had fewer press conferences than any president since Herbert Hoover. Theodore White even went so far as to say that the president lived and worked "behind a palisade of privacy more impenetrable than had any president of living memory" (White 1973, 220).

According to Michael Genovese, this type of organization—one that Nixon's fears and insecurities desperately required—nurtured the negative aspects of the Nixon personality, the darker side, the paranoid style. Within a few months of his taking office, an "us versus them" attitude pervaded Nixon's White House. Soon the president and "his men" were acting on that paranoia, indulging in such activities as developing the infamous White House "enemies list." This list was kept by the president's special counsel Charles Colson and contained 575 names, ranging from Walter Mondale to Barbara Streisand and Joe Namath. These were the enemies that Nixon and his men believed that they needed to destroy at any cost to protect the president. The

White House tried, for example, to get the IRS to audit the taxes of a number of the "enemies" on the list.

Nixon and the Congress

When Richard Nixon took office in 1969, he was the first president in over one hundred years to face opposition majorities in both houses of Congress; Nixon faced a Congress controlled by the Democrats 57 to 43 in the Senate and 242 to 190 in the House. When he returned to Washington after campaigning for Republicans in the 1970 elections and after his own reelection in 1972, he did not face Congresses that were much friendlier. In 1972, in fact, the Republicans actually lost two Senate seats!

Richard Nixon started out with that score against him, and his relationship with Congress went downhill from there. First, the president did not have much of a plan for domestic legislation when he first took office. His real agenda was in foreign policy, where he had big plans and where (as we will see in chapter 4) he met with substantial success, including détente (or relaxation of tensions) with the Soviet Union and rapprochement (or a cordial relationship) with China. The extent to which Nixon favored foreign policy at the expense of a domestic agenda is reflected in a statement that he made to Theodore White in 1967: "I've always thought this country could run itself domestically without a president, all you need is a competent Cabinet to run the country at home. You need a president for foreign policy" (as cited in Evans and Novak 1971, 11–12).

In the early days of his presidency, Nixon gathered around him a group of free-thinking men, often ideologically at odds, to discuss and develop programs and policies. This group included strong and vocal conservatives such as Patrick Buchanan and tempestuous, flamboyant liberals such as Daniel Patrick Moynihan. Since the Nixon administration thus began by working to develop a domestic agenda, the president failed to get legislative proposals before the Congress during the "honeymoon period"—that time at the very beginning of a new president's term when Congress is most likely to embrace and enact his policy proposals. In addition, scholars such as Theodore White (1973) say that Nixon was uncomfortable with the relationship of cajoling and persuading, as well as with face-to-face confrontations, that a president must have with members of Congress to be successful, and his White House staff had little congressional experience or knowledge of how things worked in Washington. Thus, as Michael Genovese argues, Nixon failed to use the Republican leaders in Congress as advocates for his proposals, and he made little effort at communication and cooperation with the legislative branch. In fact, Evans and Novak have written that Nixon's profound "lack of interest in Congress" led to his "tendency to use it as a whipping boy" (1971, 106). It is no surprise then that President Nixon's legislative proposals did not fare particularly well.

Nixon's Legislative Agenda

President Nixon finally introduced his major plan for domestic legislation on August 8, 1969. In a television address, the president unveiled his "New Federalism" to the American people, explaining in a message to Congress a few days later that after many years of power flowing from the people to the Capitol, it was time to have power flow from Washington to the people. The two most important, and certainly the boldest, elements of this plan were General Revenue Sharing (GRS) and the Family Assistance Plan (FAP). Interestingly, these two initiatives seemed to be ideologically at odds with each other—one a decentralizing policy and the other a centralizing one. This fact is merely a testament to Nixon's faith in pragmatic and politically driven leadership.

General Revenue Sharing was a clear attempt at decentralization that fit nicely with the New Federalism. It was Nixon's way of responding to a crisis that was taking root in America's cities. As the responsibilities of state and local governments had grown over the years, their costs had of course increased substantially. Especially in local jurisdictions—the cities—more and more services were required by the needy people who lived in them. At the same time, however, the revenues (money!—most of which was drawn from local property taxes) available to pay for these increased services had not grown. Thus many state and local governments found themselves in a crisis situation, unable to provide their residents with desperately needed services. Nixon's plan was to come to the rescue by sharing revenue and responsibility with state and local governments. He thought this would relax the squeeze on those jurisdictions and resolve the crisis.

In practical terms, General Revenue Sharing created a program whereby the federal government would allocate funds to states and cities without any restrictions on how that money could be spent. Initially, the president asked

Congress to immediately send back to state and local governments one-third of 1 percent (about $500 million) of all moneys raised from personal income tax. This percentage was then to steadily rise, until by 1976 a full 1 percent of all taxes collected could be returned to the states. Although Congress was not thrilled with the proposal as drafted, GRS was naturally popular with state and local officials. They got activated (particularly Governor Nelson Rockefeller of New York) and began promoting GRS in Congress, and the White House pushed hard as well. In fact, it was the only piece of domestic legislation that Nixon personally campaigned for during his tenure. After a long and complicated fight, the State and Local Fiscal Assistance Act of 1972 became law. While GRS never fully met the grand hopes of its proponents, according to Michael Genovese (1990), it was a bold and revolutionary change in intergovernmental relations. Indeed, Joan Hoff reports that the program ultimately distributed $83 billion to state and local governments between 1972 and 1986.

On the other hand, the Family Assistance Plan (FAP) never really got off the ground. The FAP was essentially a plan for welfare reform that was surprisingly liberal for the conservative Nixon. However, the president promised the American people in his television address that it was "workfare" not welfare. Nixon himself preferred to call the program a negative income tax—a great example of what Evans and Novak (1971) argue was an oft-used Nixon strategy of masking progressive policies in conservative rhetoric so that the conservative majority that had elected him in 1968 would not be alienated. Even with the conservative rhetoric, however, this proposal, too, was revolutionary: it provided for what amounted to a guaranteed income for all heads of poor households, anywhere from $1,600 to $2,500 annually for a family of four. The states were expected to supplement this amount, and all able-bodied heads of recipient families, except mothers with preschool children, would have to work or accept training. If the parent refused to work or accept training, only the parent's payment would be withheld. Thus, according to Joan Hoff (1994), the FAP unconditionally guaranteed children an annual income and would have tripled the number of children being aided.

Revolutionary as it was, the initial response to the president's proposal was positive, with columnists from both the Left and the Right loudly applauding the planned reform. But once the legislative proposal itself was submitted to Congress, the president did not pursue it, and as often happens in such cases, vultures from both sides of the aisle descended on the vulnerable proposal. At best, as Evans and Novak (1971) argue, the Nixon team mustered a conscious lobbying effort on behalf of welfare reform sporadically during its trip through the legislative process, but their effort was not consistent enough and the FAP was attacked mercilessly. As Nixon himself wrote in a memorandum to Ehrlichman in August of 1972: "The way I look at most of our domestic programs is that we have done an excellent job of conceiving them and a poor job of selling them. . . . Great ideas that are conceived and not sold are like babies that are stillborn" (1978). Although the House did pass Nixon's Family Assistance Plan, it was voted down in the Senate Finance Committee on October 8, 1970, with all six Republicans voting against the president's bill. Although Nixon later resubmitted the FAP, the president's highest domestic priority of welfare reform was dead in Congress.

Nixon had similar problems with Congress on other domestic initiatives. In 1971, for example, the president outlined a program for a National Health Insurance Partnership that would include private insurance, employment-related insurance, government-sponsored insurance for low-income families, and health maintenance organizations. Although Congress took Nixon's plan under consideration, no legislation ever emerged from congressional hearings. The president resubmitted the plan in 1973, but according to Joan Hoff (1994), it quickly became victim to the Watergate scandal, intense partisanship, and heavy lobbying by the American Medical Association.

Even with these defeats on bold and large-scale domestic initiatives, Richard Nixon did have substantial influence on the domestic front, not just in foreign policy, as is often asserted. The areas where the president was particularly influential include assisting Native Americans in pursuing self-determination without the threat of eventual termination, postal reform, the Philadelphia Plan (affirmative action), as well as creation of the Environmental Protection Agency, the Domestic Council, and the Office of Management and Budget.

Supreme Court Nominations

Unfortunately for Richard Nixon and his relationship with the legislative branch, some of his attempts to shape the Supreme Court did not fare much better in the Senate than his Family Assistance Plan had. The president's first opportunity came with the appointment of Warren E. Burger as chief justice, who was easily and quickly confirmed by the Senate. Then another seat was vacated, this one by Abe Fortas. Fortas decided to step down, according to Joan Hoff in her 1994 book on Nixon, only after Nixon and his attorney general, John Mitchell, presented information to the chief justice that Fortas had been accepting $20,000 a year from a man who was being investigated by the Securities and Exchange Commission. With the seat suddenly open, Nixon decided to pursue the "Southern Strategy" developed by campaign staffer Kevin Phillips in his 1969 book, *The Emerging Republican Majority*. The president would woo white conservative Southerners by appointing one of their own to the Supreme Court—thereby repaying his debt to the South for what it did to get him nominated and elected in 1968 and for welding together the Nixon and Wallace votes of 1968 for the 1972 election. The president's first candidate was Clement F. Haynsworth. Almost immediately following his nomination, however, problems emerged with Haynsworth's candidacy, and the administration badly botched efforts to defend him, using what John Robert Greene calls "bludgeoning tactics" (1992, 41) that greatly angered the senators. On November 21, 1969, the Senate rejected Haynsworth by a vote of fifty-five to forty-five, with seventeen Republicans opposing the president's choice.

Nixon was angry at the rejection, and out of stubbornness and a determination to stick to his "Southern Strategy," he nominated G. Harold Carswell three months later. But history was made—to Nixon's unbridled fury—when for the first time ever an American president was turned down twice in a row on Supreme Court nominations. Carswell was at best a weak candidate, and once the details emerged, he did not stand a chance. The first bad news was a 1948 speech in which Carswell proclaimed, "I am a Southerner by ancestry, birth, training, inclination, belief, and practice. I believe that segregation of the races is proper and the only practical and correct way of life in our states. I have always so believed and I shall always so act . . . I yield to no man . . . in the firm, vigorous belief in the principles of white supremacy" (as cited in Trager 1992). The speech, coupled with later revelations of Carswell's high reversal record and his involvement in the transfer of a golf course from municipal to private control in an effort to evade a Supreme Court integration ruling, spelled disaster for the nomination. The full Senate rejected him by a fifty-one to forty-five vote.

Nixon's response to the rejection was infamously harsh, sympathizing with the "bitter feelings" of millions of American Southerners about what he called an act of "regional discrimination" (as cited in Genovese 1990).

Nonetheless, Nixon had demonstrated his loyalty to the South and had effectively furthered the cause of his "Southern Strategy," something that would come in handy in the 1972 campaign. In addition, Nixon ultimately had the opportunity to fill four of the nine slots on the Supreme Court—appointing Harry Blackmun, Lewis Powell, and William Rehnquist, in addition to Warren Burger. These appointments gave the president an incredible ability to leave his mark on the judicial branch. Indeed, according to Michael Genovese (1990), the "Nixon Court" did begin a measured retreat away from some of the policies of the earlier Warren Court, demonstrating markedly less sympathy for the rights of accused persons, for charges of racial discrimination, and for civil liberties and the rights of the press.

The Burger, Blackmun, Powell, and Rehnquist nominations were all easily confirmed by the Senate, but Richard Nixon was a man who "collected injustices," and he could not and would not forget the humiliation the Senate had inflicted. Unfortunately, the rejection of two of Nixon's Supreme Court nominees by the Senate was just the beginning of the deterioration of his relationship with the Congress.

Governmental Relationships Deteriorate

Nixon's relationship with Congress worsened for a variety of reasons: he found his administration could not get its domestic programs passed, the Senate rejected two of his Supreme Court nominees, and he was also having problems getting it to ratify the Antiballistic Missile Treaty (ABM). In addition, whatever trust in Nixon the Congress might have had at the beginning of his presidency was shattered by his decision to invade Cambodia in 1970. As time passed, the president's anger, resentment, and frustration grew, and so he made less and less effort at cooperation and communication with the legislative branch. Each year of his presidency, in fact, Nixon's contact with Congress declined, and ultimately he turned away from Congress and legislative solutions. Although the president had never shown any great interest in domestic issues, by 1972 he was even more removed from them. Instead, Michael Genovese (1990) argues that he focused his energies on foreign policy and his reelection campaign.

According to Evans and Novak, the president and his men "saw Congress as an awkward and obnoxious obstacle, a hostile foreign power" (1971, 108), and they became engaged in a search for ways to get around the legislative body. Michael Genovese has called this Nixon's "independent strategy," which included vetoes, impoundment of funds, and use of administrative discretion, executive orders, secrecy, and bureaucratic reorganization (1990). While other presidents use these devices on occasion, Nixon made them a part of a broad attempt to circumvent entirely the legislative process. For example, by the end of his term, Nixon had impounded nearly $20 billion in congressionally authorized funds. In other words, the president refused to spend moneys (impounding them) that Congress had allocated for programs that he did not support. He often used this power for purely political purposes. In fact, there were several cases in which Nixon vetoed a piece of authorizing legislation passed by Congress, Congress overrode his veto, and then the president impounded the funds for the program anyway. Clearly, Richard Nixon was engaged in a practice that blatantly disregarded the legislative process! The Supreme Court and several lower courts recognized Nixon's impoundment of such funds for what it was: an illegal attempt to circumvent the balances contained in the Constitution (see *Train v. City of New York*). Eventually, the courts ordered the release of the funds.

But Nixon's deteriorating relationships were not confined to the Congress; the president also saw the bureaucracy as an enemy to be controlled and circumvented. Nixon had a profound distrust and dislike of those in the civil service, as evidenced by the fact—according to William Safire—that he used "government" and "bureaucracy" as "half words," which were complete only when preceded by the expletive "damn," as in "damngovernment" and "damnbureaucracy" (as cited in Hoff-Wilson 1988, 170). Because of this distrust and dislike, according to Richard Johnson in his 1974 book on Nixon's management of the White House, the president became almost obsessed with the notion of getting "working control of the Executive Branch of the federal government (201)." The president and his staff therefore decided that they would have to do battle with most of the bureaucracy, and Nixon planned to concentrate executive branch power in the White House and to reduce the role of the bureaucracy by reorganization.

First, on advice from the president's Advisory Council on Executive Organization (headed by Roy Ash, founder and CEO of Litton Industries), the president reorganized the Bureau of the Budget into the Office of Management and Budget and established a Domestic Council. Congress—which must approve executive branch reorganization—accepted this proposal, and it went into effect in 1970 and remains one of the most influential management changes initiated by President Nixon. Then the president presented an even more ambitious plan in his 1971 State of the Union Address. This plan called for collapsing traditional cabinet departments along functional lines, Joan Hoff argues, in order to increase White House control over the bureaucracy: State, Treasury, Defense, and Justice would remain intact while the other eight would be consolidated into four super-cabinet offices (Human Resources, Community Development, Natural Resources, and Economic Development).

Congress rejected this plan, but Nixon was not to be deterred in pursuing his corporate ideal. The day after his landslide reelection victory in 1972, the president took matters into his own hands and implemented reorganization by executive prerogative: he called for the resignation of his entire cabinet. Some of those officials, those perceived as Nixon loyalists, were later reinstated, but the independent professionals were out of a job. This move—later characterized as having a chilling effect on morale and appearing cold-blooded and ungrateful—was to pave the way for Nixon's "Six-Pointed Presidency." This new structure would consist of the four super-cabinet officers, Henry Kissinger as head of Foreign Affairs, and John Ehrlichman as head of the Domestic Council. Together they were to serve as deputy presidents, essentially running the government and freeing the president's time for "big issues" (Genovese 1990).

Nixon's grand plan for grabbing power and concentrating it in the White House died before it could get off the ground when the Watergate crisis exploded. Yet what would have happened if Watergate had not intervened? During this period in which his relationships with the other institutions of government were disintegrating (about 1972 on), the president sought to prevent Congress and the bureaucracy from getting their way by using the administrative powers of his position. Nixon successfully used vetoes, reorganization, executive orders, and the impoundment of funds to achieve his policy goals, *outside of the traditional structures of government*. In essence, the sacred system of checks and balances was abrogated as the president refused to share power with the other branches and strove to ignore, belittle, and dismantle constitutionally mandated structures of government.

The Long (and Short) Road to Watergate

As the White House's external relationships with the other institutions of American government were deteriorating as a result of Nixon's attempt to concentrate and personalize his power, the internal barriers protecting against such attempts were simultaneously disintegrating. Early in his first term, Richard Nixon had already begun to use the power of the federal government against those he saw as his "enemies" and for his own personal gain. As former White House legal aid John Dean wrote in a memo in August 1971: "This memorandum addresses the matter of how we can maximize the fact of our incumbency in dealing with persons known to be active in their opposition to our Administration. Stated a bit more bluntly—how can we use the available federal machinery to screw our political enemies?" (as cited in Genovese, 181).

Almost from the start of his presidency, for example, Richard Nixon was excessively concerned about leaks of sensitive information to the press. The president and his national security advisory, Henry Kissinger, were both afraid that such leaks would endanger national security and undermine the administration's position on such issues as Vietnam. Then in May of 1969, the *New York Times* made the damning revelation that the Nixon administration had been secretly bombing Cambodia. The administration's justifiable concern about national security coupled with Nixon's paranoia and anger made the president and Henry Kissinger ready to do whatever it took to plug up such leaks. Their solution? Wiretaps. As the president wrote, "It was decided that when leaks occurred Kissinger would supply [FBI Director] Hoover with the names of individuals who had access to the leaked material and whom he had any cause to suspect. I authorized Hoover to take the necessary steps—including wiretapping—to investigate the leaks and find the leakers" (1978, 387–88).

Reporters (including Hedrick Smith and William Beecher of the *New York Times*, Henry Brandon of the *London Sunday Times*, and Marvin Kalb of CBS News) and staff members of the National Security Council and the State and Defense Departments were all tapped. Not a single one was installed with a warrant, although according to Joan Hoff (1994), Nixon's invocation of national security made them legally permissible at the time. Nonetheless, the mess in Vietnam had already prompted the administration to act in very questionable ways.

Vietnam and Dissent at Home: The Beginning of the Journey

But the wiretaps were just the beginning. As we know, Richard Nixon won the 1968 election on promises of peace in Vietnam, and hopes were high that he would bring a quick end to the war. However, the war dragged on and on, and that hope soon gave way to frustration and anger. When the president announced to the public at the end of April 1970 that he had expanded the war into Cambodia, he further destroyed those hopes and betrayed the trust of the American people as it seemed the war was escalating instead of ending. The antiwar movement grew in numbers and in ferocity with each passing day, and the response to the expansion of the war was an eruption of more campus protests and riots. In 1970, for example, the FBI reported three thousand bombings and fifty thousand bomb threats! Nixon's comment on May 1 about "bums blowing up campuses" was published and further fired-up the already outraged protesters.

Campus opposition finally resulted in the tragedy at Kent State: one thousand students rallied at noon on May 4 to protest the widening of the war, and National Guardsmen who sought to clear an area of rock-throwing demonstrators opened fire on both protesters and bystanders without warning. When the guns had stilled, eleven people were wounded and four were killed, including two women. The president's response was brief and did nothing to heal the wounds: he said through a spokesperson, in part, that "this should remind us all once again that when dissent turns to violence, it invites tragedy" (as cited in Evans and Novak 1971, 276–77). On May 9 more than two hundred fifty thousand demonstrators descended on Washington. Less than two weeks later, two more students were killed at Jackson State College in Mississippi. In August, University of Wisconsin students protesting the university's participation in government war research blew up a campus laboratory, killing one research graduate student, injuring four others, and destroying a $1.5 million computer.

By now, President Nixon was reaching the breaking point: he was unable to bring peace in Vietnam and the pressure of the antiwar protests was growing unbearable. His predisposition to paranoia and to seeing adversaries as enemies exacerbated the pressure. In addition, the president's insecurity and his fear that he would be done in by Vietnam just as Lyndon Johnson had been all led him down the path toward Watergate. Joan Hoff argues that Nixon believed that the protest movement, the thorn in his side, was being financed from abroad, was perhaps even receiving instructions from Communist groups in China and Cuba. Although neither Nixon's staff nor the CIA was ever able to find any evidence of such a connection, it was only a small step for the president to justify breaking the law in order to protect the nation from those he saw as traitorous protesters. Soon, that was exactly what the administration was doing.

The Huston Plan probably best exemplifies the mentality of the members of the Nixon administration at that time. On June 5, 1970, a group called the Intelligence Evaluation Committee—consisting of the chiefs of the main branches of the American intelligence community (CIA, FBI, National Security Agency, and Defense Intelligence Agency) along with Haldeman, Ehrlichman, and the president—met to coordinate their activities against the demonstrators. After several more meetings, the group came to endorse the Huston Plan, which called for opening mail and tapping telephones without warrants, breaking into homes and offices, and spying on student groups through electronic surveillance and campus informants. Although they discussed that, according to Johnathan Schell in his 1976 book called *The Time of Illusion,* "covert [mail] coverage is illegal and there are serious risks involved," and that surreptitious entry "is clearly illegal; it amounts to burglary" (111–16), the president approved the plans on July 14 because he "felt they were necessary and justified by the violence we faced" (Hoff 1994, 293). Luckily for Nixon and the Intelligence Evaluation Committee, J. Edgar Hoover soon raised objections that the risks were just too great, and the president withdrew his approval.

Unfortunately, that approval was withdrawn only for the Huston Plan; the idea of creating the White House's own domestic intelligence operation was alive and well. Soon the Justice Department and Attorney General John Mitchell had formed a new Intelligence Evaluation Committee, and the Nixon administration began to expand the use of a program called "Operation CHAOS." Operation CHAOS was created with President Johnson's approval in 1967 to ferret out foreign support for dissident groups in the United States. However, most scholars, including Joan Hoff and Michael Genovese, say that Richard Nixon and his associates expanded CHAOS into a massive domestic spy system that utilized the CIA as a tool for obtaining information on domestic dissident groups. Of course, domestic intelligence on the part of the CIA is illegal under its charter, and so the web of illegal activities that the Nixon administration was involved in grew further. It was well on its way to Watergate.

Then in May of 1971, a year after the Kent State deaths, members of the protest movement planned a demonstration for the Capitol that would stop the government. On instructions from the president, who was out in San

Clemente, Attorney General Mitchell was put in charge of dealing with the protesters, and 7,200 people (not all of them protesters, either) were incarcerated, the most ever in the United States in a single day. In fact, 13,400 people were arrested over a four-day period! There were so many that almost 2,000 of them had to be taken to the practice field around RFK Stadium, where they were locked up. It was a disaster: few were read their rights, many were never charged with a crime, and others had their civil rights abridged (kept locked-up for over twelve hours without access to a toilet, unable to make any phone calls, unable to contact lawyers). Ultimately, Michael Genovese (1990) reports, all but about 24 of the more than 13,000 arrested had their cases dismissed (128).

Nixon returned to the White House from San Clemente in the middle of the May Day demonstrations. While the demonstrators were being arrested en masse outside, the president and his staff were inside the White House discussing ways to handle the problem. On May 5, President Nixon and Chief of Staff Haldeman held a terrifying conversation in which the president endorsed the idea that "thugs" from the Teamsters' Union could be used to attack and intimidate demonstrators. According to the president, the Teamsters were to "go in and knock their heads off." "Sure" replied Haldeman, "murderers. Guys that really, you know, that's what they really do . . . and then they're gonna beat the [obscenity] out of some of these people. And, uh, and hope they really hurt 'em" (as cited in Hersh 1981, 1). It was only three weeks later, on May 26, that President Nixon met with a group of construction workers and longshoremen who had attacked protesters in New York. Even though the president told the group that he found their actions "very meaningful," there is still no concrete evidence that the president or his chief of staff ordered the attack on the marchers (Genovese 1990, 128–29).

The Pentagon Papers

On June 13, 1971, slightly more than a month after the May Day mess, the Nixon administration was hit hard by another shock, and the public by another betrayal: the Pentagon Papers. On that day, the *New York Times* began to publish excerpts of a top secret study initiated by Secretary of Defense Robert McNamara in 1967. The four thousand pages of classified documents detailed the origins and conduct of the Vietnam War, including an account of how President Johnson had misused his power and misled Congress and the public. A former employee of McNamara's named Daniel Ellsberg had, as Henry Kissinger described it, "flipped [from a] hawk to a peacenik," and he turned the documents over to the *Times* (Hoff 1994, 295). The Nixon administration, concerned with the damage that publication of the Papers might do to its own war effort, used the Justice Department to obtain a temporary injunction. The injunction forced newspapers to cease publication of stories based on the Pentagon Papers. However, the case made its way to the Supreme Court in short order, and on June 30 the Court rejected the Nixon administration's claim that it had the power to prevent publication of material on national security grounds. In a six-to-three vote, the Court allowed the publication of the Pentagon Papers (Genovese 1990, 129–30). Once again the Nixon administration was attempting to justify extreme measures—even the annulments of rights and freedoms—by invoking national security.

So it was that with the revelation of one betrayal of the American public— the Pentagon Papers—an even bigger and more devastating betrayal was born. For as the administration was going to court to try to censure the press and block the publication of the Pentagon Papers, a simultaneous but highly secret effort was begun to damage and discredit Daniel Ellsberg in any way possible. Only four days after the *New York Times* published its first story about the Pentagon Papers, according to Michael Genovese in his 1990 book on the Nixon administration, the president and his most loyal staffers decided to take matters into their own hands. Frustrated by the FBI's inability to stop information leaks and generally unhappy with the lack of response on the part of the FBI, the CIA, and other agencies on security matters, the White House created the White House Special Investigative Unit, a group that came to be known as the "Plumbers."

This group was to be the administration's very own intelligence-gathering, covert-operations team, housed in Room 16 in the basement of the Executive Office Building, where they had a private telephone line that by-passed the White House switchboard. David Young and Egil Krogh were chosen to lead the unit, as their loyalty was unquestioned. Young and Krogh quickly hired more-experienced hands such as E. Howard Hunt of the CIA and G. Gordon Liddy of the FBI. Although the main mission of the Plumbers was to stop leaks, they went so far as to discuss such activities as firebombing the Brookings Institution. In fact, Michael Genovese (1990) reports that their very first action was to forge top secret State Department cables in an attempt to create a link between President John Kennedy and the assassination of South Vietnam's President Ngo Dinh Diem.

However, the Plumbers are probably most infamous for their effort to undermine and destroy Daniel Ellsberg. In search of damning information on Ellsberg that could discredit him, Hunt and Liddy (and three Cubans) went to Los Angeles in late August and broke into the office of Ellsberg's psychiatrist in hopes of finding some dirt on the man who had turned over the Pentagon Papers to the press. Nothing of use was found, but this action pushed the Nixon administration that much further down the road of illegal, inappropriate, and abusive activities. While we may never really know whether Nixon ordered the break-in or not, few will argue the point that the moral and legal tone set in the White House permitted, perhaps even encouraged, such blatant disregard for the Constitution. The activities of the Plumbers, in turn, set a precedent for those who went on to work for the Committee to Re-Elect the President (CREEP): Genovese (1990)argues that they thought this was appropriate conduct. Nixon himself told interviewer David Frost in 1977 that "When the president does it, that means it is not illegal" (as cited in Genovese 1990, 137). Clearly, the president's beliefs about the limits of his power, or the lack thereof, set him and his entire administration on a collision course with disaster. It was only a matter of time before Watergate, or something like it, would be discovered.

The Break-in at the Watergate

The affair that was to grow into the greatest constitutional crisis in United States history had its beginnings at two o'clock in the morning on June 17, 1972, when D.C. police, alerted by security guard Frank Wills, arrested five men inside the Democratic Party national headquarters in Washington's Watergate complex. Wills was making his rounds when he discovered a piece of tape horizontally covering the lock on the door. He removed the tape and went on with his duties. However, when he came by again, he discovered another piece of tape on the same door, and he called the police. Bernard Barker, James McCord, Eugenio Martinez, Frank Sturgis, and Virgilio Gonzalez were then arrested. All of the men were wearing rubber gloves and carried cameras and electronic surveillance equipment.

The placement of the tape over the lock in such a way that it was noticeable—not once, but twice!—began the unraveling that we now call Watergate. The wiretappings, the Plumbers, the break-in of Ellsberg's doctor's office only came to light because of the botched "burglary" attempt at the Watergate. Because the intruders on the sixth floor of the Watergate complex got caught, we now know of the money laundering and dirty tricks used to ensure the reelection of Nixon in 1972. Because the break-in was discovered, the president and his men attempted to cover up their connection to the mess—to all of it—by destroying evidence, committing perjury, and defying subpoenas. Taken all together, these events are "Watergate"—the crimes and acts of Nixon and his associates that led, finally, to the president's downfall.

Thus, the break-in at the Watergate was only one tiny piece in the overall scheme that was to ensure the reelection of the president in 1972. Things looked good going into the 1972 election cycle: summits were planned with China and the U.S.S.R., negotiations with the Vietnamese to bring an end to the war were ongoing, and the economy was getting pumped-up in time for the election season. But Nixon's defeat in 1960 and his victory in 1968 had been razor thin. This fact, coupled with the president's fear and insecurity, particularly about being outspent by his rivals, forced the Nixon team to take nothing for granted. They were determined to make sure Nixon won by both raising enormous amounts of money in support of the president and by attacking the Democratic front-runners in the field so that Nixon could face a weak challenger in the fall.

Raising Money

"Remember 1960," Nixon told Haldeman, "I never want to be outspent again (as cited in Genovese 1990, 179). In response, the Nixon team, led by former Commerce Secretary Maurice Stans, collected and spent more than $60 million. If it sounds like a lot, it was: more than any campaign in presidential history up to that point. Unfortunately, it was not long before the enthusiasm for raising money for the president resulted in illegal activities. Some of those violations occurred because of changes in campaign finance laws. President Nixon had signed the U.S. Federal Election Campaign Act on February 7, 1972, and the new law limited campaign spending in the media to 10¢ per person of voting age in the candidate's constituency and required that all campaign contributions be reported. Both parties, but especially the Republicans, worked extra hard to bring in contributions before the new law took effect on April 7 (Trager 1992). Even so, some of the money came in "late," including $200,000 given to the Nixon campaign by Robert Vesco, an international financier who was also a fugitive from American justice. The Nixon campaign treated it as pre-April 7 money.

Equally illegal but more egregious was the tactic taken by Stans of soliciting contributions from corporations, particularly those depending upon a close relationship with the government. Although blatantly illegal, Michael Genovese (1990) reports that this ploy was effective in netting the Nixon team millions in contributions from some of the biggest companies in the nation, including $100,000 each from Gulf Oil, Ashland Oil, and Phillips Petroleum. It also received $150,000 from Northrop, $55,000 from American Airlines, and $40,000 each from Braniff Airlines and Goodyear Tire. When the contributions were discovered, all of these companies were ultimately convicted of violating campaign finance laws. To make matters even worse, since the contributions were illegal, all of the money the Committee to Re-Elect the President received from the corporations had to be laundered in Mexico!

Even before the election, however, there was evidence that the Nixon people were up to no good. On February 29, 1972, a "confidential" memorandum was released to the major newspapers by columnist Jack Anderson that was quite damaging: the memo linked a Justice Department settlement favoring ITT Industries, Inc. in pending antitrust suits to an ITT commitment to supply funds for the Republican National Convention to be held at San Diego (Trager 1992). Later it became known that favorable governmental decisions followed contributions to the president's campaign in other cases as well, including the Vesco and Dairy cases. There seemed to be nothing that the Nixon campaign people would not do to make sure their president was not outspent! In fact, Genovese (1990) reports that they even went so far as to "sell" ambassadorships by promising big donors a post in exchange for campaign contributions. We know now, for example, that at least four big donors gave a total of more than $750,000 for such posts as ambassador to Jamaica, Great Britain, and Luxembourg.

Dirty Tricks

The Committee to Re-Elect the President was loaded with cash, and it was looking for ways to spend it. Early on, it used some of those funds to sabotage the stronger Democrats who planned to run for president in 1972 so that Nixon could face a weak competitor in the general election. Eighteen months before the election, the "dirty tricks" campaign was well under way, and Nixon's appointment secretary, Dwight Chapin, hired a friend of his from college, Donald Segretti, to be in charge. Edmund Sixtus Muskie—junior senator and former governor of Maine—was the first target, since he was the strongest challenger on the Democrat side. He was popular and experienced, and his poll numbers were competitive with the president's—sometimes even leading Nixon in the polls. Throughout his short campaign, Muskie was the victim of a variety of dirty tricks, including such things as late night phone calls to voters in New Hampshire the night before the primary from people claiming to represent the "Harlem for Muskie Committee" and having smoke bombs thrown into Muskie headquarters. According to John Robert Greene in his 1992 book on Nixon, a girl was even paid to stand outside Muskie headquarters naked and yell, "I love Ed Muskie."

Probably the most damaging trick took place just prior to the New Hampshire primary. A conservative newspaper called the *Manchester Union Leader* (the primary daily paper of 40 percent of New Hampshire's population) published a letter accusing Muskie of laughing at a description of Canadian Americans ("Canucks") and claiming that Muskie's wife was an alcoholic who would drunkenly walk up and down the aisles of planes and encourage people to "tell dirty jokes." Muskie stood on the steps of the newspaper building and denied the charges. As he was defending his wife, he publicly shed tears. The following day, just a week before the primary, there was Edmund Muskie on the front page of the nation's newspapers and on television, his voice breaking with emotion, crying. As Muskie himself said later, "It changed people's minds about me . . . they were looking for a strong, steady man, and here I was weak" (as cited in White 1973, 81–82).

Even though every attempt to locate the alleged author of the letter failed, the Nixon team's dirty tricks campaign was a great success. Muskie dropped out of the race shortly after the New Hampshire primary. The other main contenders—Jackson, Humphrey, and the rest—followed suit until Senator George S. McGovern of South Dakota, the man Nixon considered the weakest of the candidates, was the one to receive the Democratic nomination for the presidency at that party's Miami convention.

Although Nixon and his team had secured what they wanted—the nomination by the Democrats of the man they considered the president's weakest rival—the dirty tricks and sabotage continued. G. Gordon Liddy, who had held such an important post in the Plumbers, was now chief legal counsel for the CREEP. In that role, according to Michael Genovese (1990), Liddy devised what came to be known as the "Liddy Plan" or GEMSTONE. The Liddy Plan went through three incarnations because the first plan, costing $1 million, was deemed too expensive by then-Attorney General John Mitchell (the highest-ranking law enforcement official in the United States). That plan called for a variety of illegal and inappropriate acts, including employing prostitutes to lure prominent Democrats onto a yacht equipped with hidden cameras, break-ins to obtain and photograph documents, and mugging squads to beat up demonstrators at the Republican Convention. Ultimately, Mitchell (who resigned as attorney general and became director of the CREEP) approved a scaled-down version of the Liddy Plan that cost $250,000—money that would be spent on, among other things, breaking into the Watergate offices of the Democratic National Committee.

Within a week of Mitchell's approval of the scaled-down plan on February 4, 1972, Liddy had received $83,000 in cash from the CREEP's Finance Committee and had purchased bugging equipment. He was planning the first break-in of the Watergate, and his target was (allegedly) Larry O'Brien, chair of the Democratic National Committee. The White House had an "insatiable appetite" for political intelligence, according to former White House legal aide John W. Dean III, and the predominant theory is that the Nixon people feared that O'Brien might have information that could be damaging to the president. Jeb Magruder, then the deputy director of the CREEP, has indicated that the "primary purpose of the break-in was to see if O'Brien had embarrassing information linking President Nixon's close friend Bebe Rebozo to loans from Howard Hughes" (as cited in Genovese 1990, 185). This theory has been challenged by several others regarding the motivation behind the break-ins. While we may never know the real reason that prompted them, we do know that Liddy and his accomplices broke into the Watergate offices first on May 26, 1972, but were forced to abort the mission, leaving Hunt to spend the night locked in a closet. Their attempt the next night also failed because Gonzalez had not brought the proper tools. Finally, on May 28, the conspirators broke into the DNC headquarters, used two rolls of film to photograph material from O'Brien's desk, and installed bugs on two phones. When the bugs did not work properly, they had to go in again. This time, however, they got caught.

After the Break-in

Meanwhile, George McGovern was having nothing but trouble. He had selected Senator Thomas Eagleton of Missouri as his running mate, but he was forced to switch to former Peace Corps director R. Sargent Shriver Jr. (his sixth choice after Eagleton) when it was revealed that Eagleton had been treated for manic depression (including electric shock therapy). The whole Eagleton affair made McGovern look like a fool and raised serious questions about his reputation for candor and trust. The American Federation of Labor and Congress of Industrial Organizations (AFL-CIO) refused to endorse the Democratic candidate (for the first time in twenty years), and then it was revealed that McGovern had been secretly negotiating with Hanoi to end the Vietnam War. First he denied it but then confirmed it, again—according to Theodore White (1973)—calling into question his honesty. Add to this Nixon's foreign policy successes, including promises of a near end to the war in Vietnam, and McGovern's chances looked slim. The elimination of George Wallace from the campaign when he was shot on May 15, 1972, in Maryland nearly assured the reelection of Richard Nixon. Things were going well for the president.

They continued to go well even after the strange incident at the Watergate. Among the five men that were arrested that fateful night was James McCord. He was a former CIA employee and the security chief for the Committee to Re-Elect the President. In short order both E. Howard Hunt and G. Gordon Liddy were also linked to the crime; Hunt was a former CIA operative and a consultant to presidential counsel Charles Colson while Liddy was general counsel to the CREEP. Nonetheless, President Nixon's campaign manager John Mitchell stated on June 18 that the men were not "operating either on our behalf or with our consent" (Trager 1992, 1036). Although Nixon's office confirmed on June 19 that Barker, one of the five arrested at the Watergate, had met earlier in June with Howard Hunt, the public and the press alike seemed to take little notice. In fact, Nixon had the support of 753 U.S. daily newspapers in his bid for reelection, while only 56 endorsed McGovern.

So on November 7, 1972, Richard Nixon was reelected in a landslide. George McGovern carried only Massachusetts with its seventeen electoral votes. President Nixon received forty-seven million votes—five hundred twenty-one electoral votes—to twenty-nine million for McGovern in the most one-sided presidential election since 1936.

The Cover-up

The public and the press took little notice, at least in part because within days of the incident at the Watergate, the president and his men had embarked upon an elaborate if disorganized cover-up of their connection to the break-in. In Jeb Magruder's words, the coverup "was immediate and automatic; no one even considered that there would not be a cover-up. It seemed inconceivable that with our political power we could not erase this mistake we had made" (as cited in Genovese 1990, 187). According to Genovese, Jeb Magruder and Gordon Liddy immediately removed files from their CREEP offices, and one of Haldeman's assistants used the White House shredder to destroy documents. E. Howard Hunt's name was expunged from the White House phone directory, and Hunt himself removed $10,000 from his White House safe. By June 19 top CREEP officials—including Magruder, John Mitchell, and John Dean—had decided that they would deny any connection to the break-in and had agreed upon false stories. By June 23, the president himself had ordered Bob Haldeman to make sure L. Patrick Gray, acting director of the FBI, was pressured into limiting the FBI investigation into the Watergate affair. That same day, Gray agreed to comply with the request. So within just a week, the president and his men were already deeply involved in obstructing justice as they worked to protect themselves. After a week or two more, the conspirators had decided to buy the silence of the Watergate defendants by promising executive clemency and money. Indeed, Genovese (1990) reports that beginning just twelve days after the break-in, the Watergate defendants were paid more than $450,000 to ensure their silence.

The Nixon Administration and the Press

While *Washington Post* reporters Bob Woodward and Carl Bernstein were beginning to crack open the Watergate affair, the Nixon administration was working just as hard to put Watergate on the back burner by intimidating the press. On August 1, 1972, the *Post* reported a financial link between the Watergate break-in and the CREEP. On September 16 they reported that campaign finance chairman Maurice H. Stans and CREEP aides controlled a "secret fund," and on September 29 they reported that former Attorney General John Mitchell was the one who had actual control of the money. The Woodward and Bernstein story in the *Post* on October 10 began: "FBI agents have established that the Watergate bugging incident stemmed from a massive campaign of political spying and sabotage conducted on behalf of President Nixon's reelection and directed by officials of the White House and the Committee for the Re-Election of the President" (Trager 1992, 1038).

White House spokespeople denounced the *Post* stories as "shabby journalism," "mud-slinging," "unfounded and unsubstantiated allegations," and "a political effort by *the Washington Post,* well conceived and coordinated, to discredit this administration and individuals in it" (as cited in Trager 1992, 1038). Meanwhile, inside the White House they were cooking up ways to retaliate and to get the *Washington Post* to cool off on the Watergate stories: the Federal Communications Commission received three license challenges in the next three months against Florida TV stations owned by the *Post.*

Most other news organizations, including magazines and television networks, initially gave the Watergate story short shrift, dismissing it as a "caper" (Trager 1992). This was due, at least in part, to the White House's continued intimidation of the press, which it had begun in 1969. Richard Nixon and his staff had decided from the beginning that the press as a whole was yet another "enemy" of the administration, and the president's relations with the press "took on a hostility that remains unsurpassed in the history of the modern presidency," according to John Robert Greene in his 1992 book *The Limits of Power.* Greene argues that this attitude toward the press was probably rooted in Nixon's devastating loss to Kennedy in 1960, for which he held the media accountable. Perhaps it could also be traced back to his loss in the governor's race for California in 1962, after which he held his infamous "last press conference" and blasted the press for giving him "the shaft." Perhaps it went as far back as the fund scandal of 1952, which prompted the famous "Checkers" speech in which Nixon repsonded to press accusations of a secret trust fund by laying out a detailed explanation of all his finances. Whatever the root cause, news organizations were seen as adversaries, and Nixon and his staff began a concerted attack on the entire news industry and the institution of the press in the United States. As the Watergate story grew, the attacks on the media accelerated.

Even though initially the press had mostly ignored the story, it was not too long before the continuing revelations of suspicious connections and inappropriate behavior by the president and his top aides finally caught the press's widespread attention. In turn, the media reports turned the public against Nixon. At that point, all of the administration's attacks upon the press could not change the damaging impact of the facts of Watergate.

The Cover-up Comes Apart

At first, the cover-up strategy seemed to be working. On September 15, an eight-count indictment in the Watergate case was handed down. Even though the U.S. District Court judge who was overseeing the Watergate grand jury, John Sirica, had raised what Michael Genovese calls "a number of disturbing questions" (1990, 191) in July, the September charges were limited to Hunt, Liddy, and the five burglars. The president and the White House still were not being connected to the Watergate break-in. However, as their trial date approached, the president found himself being blackmailed by the Watergate defendants: they wanted more money. The threat worked, and in late November $50,000 was delivered to Hunt's lawyers. The cover-up held, and on January 11, 1973, the defendants all pled guilty except for Liddy and McCord. After deliberating only ninety minutes, the jury found both of them guilty as well.

The good news for Nixon turned sour, however, when on February 7, the Senate created a select committee to investigate Watergate and related campaign abuses. Then on February 28, the bad news for Nixon turned worse in an unexpected way. Patrick Gray's confirmation hearings to be director of the FBI began, and Gray let the cat out of the bag: he admitted that he had turned over FBI files on Watergate to John Dean, in spite of the fact that Dean and other White House officials were suspects. He also revealed that Dean had been allowed to sit in on FBI questioning of witnesses. In response to Gray's revelations, the Senate Judiciary Committee indicated that it wanted to talk to John Dean, but according to Michael Genovese (1990), he knew way too much and Nixon could not let him testify. The president withdrew Gray's nomination instead.

Then on March 23, the damn really began to break when Judge John Sirica publicly revealed the contents of a letter written to him by James McCord, who had been convicted in the Watergate burglary. McCord's letter charged that the Watergate defendants were being pressured to plead guilty and remain silent, that several people had perjured themselves, and that higher-ups were involved. Michael Genovese reports that the following week, McCord testified for four hours in a closed-door session before the Senate Watergate Committee, and he claimed that Colson, Dean, Magruder, and Mitchell all had prior knowledge of the Watergate break-in. This scared the conspirators, and on April 2, Dean's lawyers told the prosecutors that Dean was ready to cooperate. Magruder soon followed suit.

The Beginning of the End: Nixon's Tapes

On April 15, 1973, President Nixon was told by the attorney general that his closest aides, Haldeman and Ehrlichman, were being implicated in the Watergate case and should be dismissed. Two weeks later, in an April 30 television address, the president gave in and announced their resignations and John Dean's dismissal. He also denied any personal involvement in the Watergate affair and cover-up, claiming that he had been misled by his subordinates. At this point, the president named Harvard law professor Archibald Cox as a special Watergate prosecutor. As Cox was busy gathering evidence, the Senate Select Committee on Presidential Campaign Activities was slowly beginning to do its work. Finally, on June 25, John Dean appeared before the committee—and millions of mesmerized Americans watching from their homes—and began to read his 245-page statement. According to Michael Genovese, he left out few of the gory details as he described the wiretapping, the enemies list, the burglaries and break-ins, the money laundering, the Plumbers, the dirty tricks campaign, and the cover-up. The tale that unfolded seemed fictional, incredible, and unbelievable to most Americans, who still held a great deal of respect—even reverence—for the president of the United States. But here was John Dean asserting that the president was right in the middle of it all. Most of the public refused to accept what he said as true, particularly since he had no material evidence to back up this assertion. It came down to Dean's word versus the president's.

This changed on July 16, when it came out that the president had secretly tape-recorded all conversations in the Oval Office, the president's office in the Executive Office Building, the Lincoln Room, and at Camp David. Those tapes could confirm or rebut Dean's contention that the president was involved in the whole affair! The Senate immediately requested the recordings, as did Special Prosecutor Cox. When Nixon refused, they both decided to subpoena several of the tapes. Nixon rejected the subpoenas, claiming the right of executive privilege, and the battle for the tapes was engaged. The committee and Archibald Cox took the president to court, and on August 29, 1973, Judge John Sirica ruled that the president had to turn over the recordings. The president was not about to give up that easily, however, and he appealed Sirica's ruling (Genovese 1990, 209).

As if things were not bad enough in the White House, Vice President Spiro Agnew was forced to resign on October 10. Allegedly Agnew had taken bribes in exchange for government contracts while he was governor of Maryland. When all of the charges came out, the vice president decided to take a plea agreement: he resigned as vice president, pled no contest to charges of income tax evasion, and escaped a prison sentence. Two days after Agnew resigned, President Nixon named House minority leader Gerald R. Ford as vice president. He was easily confirmed, thanks to his detailed preparation as well as the reputation for integrity that he had earned from his colleagues over twenty-seven years in Congress. Ford took office on December 6, 1973.

Meanwhile, the battle for the president's tapes continued. Nixon insisted that Cox, who was technically part of the executive branch, stop pressing for the tapes. When the special prosecutor refused to back down and refused a spurious compromise offered by the president, Nixon wanted him fired. What followed on the night of October 20 has come to be known as the "Saturday Night Massacre": Special Watergate Prosecutor Cox was discharged, but only after Attorney General Elliot Richardson had resigned in protest after refusing to fire Cox and after Deputy Attorney General William Ruckelshaus had also resigned. Solicitor General Robert Bork was finally named acting attorney general, and he carried out Nixon's order to fire Cox and seal his offices so that no files could be removed. The nation went berserk over such a blatant betrayal: the tide had completely turned among the public against Nixon by now, and the president realized that he would have to respond in some way. He decided to turn over some of the tapes, and he named Leon Jaworski to succeed Cox as Watergate prosecutor on November 1, 1973.

But these actions did not mollify anyone. In fact, the release of the selected tapes only caused more outrage when it was revealed that some of them contained suspicious gaps and that the White House was claiming that two of the requested tapes did not exist. The president went on television on November 17 and claimed that he was not "a crook." Even with this forceful pronouncement, the gaps on the tapes caused a public outcry and caused Judge Sirica to recommend a grand jury investigation into "the possibility of unlawful destruction of evidence" (as cited in Trager 1992, 1040). Calls for the president's resignation began to be voiced, according to Michael Genovese, even by mainstream thinkers, writers, and politicians.

By now there was blood in the water, and the president could feel the sharks beginning to swarm about him. On February 6, 1974, the U.S. House of Representatives began a formal impeachment investigation of President Nixon. On March 1 the federal grand jury indicted seven of his top aides, including Mitchell, Haldeman, and Ehrlichman (in February of 1975 all three received prison sentences of up to eight years for their participation in the cover-up). The grand jury also secretly named Richard M. Nixon as an "unindicted co-conspirator." By now, the House, the Senate, and the special prosecutor were all trying to get the White House tapes, and finally on April 29, Nixon announced in a nationally televised address that he would supply the House Judiciary Committee with edited transcripts of the subpoenaed tapes. Although the president promised that the transcripts would provide the information that everyone wanted, they did not. In fact, according to Michael Genovese, the transcripts later proved to be both inaccurate and incomplete, and the battle for the tapes themselves continued.

When the Judiciary Committee and special prosecutor Jaworski had so much trouble getting the tapes from the president, the Supreme Court finally agreed to hear *United States of America v. Richard Nixon.* In an eight to zero decision (Justice Rehnquist withdrew from the case), the Supreme Court ruled on July 24 that the president had to turn over sixty-four of the White House tape recordings. In its decision, the Court did recognize a constitutional basis for Nixon's claim of executive privilege, a privilege not previously recognized by the courts. However, the justices also indicated that the need for confidentiality in high-level conversations with advisers could not, by itself, provide a president with unqualified immunity from all judicial processes. In the case of Nixon's tapes, which were evidence in a criminal matter, the president's need for confidentiality did not outweigh the need of the prosecutors for evidence. He would have to give them over.

The Jig Is Up

Meanwhile, the case for impeachment was moving forward in Congress. Over three days at the end of July, the House Judiciary Committee—in a bipartisan vote—recommend to the full House that it vote to impeach the thirty-seventh president of the United States. Three articles of impeachment were passed by the committee, charging the president with obstruction of justice, abuse of power, and unconstitutionally defying a congressional subpoena. Two other articles that dealt with the secret bombing of Cambodia and with income tax evasion both failed by twenty-six votes to twelve. Just six days later, the president finally released the subpoenaed tapes, and there for all the world to hear was undeniable evidence that the president had lied. It quickly became clear that Richard Nixon had begun to direct the Watergate cover-up in the first week after the break-in and that he had lied about his knowledge and involvement. By this point, impeachment was a near certainty; any support that Nixon had retained before the release of the tapes, according to Genovese (1990), now dissipated completely. A betrayed public had given up on believing in their president.

On the evening of August 8, 1974, President Richard M. Nixon announced to that betrayed public in a brief television address that he would resign the presidency. It had taken several days to bring Nixon—who reportedly was drinking heavily and wandering the halls of the White House at night, giving speeches and talking to pictures on the wall—to the point of accepting the inevitable. Even so, Michael Genovese reports that on the morning of August 9 the Nixon family went to the East Room for a farewell to the president's staff, and Nixon rambled uncontrollably about his past and his family and wept. He was the first U.S. chief of state ever to quit office.

Upon being sworn in as president later that day, Gerald Ford told the nation that the wounds of Watergate were "more painful and more poisonous than those of foreign wars" (as cited in Trager 1992, 1044). How right he was.

The Nixon Legacy: Curbing the Power of the President

Perhaps the most heart-wrenching aspect of Richard Nixon's betrayal was the hope and promise that he had once conveyed. He had been elected in 1968 on the strength of promises to heal and unite America. While stumping for the office that he so earnestly desired, Richard Nixon often proclaimed that "only through an open, candid dialogue with the people can a president maintain his trust and leadership" (Sept. 19, 1968, radio address). But instead, Nixon became the president who destroyed American notions of true leadership; he was the one who betrayed America's trust. That betrayal rocked the nation. It was to have a profound impact on the American people, shaping not only the rest of the decade but also the conduct of politics in America for the foreseeable future.

Watergate was a disillusioning experience for the American public, and trust in government declined sharply in response as cynicism toward politics and public figures increased. In fact, Carter won the presidency in 1976 at least in part because he promised the American public, "I will never lie to you." As Michael Genovese has written, "The cumulative impact of Watergate was a legacy of suspicion and distrust. It left a mark on the way we viewed and practiced politics" (1990, 224). While Joan Hoff says that "Watergate has come to represent the lawless power of lawless modern presidents during the years of the cold war" (1994, 332), John Robert Greene calls Watergate "the single most influential event in the nation's postwar politics" (1992, 129). Nixon himself told interviewer David Frost in May of 1977: "I let down the country. I let down our system of government and the dreams of all those young people that ought to get into government, but who now will think it's all too corrupt" (as cited in Genovese 1990, 225). Indeed, the 1974 elections brought out only 38 percent of eligible voters, the lowest turnout in more than thirty years.

Institutionally, the legacy of the Nixon years was the response of Congress to the overreaching of a president. In his grab for power, the president taught the legislative branch that it would have to be more vigilant in preserving the separation and the balance of power between the branches. The Congress did not miss that lesson, and the Nixon excesses ushered in a backlash of legislation designed to maintain that balance, to improve the accountability of top-level politicians, and to ensure more public access to secret or classified documents. John Robert Greene has written that in this period in the history of our nation, "Americans came to believe that there should be limits on the actions of the president and proceeded to put such limits into effect. Every moment of the following presidencies was an effort to deal with these new limits, to come to grips with a new American attitude toward government" (1992, xiv).

Probably the first and most famous action taken by Congress to limit the activities of American presidents was the Congressional War Powers Resolution, an attempt to reassert Congress's constitutional power to declare war. Although in article 1, section 8, the Constitution clearly delegates this power to the Congress, John Robert Greene argues that strong presidential moves into Korea and Vietnam had chipped away at it until the authority to make war seemed to be essentially an executive prerogative (1992). By late 1973, Nixon's popularity had begun to decline, and bolstered by Watergate, the Congress passed the War Powers Resolution over the president's veto on November 7. Essentially, the resolution limited a president's authority to commit troops in a foreign conflict without congressional approval (affirming article 1, section 8, paragraph 11 of the Constitution). It also gave Congress the authority to disengage American troops from hostilities. President Nixon said at the time that the resolution would impose unconstitutional and dangerous restrictions on presidential power and would "seriously undermine this nation's ability to act decisively and convincingly in times of international crisis" (Trager 1992, 1041), and every president since Nixon has questioned the constitutionality of the act. However, to date there has been no direct challenge to it.

Yet another important piece of legislation passed by Congress in response to the Nixon years—this one a reaction to Nixon's impoundment of nearly $20 billion in congressionally authorized funds—was the Budget and Impoundment Control Act of 1974. One month before Nixon's resignation, Congress lashed out at Nixon's practice of impounding funds that it had authorized for programs that he did not like. Although nearly every one of Nixon's predecessors also used the technique to control federal spending, Greene (1992) argues that Nixon's apparent glee in using impoundment to dismantle many of Johnson's Great Society programs so angered the Congress that the House Judiciary Committee briefly considered listing it as an impeachable offense. Instead, Congress passed the Budget and Impoundment Control Act.

This act attempted to codify and control the impoundment of funds by future presidents and created the Congressional Budget Office, whose data-gathering powers allowed Congress to submit its own draft budgets to control spending ceilings. In fact, Joan Hoff (1994) argues that the new budget process resulting from this change was one of the premier reforms of the 1970s; members of Congress heartily supported it because it diminished the president's authority over a function traditionally considered to belong to the executive branch. However, the act ultimately proved inadequate when it came to controlling impoundment actions by Presidents Ford, Carter, and Reagan. In 1985, the Supreme Court declared the impoundment control provisions unconstitutional because they constituted a legislative veto in violation of the separation of powers.

The Election Reform Act was another piece of legislation crafted in response to Nixon's presidency. Passed by Congress just hours before President Nixon's resignation, the act limited the amount that any individual could contribute to a candidate for federal office, as well as the amount that any presidential candidate could spend. It also provided for a $1 tax check-off on federal income tax returns to allow for federal funding of presidential elections, and it contained other provisions designed to minimize the impact of large-company contributions. The goal of the legislation was to prevent the kinds of abuses that had characterized the Watergate scandal (Trager 1992).

Congress made plenty of other moves to rein in the power of presidents, as we shall see in the following chapter. Other legislation passed by Congress in response to Watergate includes the Case Act (1972), the 1974 amendments to the Freedom of Information Act, the National Emergencies Act (1976), the Government in Sunshine Act (1976), the Federal Corrupt Practices Act (1977), the Foreign Intelligence Surveillance Act (1978), the Presidential Records Act (1978), and the Ethics in Government Act (1978). This last piece of legislation provided for the creation of an independent counsel to investigate wrongdoing in the executive branch of government, and it was to have profound effects on the conduct of all presidents following Nixon. In particular, President Bill Clinton came face-to-face with this specific legacy of the Nixon years, triggering yet another constitutional crisis in American government in the late 1990s.

Congress was not the only branch of government to respond to the Nixon era in an activist way. Michael Genovese (1990) reports that although the courts were at first reluctant to challenge the power and prestige of the presidency, more cases were decided against President Nixon than in any other period in American history—more than during the Civil War and the New Deal era combined. The Pentagon Papers case, in which the Supreme Court rejected a bid by Nixon for expanded power, was one of the early cases intended to curb presidential autonomy, and it was followed by a series of court decisions that restrained the president's power to impound congressionally appropriated funds. As we know, the courts also played a significant role in the Watergate affair. Michael Genovese argues that, buttressed by the support of the Congress and the public, the courts took a clear stand in putting a halt to excessive claims of presidential power during the Nixon years. Claims (and their aftermath) that were to shape the rest of the decade and, indeed, the remainder of the century.

2

Ford

The Pardoning, but Not the Healing, of America

GERALD FORD'S PRESIDENCY is not remembered by most Americans as particularly noteworthy or important, and certainly his time in office was brief. However, that time—no more than two and one-half years in all—was pivotal to the continued health of the nation and represented something of a turning point in the seventies. Gerald Ford, as a president and a leader of the American people, negotiated the dangers and pitfalls of the ambiguous time after Watergate so that the nation could "pick up the pieces" and move forward. This is not to say that Ford conducted his administration with graceful skill; in fact, his leadership style was often clumsy, and his administration failed to make up in direction what it lacked in grace! Indeed, the media view of Gerald Ford depicted (and still depicts) an awkward, bumbling man (although he was perhaps the best athlete to ever occupy the White House) who was regularly charged with being inept and less than totally competent. Ford is probably best remembered for several embarrassingly public gaffes, including an infamous misstatement in a campaign debate about the freedom of the Polish people. Nonetheless, according to Roger Porter, Gerald Ford took office with his goals firmly planted in the future instead of mired in the past, and he worked hard to bring the American people and their system of government back up out of the ashes of Watergate. Perhaps most important of all, Ford—the only president never elected to office—chose the long-term considerations of the nation's health and prosperity over personal political expediency.

Gerald Ford assumed the presidency in August 1974, and as he was sworn in on that August day, he promised the American people that "the long nightmare" was over. For a nation preoccupied with the wounds of Vietnam and Watergate—a citizenry feeling disillusioned, frustrated, and even betrayed— these words rang a note of hope once again. According to John Robert Greene (1992), the new president was quite unlike his predecessor. Gerald Ford was a comfortable man to be around, and he brought a breath of fresh air to the White House. He insisted, for example, that White House staffers keep their office doors open as much as possible and that his alma mater's "Michigan Fight Song" be played when he entered a room rather than "Hail to the Chief." He was also prone to swimming in the White House pool with an inflatable rubber duck at his side, and he urged reporters to take all the pictures that they wanted. As he himself told the world, he was a Ford, not a Lincoln.

But more than this, Ford embraced the role of emergency medical technician to a nation in dire need of help. Determined to heal the wounds of the Vietnam War even before America's involvement in Asia was completely ended, Ford announced an "earned amnesty" program for the fifty thousand American draft evaders and deserters only ten days after taking office. He did this before the most challenging audience that one could imagine: the seventy-fifth annual convention of the Veterans of Foreign Wars. One month later—on Sunday, September 8, 1974—Gerald Ford unveiled his most dramatic and his most risky attempt to refocus the nation's energies on the future: he granted Richard Nixon a "full, free, and absolute pardon" for all federal criminal acts he committed or may have committed or taken part in while in office.

The Pardon

Roger Porter (1988a, 1988b) believes that President Ford was motivated to take this risky action both by a desire to resolve the Watergate issue (which legal experts had indicated could tie up the courts for months or years) and to dispose of the issue of Nixon's fate, which consumed the lion's share of the media's attention at that time. In fact, Ford noted that he had taken the action to spare Nixon and the nation further punishment in the Watergate scandal. While his goal may have been to heal wounds, his dramatic gesture was only a start down the path to healing. Some, such as presidential press secretary J. F. terHorst, who resigned his post in protest, were not ready to step onto that path so soon. Others were (and still are) suspicious of the quick pardon—

coming before Nixon was even formally indicted of any crime. That suspicion led to questions of whether some kind of deal had been struck between Ford and Nixon over the pardon before Nixon resigned. In fact, according to Joan Hoff (1994), these questions contributed to Ford's defeat by Jimmy Carter in 1976; Ford was never able to overcome the damage done to his political credibility because of the pardon.

The suspicion makes sense in many ways. Ford was loyal to the Nixon administration in his post as House minority leader; he voted to support the president's positions and programs over 80 percent of the time. In addition, Ford was a staunch Nixon defender in Congress when Watergate first broke, and he continued to make speeches in defense of the president long after he took the job of vice president, often attacking Nixon's staff. In fact, Ford continued to state publicly that he believed Nixon was innocent of any impeachable offense until August 5, the day the "smoking gun" tape revealed that Nixon had lied, which forced Ford to break with the president. In addition, the pardon was negotiated in secret and given on terms that seemed clearly favorable to Nixon—the disgraced president did not even admit wrongdoing. Fresh from the horrors of Watergate and full of the cynicism it engendered, almost no one believed the Ford administration's strong protestations that no secret deal had been made. However, the benefits of time and the opening of presidential materials have vindicated Gerald Ford. The evidence that is currently available regarding the last days of the Nixon presidency does suggest that Alexander Haig, Nixon's chief of staff, may have attempted to finagle a deal from Ford on Nixon's behalf. However, most scholars, such as Kenneth Thompson, believe that if Haig was offering a deal, Ford clearly rejected it.

Nonetheless, Gerald Ford was already considering the option of a pardon for Nixon before he even took office, and the new president filled his first days by agonizing over the idea. Ford reveals in his memoirs (1979) that he finally came to believe that America needed to focus on recovery rather than revenge so that healing could begin. Indeed, Ford even asked Congress to appropriate $850,000 to facilitate Nixon's transition to private life (it ultimately granted him $200,000). Gerald Ford clearly did his best to get the healing process started, a monumental task in itself. However, it is doubtful that he was motivated only by the goal of national healing. John Robert Greene has argued beautifully that it is a great disservice to Ford to believe that this goal was his only one; in fact, the pardon was also an attempt to evict the ghost of Nixon from the White House and to start anew with the Ford administration. As

Ford himself has said, "I had to get the monkey off my back" (1979, 159). The Ford presidency is thus the story of healing but also the story of an administration struggling to create its own identity, to "escape the long shadow of the Nixon administration by offering its own agenda to the American people," as John Robert Greene describes it (1995, xii).

Unfortunately for Gerald Ford, the gamble of the pardon did not pay off. He held his ground after deciding to pardon Nixon, even though polls showed that almost 60 percent of Americans opposed it. Indeed, the response of the American public and of Congress to the pardon was strong and negative: letters criticizing Ford poured into the White House, some members of the administration were physically attacked by protesters, and a subcommittee of the House Judiciary Committee immediately began an inquiry into the pardon. Ford's approval rating plummeted from 71 percent to 50 percent in less than a week after the pardon. So although he tried to begin anew with his own administration and chose the long-term health of the nation over political expediency, the new president was damaged by that choice. For Ford personally the pardon could be called a grievous mistake that cost him both his "honeymoon" with the American people and subsequently the 1976 election. For many Americans, Roger Porter (1988b) argues, this single act of the pardon overwhelmed the sense of openness, accessibility, and candor that Ford had so successfully begun to establish.

Thus, John Robert Greene (1995) believes that rather than ridding himself of the Nixon taint and starting afresh with his own agenda, Ford's pardon only linked him more strongly to Nixon, sabotaging any attempt to initiate an independent presidency. As Ron Nessen, Ford's second press secretary, says, "the specter of Richard Nixon haunted the Ford White House from the first day to the last" (Nessen 1978, 29). Because suspicions remained about the quick pardon even after the 1976 elections, Ford's risky decision continued to hound him long after he had left office.

The Struggle for Direction

Ford went from being the vice president of a failing administration to the president of the United States of America quite suddenly. Normally the transition from one presidential administration to another is about sixty days; altogether Gerald Ford had less than two weeks. Added to this difficulty, according to John Robert Greene (1995), was the heavy burden that Ford carried with him on this quick flight up the political ladder: he needed to begin the healing of the nation, to construct a new administration, and to create an agenda for his presidency in a very short period of time.

Ford himself could do little to prepare before Richard Nixon's presidency ended; he certainly could not appear to be pushing Nixon out to make way for himself! Nonetheless, others were ready for the eventuality when it became a reality: a secret "transition team" had been planning for the first days of Ford's presidency without his knowledge, believing that Nixon's removal from power (one way or the other) was inevitable and imminent. Clay Whitehead, head of the Office of Telecommunications Policy, and Phil Buchen, longtime friend of Ford and former law partner, had agreed that Ford would need specific recommendations in hand from the first moment after his inauguration. With the help of three other young members of the Nixon White House— Brian Lamb, Lawrence Lynn, and Johnathan Moore—they packaged together in a binder their recommendations on the problems that they believed Ford would most likely face upon taking up the mantle of power. They hoped to get that binder to the new president immediately after his inauguration, before he fell into the "hands of others, including Al Haig and Henry Kissinger." This small and secret transition team believed that otherwise Ford would "never have a chance to be his own man" (Greene 1992, 192).

Even with the secret preparations, however, the transition was bumpy. As John Robert Greene has written, "forced into a peculiar on-the-job training, the team had had a wild, disorganized thirty days" (1992, 193). First, Ford had staffing problems. His vice presidential staff had incredible personality conflicts, and according to Kenneth Thompson (1988), both Ford and Robert Hartmann, his chief of staff, lacked managerial skills. In short order, Ford's vice presidential staff had fallen into disarray, and many feared that those problems would be tantamount to disaster if Ford continued with the same staffing arrangement when he became president. Although the secret transition team had suggested that Ford let go of Nixon's chief of staff, Al Haig, it was overridden by the formal transition team that Ford had created by adding political insiders and friends to the original group. This formal transition team believed that Al Haig and others on the White House staff should be kept on in the Ford administration in order to provide continuity. Ford agreed, writing later: "Although I wanted people to perceive that there was a big difference between the Nixon and Ford administrations, I didn't think a Stalin-like purge was the way to go about it. Besides, there were people on the

White House staff who had nothing to do with Watergate. For me to have fired them all would have tarred them with the Nixon brush" (1979, 148).

So Al Haig and others from the Nixon administration stayed on in the White House, although Haig no longer carried the politically unpopular title of "chief of staff." Instead, it was determined by Ford and his official transition team that there should be no chief of staff. In fact, during his first weeks in office, Ford indicated that he was determined to be his own chief of staff. This "spokes of the wheel" approach put Ford at the hub and his eight or nine advisers as equal spokes leading to the center. Thus, unlike a hierarchy, Ford's structure permitted the senior White House aides independent and virtually unrestricted access to the president. Roger Potter argues that this structure also projected the sense of openness and accessibility that Ford so strongly desired of his administration (1988b). However, according to Kenneth Thompson (1988), this approach also had its problems—and they were serious. For example, although Al Haig continued to run the Ford White House with the same efficiency with which he had managed the declining months of the Nixon presidency, the staff as a whole was unable to help the new president formulate a coherent policy direction for the new administration. For unlike its immediate predecessors, Ford's White House staff was just organized too loosely.

In addition, when Ford took the advice of his transition team and kept Al Haig on in his administration, as well as Henry Kissinger as both secretary of state and national security adviser, the seeds of dissension were sown in a Ford staff that was already disorganized and underprepared. According to Kenneth Thompson, Hartmann in particular begrudged Haig access to the president and believed generally that Ford's decision not to clean house and fire all Nixon appointees prevented him from ever creating his own presidency. The evidence does suggest that there were difficulties in the Ford White House in melding together the old Nixon people and the Ford people. So within a month the president was forced to ask Donald Rumsfeld, ambassador to the North Atlantic Treaty Organization, to become his "staff coordinator," essentially a chief of staff. Although the point of bringing Rumsfeld on board was to bring order to the White House and better deal with staffing problems, Rumsfeld soon earned a reputation for being heavy-handed, and the tensions among Ford's staff persisted. An image of Ford as an ineffective leader—one who could not even control his own staff—soon emerged, and the issue of a feuding and disorganized staff became one of Ford's biggest problems as president. Some scholars, such as John Robert Greene and Kenneth Thompson, even believe that it helped to cost him the 1976 election.

Feuding staff caused the new president trouble in 1976 because, unfortunately, the disorganization and tensions that characterized the transition period for the fledgling Ford administration came to roost permanently in the White House. This was not helped by the fact that the new president had to wait four months for his vice presidential nominee—Nelson Rockefeller—to be confirmed by Congress. Because they spent so much time fighting organizational troubles, the Nixon legacy, and Congress, Gerald Ford and his administration never really had the time nor the ability to find a direction for themselves. The goal of excising the Nixon cancer and starting afresh thus could not come to fruition, and Ford was never to become "his own president" (Sloan 1993).

Ford, Congress, and Three Crises

Under other circumstances, Gerald Ford might have had relatively good success with Congress—even one dominated by Democrats—as he had always been a man of legislative temperament. Indeed, John Robert Greene (1992) argues that Ford's twelve terms in Congress are a story of a steady growth of power in a variety of important areas. From his expertise on defense matters as a member of the defense subcommittee of the prestigious House Appropriations Committee to his service on the politically sensitive Warren Commission (which investigated the assassination of John Kennedy), Ford had carved out a reputation for hard work and integrity. He was young and independent, but as House minority leader he was also known as a fine leader of the "loyal opposition." Quite simply, before he became president, Gerald Ford was "respected and beloved by colleagues in the Congress" on both sides of the aisle (Thompson 1988, xi).

In addition, Ford worked hard to get his relations with Congress off to a good start. According to Greene (1995), in the first month, the new president worked the phones constantly, invited Democratic liberals (whom Nixon had banned) to the White House, and generally paid more attention in one month to presidential relations with Congress than Nixon had in six years. Ford even established a congressional hour, held every couple of weeks, that allowed members to bring important constituents to meet him. However, as he had with the American public, Ford quickly sabotaged his relations with Congress.

His "honeymoon" with the legislative branch ended abruptly with his announcement of the pardon of Richard Nixon. Congress's reaction was so outraged and so bipartisan that even the White House was surprised, and in short order Congress stopped treating Ford as one of its own and started lashing out against him.

Of course, the Republicans got hit hard in the midterm elections following Watergate; unfortunately for Richard Nixon's party—and especially for Gerald Ford—the public held it accountable for the betrayals of Nixon and his associates as well as for the severe downturn in the economy. Voters were also angry and suspicious about Ford's pardon of Nixon, and they sent a message that arrived loud and clear. Republicans lost forty-eight seats in the House and five in the Senate. This meant that the Democrats, who had already controlled Congress, now held a commanding majority. In fact, House Democrats now had one vote more than the two-thirds necessary to override a presidential veto.

Thus America gave birth to the "Watergate Babies"—the youthful Democratic leaders who rode to power in 1974 on the issues of Watergate, the pardon, and "the mess in Washington." As promised, members of Congress's new "class of '74" really shook things up. According to John Robert Greene (1992), they refused to obey the unspoken congressional rule that freshmen should keep a low profile in their first term; they trashed the long tradition of seniority by ousting members of the old guard from their strongholds as committee chairmen; and they dispersed power from the relatively few standing committees to an expanding number of subcommittees by the adoption of the "subcommittee bill of rights." Clearly, the Watergate Babies were an independent group committed to bringing about serious change in American government, and first on their list was to restore balance among the three branches of government by restraining the power of the president. It comes as no surprise then that relations between Congress and the Ford White House were strained; it was not long before the president knew to expect only opposition to his policies.

If Gerald Ford's attitude toward Congress had initially been better than Richard Nixon's, the results of his interactions with the legislative body were no better than his predecessor's. It soon became clear that Ford stood little chance of getting his own legislative package passed. Moreover, in light of the grim economic picture, the new president decided that no domestic initiatives were possible and that spending on existing programs would have to be disciplined. So Ford took on Nixon's veto strategy with a vengeance, returning legislation (particularly spending bills) to Congress at an unprecedented rate. In fact, Ford vetoed sixty-six bills during his tenure, the third-highest use of that power among all presidents and four times the yearly mean over the preceding century. Ford himself stated at a fundraising dinner in Connecticut: "Oh, I know that the veto has been described as a negative act. And I have used it 39 times and saved, in the process, the American taxpayers $6 billion. I will use it a hundred times, if necessary, to prevent excessive inflationary spending increases. And that is about as positive as you can get" (as cited in Greene 1992, 207–8). Even so, twelve of those vetoes were overridden by an unfriendly Congress.

Worse yet, "congressional oversight" of the executive branch had become the hottest new sport in Washington, and Ford's administration paid the price. The Hungate subcommittee investigation of the Nixon pardon was unprecedented, and Ford's decision to answer the committee's questions in person made him the first president since Abraham Lincoln to testify directly before a committee of Congress. Even more astounding was that during his testimony, Congresswoman Elizabeth Holtzman called the president's honesty into question, saying there were still "very dark suspicions" about a deal (Greene 1995, 57). After Watergate, a new relationship had been born between the executive and legislative branches of government, and Gerald Ford would have to deal with that new relationship.

Similarly, an investigation into the activities of the CIA initiated by Frank Church of Idaho established congressional oversight of intelligence operations once and for all. Even though President Ford had already established a commission, headed by Vice President Rockefeller, to investigate CIA activities within the United States—activities that would violate the CIA's charter— the Senate created its own Select Committee to Study Governmental Operations with Respect to Intelligence Activities, also known as the Church Committee after its chairman, Senator Frank Church. The report of the Rockefeller Commission revealed excesses committed by the CIA, including the details of Operation CHAOS (used during the Nixon administration to collect domestic intelligence against the antiwar movement) and the assistance the CIA had given to Nixon's "Plumbers." However, on the orders of President Ford that report also suppressed large amounts of damning evidence about CIA activities, including shocking and explosive revelations about assassination plots of foreign leaders that Church later released to the press.

The impact of both the committee and the commission investigations was extensive. President Ford ultimately dismissed Secretary of Defense James R. Schlesinger and CIA Director William Colby in November 1975. In December, when the Church Committee published its six-volume final report, it offered one hundred eighty-three recommendations for improving intelligence, and one of those recommendations resulted in the establishment of formal congressional oversight of intelligence affairs. In fact, the congressional investigation of the CIA ultimately resulted in the intelligence agency finding itself under the intense scrutiny of eight separate oversight committees, including a permanent Select Committee on Intelligence in each house!

John Robert Greene argues that the establishment of these congressional committees was to become one of the most important developments of the 1970s in American politics. Indeed, congressional oversight reaped benefits as early as February 1976 when an amendment to the Defense Appropriations Bill terminated CIA activities in Angola. It was the first time that covert action had been halted by order of Congress. As Greene has written, "quite clearly there had been a shift in the balance of power toward Capitol Hill" (1992, 206). Unhappily, that meant that the new president could get little accomplished without damaging fights with Congress.

The Economic Crisis

In the two decades prior to 1970, Americans had enjoyed unprecedented prosperity. World War II had left the United States in a position of economic superiority, according to Keith Nelson (1995), and American economic might was the envy of the world. However, as the seventies approached, the world economy and the American place within it were going through profound changes. The costs of the American position of hegemony proved too great for the nation to bear in the long run, and by the time Nixon was sworn in as the thirty-seventh president, U.S. economic decline was already evident. By the summer of 1971, states Robert Hargreaves (1973), the economy was in an acute state of crisis: productivity in a variety of basic industries had begun to decline; unemployment was increasing; interest rates and inflation were both on the rise; and trade deficits, unbalanced budgets, and a growing deficit were all cooling the U.S. economy.

Unfortunately, Nixon's economic policies only served to exacerbate these conditions. His New Economic Policy of 1971—with its move toward a controlled economy (wage and price controls) and its "closing of the gold window" (ending the convertibility of dollars into gold and allowing the dollar to float against other currencies)—had short-term success but harmed the economy in the long term. In addition, the Nixon administration's lack of preparation or strategy for dealing with the 1973 oil embargo by the Organization of Petroleum Exporting Countries (OPEC), imposed in retaliation for U.S. support of Israel in the Yom Kippur War, immediately boosted energy prices by 367 percent. This plunged the United States into the worst recession of the postwar era. Perhaps worst of all, Nixon's artificial overheating of the economy in 1972 to improve his own electoral chances worked in concert with his other economic policies to leave his successor with yet another ugly legacy. That legacy was a true American economic crisis.

Indeed, according to John Robert Greene (1992), Nixon's economic policies had resulted in both skyrocketing prices and more people out of work than there had been in a decade. By July 1974, for example, inflation rose to its highest level since 1919, and less than a year later, in May of 1975, unemployment reached 9.2 percent. This level of unemployment was two percentage points higher than the previous postwar high! Such economic troubles were particularly perplexing because, with inflation and consumer prices high, the United States should have been experiencing low unemployment and relatively strong business growth. Instead, unemployment was increasing and business growth was slowing. Even U.S. trade was in trouble, with the trade deficit hitting a record $1.1 billion. Simply put, according to Greene, the economy was in chaos.

Thus, the number one issue on Ford's domestic agenda when he took office was the economic crisis. Initially, Ford decided to deal with the economy by taking the conservative line and focusing on inflation. His program—which ultimately became the butt of many campaign jokes in the 1974 elections and which helped to smash the president's party in those elections—employed the slogan "Whip Inflation Now" (shortened to WIN). It called for deep cuts in government spending and a tax increase, as well as for a renewed volunteerism that urged Americans to spend less and save more. However, the country was in little mood for sacrifice; in the words of one observer: "Americans were losing their jobs, and Ford was talking about planting radishes in the back yard" (Reeves 1975, 163). The Republicans got whipped in the 1974 election, and Ford's program certainly accomplished little in terms of lowering inflation.

By 1975 it became apparent to all that the country was experiencing the worst of all economic worlds: stagflation. This meant that the nation was feeling the crunch of rising prices *and* slow economic growth, and it was clear that something had to be done. In his State of the Union Address on January 13, the president offered his package for the economy: a one-time $16 billion tax cut across the board and—to compensate for the increase in the deficit caused by the cut—a moratorium on the creation of any new federal spending program and a 5 percent ceiling on both Social Security raises and federal pay raises in 1975. The response to the president's program, according to Greene (1992), was quick and merciless: the press bashed Ford for his "flip-flop" on the economy; the conservative Right of his own party attacked him for abandoning conservative economics too soon; and the Watergate Babies in Congress virtually ignored his plan. Instead, Congress passed appropriations bills far outstripping those for which Ford had called and proposed a tax cut surpassing his request by $7 billion, all deficit financed. The president's plan for rescuing the economy was in serious danger.

In response, Ford and his economic team offered a third option in an address to the nation on October 6, 1975, this time calling for a permanent tax reduction of $28 billion, contingent upon Congress agreeing to a federal spending ceiling of $395 billion for fiscal 1977. Once again, however, Congress ignored the president and passed the tax cut without the spending ceiling. Now Gerald Ford was in an uncomfortable position: he would have to veto a bill that was extremely popular with the public. He did it anyway, and in one of the victories of his administration, Congress barely sustained the veto. It was not until early 1976—with the threat of looming elections—that both parties finally agreed to a bill that provided for a tax cut and spending limits on the part of Congress.

In the end, President Ford had no small success with improving the economy: by his last year in office, a healthy economic recovery was under way, and the consumer price index for the year rose by only 4.8 percent (Greene 1995). Ford had cut inflation in half over his time in office; 4 million more people had jobs in early 1976 than did during the low point of the 1975 recession, and by the end of 1975 real GNP was growing by 6.2 percent. However, the political damage done to the president by his fight with Congress over the economy wounded him gravely—both with the public and with his old colleagues on Capitol Hill. He had vetoed a popular tax cut, he faced an unfriendly Democratic Congress, and Ronald Reagan (the conservative Republican governor of

California) had begun to publicly attack his policies, accusing him of abandoning the Right. To say the least, Ford was taking a beating.

The Energy Crisis

Unfortunately for the president, his troubles were not limited to the crisis in the economy. He also faced other serious problems, such as the energy crisis. Ford took a lesson from Nixon on the energy issue—he was determined not to get caught unprepared—and so he bored into the issue as soon as he had dealt with Nixon's pardon. Indeed, he needed to do so: according to Anderson and Boyd (1983), the price of oil had quadrupled in late 1973 as a result of the OPEC oil embargo, and the term *energy crisis* had entered into common usage. The energy scarcity in turn fed inflation, while deficits in the balance of payments to the oil-producing nations were beginning to produce extensive unemployment in energy-related industries. Oil was no longer considered an inexpensive fuel available in unlimited quantities. Rather, questions were being raised about the security of the energy supply and about dependence on foreign imports.

Unfortunately for Gerald Ford, however, he had yet another Nixon legacy to contend with concerning energy. Because of quotas on oil imports that had been set during the Eisenhower administration, as well as a generous system of tax breaks, the U.S. oil industry was booming in 1969 when Nixon took office. Thus, Anderson and Boyd (1983) argue that Nixon paid little attention when the eighteen-member OPEC met in Venezuela in December 1970 and agreed to raise the posted prices of Persian Gulf oil and to increase taxes on the oil. His administration likewise failed to respond to the news that U.S. crude oil production capacity was declining in the years after Nixon took office while American consumption was rising sharply. It also ignored the fact that more and more of that demand was being satisfied with foreign oil, much of it coming from insecure sources in the Middle East. Instead of responding to these developments, Nixon's administration maintained the same old energy policy, refusing to budge from price controls on oil, refusing to perceive the OPEC as a serious cartel, and refusing to see that America was becoming dangerously dependent on foreign oil. The government was thus completely unprepared for the oil embargo and the resulting energy crisis of 1973. Nixon's failure to prepare and his administration's rejection of new domestic energy production in favor of foreign imports saddled Ford with a trajectory that called for a 50 percent jump in oil imports in the years after 1974.

The long-term strategy needed for dealing with this crisis was to let the price of oil in the United States rise to the world level. A sudden, staggering increase of this kind would force American consumers to recognize the need to cut their use of oil by lowering thermostats, driving smaller cars, adding insulation to their homes, and switching to cheaper fuels. So, with advice from Frank Zarb, the new head of the Federal Energy Administration, President Ford made his plan for dealing with the energy problem known to Congress and the American people in the same 1975 State of the Union Address in which he unveiled his plan for the economy. He proposed that Congress end controls on the price of domestic oil and pass a tax on oil producers. He also announced that he would raise the tariff on foreign oil by executive order. This plan was based on the idea that the immediate decontrol of domestic oil prices would be the best long-term solution to the energy problem, and that existing tariffs on Middle Eastern oil should be raised so that domestic crude prices could become competitive. Of course, this policy meant substantially higher prices for gasoline and heating oil, but Ford proposed the tax on the oil producers to take the sting out of that bad medicine. To Ford and his advisers, decontrolling prices seemed to be a moderate solution to the energy crisis compared with some of the other alternatives that were being discussed, such as gasoline rationing.

So the president was completely unprepared for the ferociously negative response to his plan. Indeed, John Robert Greene (1992) argues that Congress nearly exploded in opposition to Ford's plan to raise the tariff by executive order, calling it an abuse of presidential power. Again, the focus was shifted from the issue at hand—energy—to the battle between the president and Congress. Only a week after the State of the Union Address, the House passed a measure that would nullify Ford's executive order. Thus, on March 4, the president was forced to veto the nullification, but he agreed to hold up any further tariff increases for sixty days. With Congress in opposition to him and proposing a phased tax increase on gasoline, with summer coming, and with the presidential election looming large, Ford decided that he would have to abandon his original plan. He submitted a new one to Congress that called for a phased decontrol of oil prices over a thirty-nine-month period. Once again, however, Congress ignored the president and instead passed a bill extending the life of oil price controls. Ford vetoed the bill but agreed to another waiting period, although this time he demanded that Congress come up with a plan of its own. Finally, by early December, Congress had produced its own compromise energy bill, which rolled back the prices on domestic oil but also gave the president the authority to decontrol them over a forty-month period.

It was not exactly what Ford wanted, says Greene (1992), but with the New Hampshire primary just around the corner and fearing a damaging override, the president signed the Energy Policy and Conservation Act of 1975 and formally withdrew his plan for increases in the tariffs on imported oil. Thus, in the end Ford got an energy bill, but the price was high for him and for the nation. Personally, the president once again looked weak in the face of an energized Congress. Once again he was forced to abandon his original plan and compromise on Republican principles. Once again, Ronald Reagan had fuel for his fire.

For the nation, however, the price was ultimately even higher. As a result of the maintenance of Nixon's price controls on oil, according to Anderson and Boyd (1983), American consumers continued to believe that they were somehow entitled to protection from the world price of oil, and they continued to use oil with apparent abandon. By now, two-thirds of the oil consumed in the United States was produced at home, and the price on most of it was frozen at less than half of the world price! Unfortunately, the piper would eventually have to be paid.

New York's Fiscal Crisis

New York City was in a bad way. For years, it had spent and borrowed more than it had taken in in revenues. In fact, since 1965 its operating budget had more that tripled, with expenditures increasing by an average of 12 percent a year while revenues increased by less than 5 percent! To meet its bills, New York had borrowed millions of dollars in the tax-free municipal bond market. By the time Ford took office, however, the city did not have the money to meet its obligations on the bonds. By April 1975 its credit rating was so bad that several banks told the city that it could no longer borrow in the market, and the city was threatened with default. It was also facing the fact that it might have to shut down many of its necessary services for lack of funds. So the state's new Democratic governor and the city's mayor went to the White House on May 13 and asked Ford for a $1 billion loan for ninety days. Although Ford told the two that he would need some time to think about it, he later told his aides that he would never support federal aid for the city (Greene 1992).

New York State advanced the city more than $300 million in aid over the summer, and in September the aid increased when the state approved a $2.3 billion aid package. Even this amount, however, could not save the city, and by October the threat of default was imminent. Still Ford refused to support any federal aid to the city, declaring in a speech on October 29 at the National Press Club that he would veto any bill providing for a federal bailout of New York City. The next day's headline in the *New York Daily News* read: "Ford to City: Drop Dead."

With the presidential election season nearly upon him, the president could not afford the negative publicity. He also needed the support of New York senator James Buckley, who was labeled by Ford's political team as a swing vote at the upcoming Republican National Convention and who also hinted, in meetings with Ford's congressional liaison team, that "given certain considerations" he could support Ford (Greene 1995, 95). With the deck stacked against him, the president blinked: on November 11, Ford totally reversed himself and agreed to a modified bailout. The federal government would loan money to New York City with the stipulation that at the end of every fiscal year, the city would repay the entirety of the principal, plus an amount of interest that was 1 percent greater than the prevailing market rate. While the city got what it wanted and needed, Gerald Ford had again allowed events to lead him rather than the other way around.

Ford and Foreign Policy:
The Caretaker President Who Couldn't

Unlike Nixon, Ford enjoyed the challenges of domestic policy and wanted to concentrate most of his attention as president to pressing domestic problems such as the economy and the energy crisis. In the arena of foreign policy, however, Ford probably would have preferred to be a true "caretaker" president, simply continuing along the road that Nixon had built and settling into what he later called "quiet diplomacy" with the Soviet Union (Thompson 1988, 102). Unfortunately, that was not to be. As we shall see in greater detail in chapter 4, détente had already begun to unravel when Ford took office in August 1974, and he was soon faced with a series of crises that threatened to force the United States to once again square off against the Soviet Union in dangerous confrontations. As with domestic policy, Ford quickly became embattled in foreign policy, fighting the Nixon legacy, Congress, the Republican Right, and his own feuding staff. According to John Robert Greene (1992), not only did Ford fail to sustain Nixon's foreign policy triumphs, but he also proved unable to navigate a new and coherent course for his own administration.

Once again Ford was blocked from accomplishing his goals by the Nixon legacy of distrust of presidential power, faring little better with Congress on foreign policy than he had on domestic issues. Perhaps the best example of the new limitations imposed on presidents in the post-Watergate era is the first crisis that Ford faced in office: the Turkish invasion of Cyprus. Cyprus—a small island located fifty miles from the Turkish coast—was inhabited by both Turks and Greeks, and so it had long been a pawn in Mediterranean politics. The situation came to boiling point in June 1974 when a group of Greek Cypriots backed by the military junta in power in Greece overthrew the government of Cyprus and declared a union with Greece. One month later, Turkey invaded Cyprus, using NATO weapons that had been supplied by the United States. Henry Kissinger soon managed to initiate peace talks, but they broke down only four days after Ford took office. When Turkey then invaded the northern part of Cyprus, the Greek Cypriots blamed the United States and stormed the American embassy, killing the American ambassador in the attack. The Ford administration sided with Turkey, an old ally that allowed U.S. missiles and military bases on its soil. However, many Americans—particularly Greek Americans—thought that the United States had taken the wrong position, and Congress soon agreed. Within just a few months, the legislative branch had forced the president into a compromise that resulted in an embargo of Turkey, causing an old ally to close all but one NATO air base and all U.S. military and intelligence facilities. Turkey also instituted restrictions on American ships using Turkish ports and on military overflights. Ultimately, American-Turkish relations were weakened by the actions of Congress regarding Cyprus according to George Lenczowski (1990), and Turkey soon established closer ties with the Soviet Union.

The crisis in Cyprus quickly and clearly outlined the new relationship between the executive and the legislative branches in foreign policy; for the first time in two decades, Congress was the initiator of a foreign policy that was clearly contrary to the wishes of the White House. The legislative branch had won. As Gerald Ford later wrote, "Congress was determined to get its oar deeply into the conduct of foreign affairs. This not only undermined the chief executive's ability to act, but also eroded the separation of powers concept in the Constitution" (1979, 146).

Its victory over Ford concerning Cyprus bolstered the faith of Congress in this new foreign policy role and led to more trouble for the president. The final rounds of the Vietnam War demonstrated that trouble. Although the United States had helped to bring about peace in Vietnam during Nixon's tenure, the North Vietnamese Communists were still as threatening to the South as they had ever been. While it was clear that the American public would never allow a recommitment of U.S. forces in Vietnam to stop the North, Ford wanted to support this U.S. ally with money. However, Congress would not cooperate, allocating for Vietnam only half the amount Ford had requested in his budget proposal for 1975. The South Vietnamese were now desperate and the North Vietnamese knew it; they invaded the South once again in December. Although the president immediately asked Congress for emergency aid for the South, Congress was at first stingy with the funds and later denied completely any further military aid for either South Vietnam or Cambodia. John Robert Greene (1992) believes that, in the end, Ford's inability to get congressional funding sealed South Vietnam's fate; it surrendered to the Communists on April 30. Ironically, Ford was blamed by conservatives for abandoning an American ally in the fight against Communism.

Those same conservatives despised Nixon's détente, and they now blamed Ford for perpetuating the policy that allowed the United States to "go soft" on Communism. This criticism was leveled at Ford, according to Firestone and Ugrinsky (1993), even though the president had fought for increases in defense spending and had managed to negotiate a framework agreement for the Strategic Arms Limitation Talks (SALT) II Accords at Vladivostok (the agreement was never ratified). Again, Ford was forced to fight with a Congress determined to block presidential power, first scuttling a trade bill with the Soviets and then forcing Ford to place an embargo on all overseas shipments of wheat and corn, angering Soviet leader Leonid Brezhnev. And again, Ford had to face angry conservatives when he returned from signing the Helsinki Accords. While the agreement at Helsinki was historic in many ways and included a Soviet commitment to follow a more liberal human rights policy, Ford was battered for agreeing to accept as permanent the postwar boundaries of the Soviet Union and its Eastern European satellite countries. Ford tried to limit the damage by telling reporters that the agreement was not legally binding, but it was too late. Hundreds of letters flooded the White House, scouring the president for apparently writing off Eastern Europe. Of course, Ronald Reagan immediately attacked the agreement in the press, and it became obvious to all that détente would become a major issue in the upcoming presidential elections.

The 1976 Elections and the President Who Was Never Elected

It was also clear to all that Reagan was readying himself to challenge Ford in the 1976 presidential primaries. His entry into the presidential race in 1968 had indicated his higher ambitions, and he was merely waiting for the time to be ripe. Once Nixon had fallen, according to John Robert Greene (1992), Reagan saw his opportunity and by the end of 1974 had become the most outspoken critic of the Ford administration.

With Reagan continuously bashing Ford for abandoning the conservative Right, Ford attempted to make amends before the primaries. In what has become known as the "Sunday Morning Massacre," President Ford completely rearranged his staff, demoting Henry Kissinger, dismissing Secretary of Defense James Schlesinger, and removing the liberal Nelson Rockefeller from consideration as his running mate in 1976. Unfortunately, this grand strategy did not work. The removal of Rockefeller from the ticket was particularly problematic, making many feel that Ford had been duplicitous and disloyal, traits that were particularly dangerous in the post-Watergate era.

This difficult start to Ford's campaign was one of the many factors that led to the closest race for the Republican presidential nomination since 1952. Reagan hit Ford hard, attacking détente and Ford's conduct of foreign policy, accusing the president of backing down to blackmail on the Panama Canal, and casting himself as an outsider. The contest was close: as the primary season ended, in fact, Reagan held the lead with 178 committed delegates followed by Ford's 114. Sixty-four were uncommitted, and more than 270 delegates were yet to be chosen in states that employed nominating conventions or caucuses rather than primaries. In the race for these latter delegates, Ford surged ahead, and by the time the convention opened in Kansas City, he had the most committed delegates, although he was 28 short of having enough to win the nomination. In the end, the president won a first-ballot victory by a razor-thin margin of 1,187 to 1,070 votes. He was finally the Republican presidential nominee for the 1976 elections.

Going into that 1976 race, however, Gerald Ford was damaged goods. First of all, he was a Republican, the party of Watergate, and he was sure to be swept from office on that fact alone. Added to this were his unpopular pardon of Nixon, his administration's apparent weakness in the face of an activist Congress, the problems in the economy, and the dissatisfaction with détente. Ford was weak, and Reagan's challenge had made him even weaker. Finally, new campaign finance laws created a situation in which, for the first time in recent memory, the Republicans did not have a sizable advantage in fundraising. The president decided to campaign by being "presidential," staying in Washington and attending to his responsibilities as president while his running mate, Robert Dole, went on the attack. But this strategy was a mistake; Ford's administration had become synonymous with the "mess in Washington" in a year in which being an outsider and a political neophyte was a blessing. Jimmy Carter was the epitome of that outsider, and he wisely played that card for all it was worth.

Carter also played a political card that had stayed in the deck for nearly the entire postwar period: that of a moralist. In post-Watergate America, Carter's most famous speech line, "I'm Jimmy Carter and I'm running for president. I will never lie to you," was a winner. The candidate repeated his winning line over and over, throughout both the primaries and the fall campaign, and the American public liked what they saw. By August, Carter had a twenty-point lead in the polls. Even a tasteless Carter interview with *Playboy* was not enough ammunition for Ford to knock out his rival, as Ford himself and his administration were dogged by their own scandals (including allegations that Ford had received illicit money from labor unions while he was a member of Congress). The final blow was the infamous misstatement Ford made during a televised debate with Carter in October: the president essentially said that the Soviet satellite countries of Eastern Europe were not under Russian domination. To make matters worse, he refused to acknowledge his mistake and did not issue a formal clarification until six days after the debate.

In an election with the lowest voter turnout since 1948, the political outsider and moralist won the day by a slim margin—only fifty-six electoral votes. A new day had dawned in America.

The Ford Legacy: A Pardon, but No Healing?

Gerald Ford became president in 1974 with the intention of healing the wounded nation, and he decided early in his presidency that to save the nation further pain and begin the healing process, Richard Nixon would have to be pardoned. With this action, the new president undoubtedly also hoped to get the Nixon "monkey" off his back—to clear the air in the White House, to clear away the shadows of the Nixon legacy, and thus to make his own mark and engineer his own presidency. However, Gerald Ford was wrong in that decision. His pardon of Nixon, at least at the time, did not bring healing. *Time* magazine charged in 1974 that by "taking such a sweeping action so soon, Ford damaged his efforts to restore confidence in the U.S. presidency and opened his own credibility gap" (10). And J. F. terHorst, the original press secretary for the Ford administration who resigned in protest over the pardon has said of it, "The president had not prepared the country for this and therefore the country was unable to do what Mr. Ford hoped—put Watergate behind it. In many ways, the pardon tore the scab off the Watergate wound just as it was beginning to heal" (as cited in Thompson 1988, 214).

So while Ford's pardon did not bring a resolution to Watergate for most of the American public, neither did it enable the president to break free of the Nixon legacy and get his own administration off the ground. There was not enough time, there was too much of the Nixon legacy to fight, there were too many squabbles among Ford's staff, Congress was in no mood to be friendly to Nixon's successor, and the new president was really unprepared in many ways to establish his own presidency. As administration critic Adlai Stevenson III has said, "[Ford had] no strong views of where the country should be going, no strong understanding of history and the world" (as cited in Greene 1995, 191). Even Ford's old colleagues in the house had damned him with faint praise by describing him as, "solid, dependable, loyal—a man more comfortable carrying out the programs of others than initiating things on his own" (*Congressional Quarterly* 1973, 2762). At least one Ford observer also believes that Gerald Ford was the author of self-imposed limitations on his role as president, as a result of his constant awareness that he had come into office via a constitutional amendment rather than through election by the people. Lou Cannon of the *Washington Post* has said of Ford, "he was very conscious that he had not been elected. He was extraordinarily conscious of the constitutional process. He knew he was in there on a pass, and it hobbled him in ways that it shouldn't have" (Thompson 1988, 353).

Perhaps more than anything, however, Gerald Ford was hobbled by the Nixon legacy. He and his administration—in fact the presidency as an institution—were the greatest victims of Watergate. The circumstances that propelled Ford to the presidency, an office he did not seek and which he had not expected to attain, were the same circumstances that made it impossible for him to govern effectively. The excesses that led to Nixon's downfall also created a Congress (and perhaps a press and a public) intent upon shackling the president. Gerald Ford had long ago made up his mind that he did not want to be president (his goal in politics was to become Speaker of the House of Representatives), which made him perhaps the best president the nation could ask for in the troubled post-Watergate seventies. No, the pardon did not heal, did not wipe the slate clean, did not magically allow Ford to establish his own presidency. However, what he could not do by conscious decision, Ford did accomplish, at least in part, just by being himself. The example he set—his integrity, his openness, and his willingness to put the nation's long-term health before personal political expediency—was just what the doctor ordered for an ailing nation, a nation feeling the pain of betrayal and the empty depression born of cynicism and distrust.

Time and time again, Ford chose the needs of the nation over his personal political benefit. One time it was his choice to continue the administration's work in dealing with trouble in South Africa, even when his advisers told him that it would hurt him in the Texas primary during the 1976 campaign. Sure enough, Ford did not win a single delegate in Texas. Faced with another momentous decision, Ford chose Nelson Rockefeller as his vice president in 1974, believing that having a man of Rockefeller's stature would reassure the country and the world. What would have been far better for Ford would have been the obvious, hard-nosed political choice: Ronald Reagan. With Reagan as vice president in 1974, Ford would have appeased the conservative Right of the Republican Party and would have removed Reagan as his primary challenger in 1976. But as Richard Cheney, Ford's chief of staff, later reminisced, "I don't think when he made that decision . . . that he gave any thought at all to the 1976 election" (Thompson 1988, 85). Nor did Ford give thought to his 1976 race for the presidency when he decided to pardon Richard Nixon, telling his aides, "I don't care what the polls say, it's the right thing to do" (Thompson 1988, 85).

Gerald Ford was not even Nixon's first choice for vice president, but Nixon chose him because of his acceptability to Congress (whoever was chosen would need to be confirmed by both houses) and his reputation for integrity: the traits that allowed Ford to keep American government going after Watergate had nearly destroyed it. As Ford's longtime friend and adviser Philip Buchen would later say: "he was friendly and straightforward. He had an almost earnest demeanor, and he never showed glibness or arrogance or pompousness. I think he had the reputation for honesty and trustworthiness which helped restore the presidency at a time when it needed some restoring. He was . . . a fortunate choice at the time for this reason . . . you'd be hard-pressed to find anyone else who could have done the job or served that purpose at the time as well as he did" (in Thompson 1988, 35). Similarly, Robert Hartmann, another Ford friend and adviser, claims: "I cannot say that he was the man for all seasons. I *can* say that he was the man for *that* season, when he restored the faith of a troubled people in their constitutional government and in the honor and decency of the presidency" (in Thompson 1988, 92).

Although Gerald Ford's presidency did not bring about the healing that he so proudly claims as his legacy, he did reset the nation's ethical compass and put the ship of state back on course. He did begin the healing process—not with his pardon, but with his person. As Kenneth Thompson wrote in his 1988 book on the Ford presidency,

> We have forgotten how desperate the true State of the Union was when he took office. It was not, as in 1860, a case of certain states threatening to secede and defy the federal government in Washington. It was worse; a threat of millions of individual Americans—young and old, black and white, rich and poor, urban and rural—threatening to secede from the social compact that binds us together as a nation. This unspoken understanding had been twice shattered, first by the duplicities of Vietnam and later by the deceptions of Watergate. The fundamental consent of the governed had been rudely overridden, not once but twice. The contract of confidence between ordinary Americans and their leaders in Washington was almost abrogated. Jerry Ford, simply by being what he was, turned this trend around (in Thompson 1988, 92).

3

Carter

America's Outsider Can't Make Good

IN JANUARY 1977, as he began his inaugural address, Jimmy Carter turned to Gerald Ford and said, "For myself and for our nation I want to thank my predecessor for all he has done to heal our land" (Trager 1992, 1060). While Carter was right to show appreciation for all that Ford had done to heal the nation, the task had only really just begun. Ford's depth of character and his political self-sacrifice had allowed the healing to begin, scabbing over the most gaping national wounds. Yet, as Carter observed in his memoirs, "in spite of Ford's healing service, the ghosts of Watergate still haunted the White House" (as cited in Greene 1995, 192). John Robert Greene also writes in his 1995 book on the Ford administration, "Although Ford's fundamental decency restored much of the luster to a badly tarnished presidency, one should not conclude that at the end of his tenure the nation had fully regained trust in its government" (192). The harm of Vietnam, of Watergate, and even of Ford's pardon of Richard Nixon continued to generate cynicism in the battered nation.

The nation's trust of public officials and presidential power had decreased dramatically during the early 1970s, from 61 percent in 1964 to 22 percent in 1976. That distrust, coupled with demands for accountability in government, were the tickets that assured James Earl "Jimmy" Carter—the honest, truthtelling, anti-Washington outsider—his ride to the White House. The year 1976 was the year of the outsider, a new type of candidate that caught the imagination of the American voter. These candidates were inexperienced in national politics, but in 1976 this was an asset rather than a handicap: John

Robert Greene (1992) argues that they played up their distance from the federal government and attempted to corner the market on virtue. Further, Jimmy Carter was the ultimate outsider: when the Georgia governor announced his candidacy in December 1974, he was virtually unknown and a long shot at best. In fact, when he told his mother that he was going to run for president, she asked, "President of what?" (Kaufman 1993, 15).

Educated as a nuclear engineer, Carter had become a peanut farmer in rural Plains, Georgia. His political experience at the state level was minimal and at the national level, nonexistent. Although he had been a Democrat his entire life, he was unknown in Democratic Party circles. And it was hard to tell what the man's true ideology was: he seemed clearly liberal on civil rights issues, decidedly ambivalent on other social issues, and strongly conservative on most economic issues. To top it off, Jimmy Carter was a moralist, a "born-again" Christian who taught Sunday School and prayed in public.

This was the kind of man that America thought it wanted, someone the people could trust. Jimmy Carter was that man. According to detailed analyses of Carter's personality, personal life, and presidency, he was honest. His goals were always to do what he believed was right, no matter whether it was politically acceptable or not. He was a man who saw politics as a moral activity; he practiced humility, charity, forgiveness, and tolerance as political virtues. This moral political compass, coupled with his extremely intense drives for achievement and independence, according to Erwin Hargrove (1988), brought Carter to conceive of the political leader as a "trustee for the public interest": he believed that the essential responsibility of leadership was to articulate the good of the entire community rather than any part of it. Indeed, he embarked on the quest for the presidency with the self-confident belief that he could resolve the nation's problems.

To assure the public that he could indeed solve those problems, this peanut farmer from Georgia was willing to work long hours in preparation, to campaign until he was ragged, and to put his family's business on the line. With the assistance of a crack campaign team (including Hamilton Jordan and Jody Powell), Carter soon made a phenomenal rise from dusty obscurity to the bright lights of the national scene. The governor was assisted in this by his service as campaign coordinator of the Democratic Party's fund drive for the 1974 congressional and gubernatorial elections. This post took Carter all over the nation, helping him to establish valuable contacts with local politicians, state party leaders, and the heads of important interest groups. Carter also had the benefit of his membership in the prestigious Trilateral Commission, an exclusive group of top bankers and businesspeople in the United States, Western Europe, and Japan. Membership in this group assured Carter of access to the corporate elite in America (who supported him strongly throughout his campaign). It also provided him with foreign policy credentials and experience. The Federal Election Campaign Act Amendments of 1974 also helped Carter garner the national recognition that he needed as well, with the federal treasury picking up about half of the cost of running.

All the while that he was running for president, Jimmy Carter smiled his trademark smile, one that was wide and open, showing lots of teeth and lots of caring, one that portrayed honesty and integrity. Along with that open smile, Carter offered lots of promises. He promised Americans that he would eliminate the kind of secrecy in government and diplomacy that had produced Vietnam and Watergate. He vowed that he would open up government to the average citizen, protecting and promoting the public good of all citizens over the private interests of the special few. He said that he would fight for equity, efficiency, and competency in government. To seal the deal, Carter wisely selected Walter Mondale as his running mate, providing the balance of someone who was familiar with the federal government and, particularly, with Congress.

Backed by a Democratic Party united for the first time in a long time, Carter soon began collecting endorsements—the AFL-CIO, the National Education Association—and took a substantial lead against Ford in the polls. In fact, a Harris poll conducted immediately following the convention showed Carter leading Ford by a margin of 66 percent to 27 percent. Although the rest of the campaign season saw that lead whittled away by President Ford, the economy, the pardon, and Carter's outsider status were enough to make him the thirty-ninth president of the United States. He won with a mere 297 electoral votes (only 51 percent of the popular vote) to 240 for President Ford, making him the first Southern president since the Civil War.

The Carter Administration: How Does an Outsider Succeed in Washington?

Jimmy Carter moved as quickly as President Ford, though more boldly, to change the atmosphere at the White House—to make it clear that he was an open and honest president, a regular guy, an outsider. According to Garland

Haas in his 1992 book on the Carter administration, the new President banned the playing of "Hail to the Chief," wore blue jeans around the White House, and exchanged the mammoth presidential limousine for a more modest sedan. Carter also liked to be seen carrying his own bags from the presidential helicopter, and he made efforts to interact with the public directly through "town hall meetings" and call-in radio talk shows. After his first six months in office, he had great approval ratings, with Gallup reporting that 66 percent of the American public approved of his overall performance.

During the campaign that finally brought him to power in 1976, Jimmy Carter had often promised not only to be an outsider but also to bring new faces to Washington with him. As the new president worked to keep this promise, however, it often worked to his detriment. When he made his cabinet appointments, for example, he ignored the major interest groups making up the Democratic Party and instead drew most of his appointments from the Trilateral Commission and the Brookings Institution. As for the White House staff, Carter brought a group of unknown outsiders from Georgia—soon known as the "Georgia Mafia"—to the White House with him. Thus the new president quickly alienated his main constituencies and staffed several key posts with outsiders who were not fluent in the language of Washington.

In addition, Carter, like Ford, rejected the idea of the Nixonian type "palace guard" in staffing his White House. He had made this a central theme of the 1976 election campaign, conveniently ignoring Ford's dismantling of the Nixon White House staff structure. Carter promised not to appoint a chief of staff to oversee the work of other aides, says Erwin Hargrove (1988), preferring a "collegial" style of decision making—working with small groups of trusted advisers with minimal formal structure. Thus he established the old "spokes of the wheel" staff structure in the White House, with himself at the center and advisers equally arrayed around him in a circle. Very quickly, however, the new president (like his predecessor) found that this approach was extremely disadvantageous, fostering divisive staff rivalries and plenty of confusion as cabinet members (who had been charged with policy development and administration) and White House staffers went off in different directions (Haas 1992). In his attempt to create a real "cabinet government" (Hargrove 1988, 182), the president even prohibited a strong White House coordinating role in policy development. Carter believed that intelligent people could solve problems without elaborate machinery or formally delineated relationships, a belief that badly underestimated the complexity of the task of governing.

After Carter's first several months in office, according to Burton Kaufman (1993), the White House remained in an organizational tangle, with such fundamental questions as the delegation of authority and the administrative structure of the staff still unresolved. In addition, by essentially acting as his own chief of staff, Carter's penchant for becoming overly absorbed with details was allowed free reign. This obsession with details, coupled with his difficulty in delegating responsibility to others, created a situation in which Carter (and his desk) soon became overwhelmed with minutiae, seriously hindering quick and coherent decisions. So, as had President Ford, Jimmy Carter was ultimately forced by staffing problems to appoint a chief of staff.

However, Carter chose his controversial political adviser, Hamilton Jordan, to take the post. Although the president promised that this new arrangement would expedite decision making and free him to attend to larger issues, it only created more problems for the president. The Democratic leadership in Congress, with whom Jordan had to work, had no love for the man. Many in Congress did not know Jordan, and he remained aloof from both political and social contact with members of Congress. In addition, rumors soon surfaced that Jordan had sniffed cocaine at Beverly Hills parties and at the Studio 54 disco in New York, seriously embarrassing President Carter, the leader who had come to Washington promising morality, honesty, and the benefits of having an outsider president.

Carter and Congress: The Outsider versus the Insiders

Such problems notwithstanding, everyone hoped and expected that the new president and Congress would have a better relationship than the previous administration. Members of Carter's own party swept the Congress in 1976, regaining many of the seats once regarded as forever lost to Republicans: House Democrats outnumbered Republicans 292 to 143, establishing a two-thirds majority in the House of Representatives and a nearly two-to-one margin in the Senate. Even after the midterm elections in 1978, when the president's party typically takes a beating, the Republicans only gained 3 seats in the Senate and 11 in the House, leaving Carter a Congress that was still controlled by his own party. Moreover, the congressional leadership seemed ready to assist the president in carrying through his program; according to Garland Haas (1992), Thomas P. "Tip" O'Neill, the newly elected Speaker of the House, promised his full support.

Unfortunately, however, relations between Jimmy Carter and the legislative branch were not as good as everyone had expected, and Carter endured endless frustrations in his attempts to lead the Democrats. Carter faced the same trouble in Congress that had confronted Gerald Ford: a legislative body intent on reining in the power of the president and expanding its own role. For Carter as for Ford, the root of this trouble with Congress was the class that rode to power in 1974 after Watergate, the "Watergate Babies." Young, aggressive, and the most independent-minded legislators ever elected, most of the Watergate Babies were not inclined to submit either to presidential authority or to party discipline. By the time the ninety-fifth Congress had convened after the 1976 elections, two groups had emerged in Congress that effectively destroyed party unity and discipline: the "Boll Weevils" and the "Gypsy Moths." The Boll Weevils were the more destructive for Carter, as they were boring from within the Democratic Party, just as boll weevils bore from the inside of the cotton boll. About fifty Southern, conservative Democrats made up the Boll Weevils, and they had clashed for some time with their national party leaders, particularly over defense spending and budget deficits. They were not about to fall in line now just because Jimmy Carter was also a Democrat from the South. Although the Gypsy Moths—about fifteen or twenty liberal Republicans from the Northeast and Midwest—habitually joined ranks with centrist Democrats, they likewise had no intention of supporting Carter.

With the climate of independence in Congress at its peak in the late 1970s and party unity at an all-time low, Carter was bound to have trouble with Congress. In addition, Carter had won his nomination and the presidency itself by campaigning as an outsider, vigorously criticizing Washington and all of its insiders—the men and women in Congress that he would now have to work with. As Hamilton Jordan put it: "There was a subtle but strong feeling when we arrived in Washington that 'Well OK, you Georgians won the big prize through gimmicks, good fortune, and by running against Washington. But now we are going to show you who's boss in this town' " (1982, 171). As one of the members of Carter's congressional liaison team later said, "You don't spend a year and a half running against Washington, then come to

Washington, and not have to pay for some of that rhetoric" (Jones 1988, 107).

Perhaps the biggest cause of many of Carter's problems with Congress was the fact that not only had he campaigned as an outsider, he *was* an outsider. He was a man with no experience in Washington and no appreciation for the intricacies and realities of how Washington worked. Carter and his staff were painfully unaware of—or just did not care about—the necessary elements for a good relationship with the legislative branch, and they were woefully unprepared for the fact that the president can accomplish little without the cooperation of that branch. As one of his advisers remembers it, Carter made little initial effort to get along with Congress because he did not think it was necessary (Hargrove 1988, 17).

The Carter administration even failed to comprehend that members of Congress were important players in their own right. The executive branch failed to understand that members of Congress had their own political concerns beyond passing the extremely long legislative agenda of the president. This was particularly true of Carter's agenda, which was overloaded to begin with and also included such highly controversial (and thus for a congressperson, best avoided) issues as the Panama Canal, deregulation, tax reform, Social Security reform, and welfare reform. Instead, as Garland Haas has put it, the president simply "dismissed the members of Congress as bothersome claimants for presidential attention and resources, rather than seeing them as instruments of political action" (1992, 66). Erwin Hargrove relates that Carter could not "easily align himself with congressional politicians because . . . he saw them as preoccupied with particular interests rather than being trustees for the public interest, as he sought to be" (1988, 16). In fact, Carter believed that for this reason Congress lacked the capacity to govern the nation, and that it was his responsibility to be the national leader—to stand fast in the face of specialized interests.

So when offers of help came from old Washington hands, Carter spurned them. His staffers frequently failed to return members' phone calls. The official line on different policies was often unclear, as cabinet officers endorsed positions independently of the White House. According to Charles Jones (1988), the president also had the habit of taking trips without informing legislators whose district he was visiting, and reporters who traveled with him on these trips said that he seemed incapable of saying nice things about members of Congress even as he traveled among their constituents. Even more troubling, legislative packages were announced by the White House without consulting with members beforehand. As Carter himself later said, "[I] was more inclined to move rapidly and without equivocation and without the long interminable consultations and so forth that are inherent, I think, in someone who has a more legislative attitude, or psyche, or training or experience" (in Hargrove 1988, 15). Of the ten candidates who ran for the presidency between 1960 and 1976, Jimmy Carter was the only one without any congressional experience.

Worst of all, says Garland Haas (1992), people on the Hill complained bitterly that they had no clear sense of the administration's priorities, such as which policies would be compromised to ensure the adoption of other policies. This was because Carter first overloaded the agenda with nearly every issue that he believed needed attention and then insisted that they were all top priorities. Refusing to admit that it was impossible to get everything that he wanted, he rejected any conception of leadership through compromise. He simply was not willing to bargain—the stock-in-trade of anyone attempting to get the cooperation of 535 independent legislators. As Cyrus Vance, Carter's secretary of state, later explained it: Carter "was hindered, not only by a lack of knowledge of the Washington scene and the Congress, but by almost a contempt for the Congress which members of Congress felt and which made it difficult to carry through difficult political issues where you needed the Congress's help if you were ever going to get your program put into effect" (1990, 139–40). So time and time again, Carter refused to budge on some element of an issue for the sake of the larger victory. Time and time again, he watched his proposals go down to defeat.

The members of Congress did not subscribe to Jimmy Carter's moral view of politics, and they felt bitter and threatened by his presidency, believing that following his lead would bring about their own defeat. They held that his brand of trusteeship politics ignored the realities of the electoral connection that kept them in office. As Erwin Hargrove has so eloquently argued, Carter believed that the point of presidential leadership was good policy. In a political system tilted in favor of policies that were expedient, constituency-oriented, costly, and good for the short run, Carter believed that it was the president's job to "push for policies that were problem-solving, goal-oriented, cost effective, and best in the long run" (1988a, xx). Although a noble goal, it was simply not a goal realizable in the Washington of the late seventies. Carter the outsider would not play the legislative game, and the result was that he could rarely win when the stakes were high.

Gerald Ford's successful achievements in restoring some of the public trust in the office of the presidency and reestablishing political stability in the nation had been essential for the nation's health. But according to Firestone & Ugrinsky (1993) they also obscured more mundane but equally pressing issues such as the economy, foreign policy, energy conservation, and environmental pollution. All of these areas demanded immediate attention, but the new president soon discovered that he was going to have difficulty in convincing the recalcitrant Congress to go along with his plans for solving them.

The Pardon, Part Two

Carter's difficulties with Capitol Hill began early—on his first day in office. On January 21, Carter issued his first executive order, pardoning virtually all Vietnam-era draft resisters and allowing those living abroad to return to the United States. Carter used the same presidential authority employed by Ford to pardon Nixon, and he got essentially the same response: immediate and strong criticism. Peace groups said that the president had not gone far enough, while veterans' groups called the pardon an insult to the millions who had served. Republican Senator Barry Goldwater of Arizona was so enraged that he described Carter's action as "the most disgraceful thing that a president has ever done" (as cited in Kaufman 1993, 30). In fact, only four days after the new president signed the order, the Senate narrowly defeated a resolution stating that Carter should not have issued the unconditional pardon.

The Bert Lance Affair

In the summer of 1977 the media revealed that Bert Lance, Carter's dear friend and director of the Office of Management and Budget, was under investigation for questionable banking and campaign practices. Specifically, it was charged that Lance had violated banking and securities laws when he was president of two different Georgia banks. The scandal quickly became the top story in the nation's capital, and Lance was forced to undergo three days of televised hearings conducted by the Senate Governmental Affairs Committee. Lance defended himself well in the hearings, and the controller of the currency found no criminal behavior. However, he did charge that Lance had engaged in "unsafe and unsound" banking practices. With Lance's image tarnished, many in Congress decided that he had been damaged enough by the fiasco that he should not be the chief financial adviser to a president who so stressed ethics and morality.

Carter himself was frustrated and angry when it became clear that Lance would not survive the scandal. Although Lance promptly resigned when Senate Majority Leader Robert Byrd told Carter that he would have to go, Burton Kaufman argues that no problem caused Carter greater grief or did more harm to his presidency in its first year than the scandal. Carter's unfailing support of his friend went well beyond the bounds of political prudence, raising questions about his political judgment and about his highly trumpeted commitment to the highest ethical standards. According to Garland Haas, in fact, "the whole affair provided one of the most damaging episodes for the Carter administration and Congress, and . . . increased the tension between Capitol Hill and the White House" (1992, 62). The president himself later wrote, "We first realized the adverse consequences of still being outsiders when we had to face the allegations raised against Bert Lance" (Carter 1982, 127).

The Water Projects: The Outsider Wins the Battle but Loses the War

Much of Carter's trouble with Congress stemmed from his vetoes of some of the Congressional Democrats' most cherished measures. In fact, before the ninety-fifth Congress had adjourned in October of 1978, Carter had vetoed nineteen different bills. Although all of his vetoes were sustained, the president nonetheless suffered a great deal of political damage as a result of his actions. His relationship with Congress, already tense, began to come apart.

One of the best examples of Carter the outsider winning the veto battle only to lose the war came about early in his term, in February 1977, when the president decided to cut water project funds from the federal budget. Without consulting any congressional leaders, he picked out eighteen of these projects and announced publicly that he had decided to cut off their federal funding. What Carter refused to understand was that several extremely powerful members of Congress (including the chairman of the Senate Finance Committee, the House majority leader, and the chairman of the Senate Armed Services Committee) had labored for years to get these projects approved and funded, and they were not about to give them up.

However, word came back from the White House that the issue was non-negotiable. From his earliest years in politics in Georgia, Carter had believed that his role was to protect the public good from powerful special interests, and he detested pork barrel legislation in any form. Therefore he refused to negotiate on the water projects, and the angry senators promptly handed Carter the first major legislative defeat of his new presidency; they simply added the water projects as an amendment to the public works bill, which the president was expected to sign. Jimmy Carter, however, would not back down, and he vetoed the bill; ultimately, half of the projects he targeted for elimination were funded. The House vote was substantially short of the support needed to override the president's veto, which he called a great victory. However, almost every Democratic leader had voted to override the president. According to Garland Haas (1992), Carter's "victory" in the fight over the water projects turned out to be a major political disaster for him; the injured congressmen soon took their revenge on his major legislative proposals—including his stimulus plan for saving the economy and his energy conservation program. As Carter himself later wrote, "The issue of the water projects was the one that caused the deepest breach between me and the Democratic leadership" (1982, 119).

Carter, the Water Projects, and the Economy

President Carter's first congressional payback came with his first major legislative initiative, an attempt to deal with the sagging economy. Although Ford had managed to cut the inflation rate nearly in half, Carter still inherited an economy in trouble. According to the polls, the state of the economy was the public's greatest concern, and for good reason. Unemployment was still above 7 percent, inflation was riding between 5 and 6 percent, and the federal government was running a $66 billion annual deficit. While Ford had focused on inflation as his primary economic target, Carter decided that unemployment was the most pressing problem, believing that if unemployment could be reduced, inflation would take care of itself.

Garland Haas reports in his 1992 book on the Carter administration that the president believed that in order to bring down unemployment, the economy had to be stimulated. So in January of 1977, he submitted his first policy initiative to Congress: an economic stimulus package amounting to $31 billion spread equally over two years. The package had several parts, including public works, public service employment, and a small but permanent reduction in taxes. The centerpiece of the stimulus for the first year, however, was something called a "rebate": a one-time cash grant of $50 for each taxpayer in the United States. The president estimated that the rebate would channel about $11 billion in purchasing power to consumers, which would increase spending and consumption, thereby creating jobs and reducing the deficit. Although key congressional leaders, as well as Carter's own treasury secretary and head of the Office of Management and Budget (OMB), disliked this proposed rebate, warning the president that it would most likely overstimulate the economy and increase inflation, they all supported it publicly.

With that support, the rebate passed the House quite easily—only to come to a screeching halt in the Senate. It had no chance of passing there without the support of the Senate Finance Committee chairman, Russell Long, and he was not about to support it; five of the water projects Carter was threatening to eliminate were located in Long's state. So Chairman Long indicated that he was delaying action on the rebate to give the president time for "thoughtful consideration" of the targeted water projects, a clear message that the president was in a losing confrontation with Congress unless he was willing to barter. However, Jimmy Carter refused the offer to trade the water projects for a vote on the tax refund. Barely three months later, the president withdrew his support for the rebate program, saying that the economy was doing better than expected and the payments were no longer needed. He ultimately did admit that political considerations were involved but refused to say that he had backed off because he feared political defeat.

Meanwhile, the Democratic congressional leaders who had supported the rebate against their better judgment had been left out on a limb by the president's actions, and they were furious. "It was a little less than fair to those of us who supported it against our better judgment and worked hard to get it passed" (Congressional Quarterly Almanac 1977, 95–96), complained the chairman of the House Ways and Means Committee. In one fell swoop, the new president had alienated most of the power structure in Congress: both those who had supported his rebate and those who had not. As one White House aide later put it, "There was where we first got the reputation—'you can't trust these people' " (Jones 1988, 134).

To make matters even worse, Carter later changed his tune on the economy. By early 1978, inflation was rising again, reaching 6.8 percent, and the president began claiming that inflation rather than unemployment was the top economic concern of the nation. This flip-flop again hurt the president. As he later wrote in his memoirs, "My advisers were right about the political damage. The obvious inconsistency in my policy during this rapid transition from stimulating the economy to an overall battle against inflation was to plague me for a long time" (Carter 1982, 77–78).

Moreover, Jimmy Carter's prescription for dealing with that inflation, which had surged to an annual rate of more than 11 percent by early fall of 1978 and was wreaking havoc on the American economy, was no help to him politically. He issued a call in October 1978 for voluntary wage and price guidelines and, acting on his belief that excessive government spending was one of the primary causes of inflation, also indicated that the budget deficit for 1979 would be held to $30 billion or less. This approach further angered and alienated both Democratic members of Congress and Democratic interest groups, who felt that the president had abandoned their traditional cause of helping the needy segments of American society by cutting spending. On both sides of the aisle in Congress Carter's cuts in defense, which amounted to $2.7 billion, were extremely problematic and controversial.

So when Carter later followed his announcement on the 1979 budget with a tax reform bill that called for a net $24.5 billion tax cut, Congress was in no mood to cooperate. The legislative body instead converted the reform bill into a reduction of the capital gains tax, sending the president a bill aimed primarily at easing the tax burden on middle- and upper-income groups. Carter signed the bill because he said it met his fiscal objectives, but unfortunately it did not slow inflation as Carter had hoped, instead stimulating the economy. By the third quarter of the year, the annual inflation rate had risen into double digits, and by the time President Carter had entered his third year in office, the rate of inflation had moved up to 13.3 percent, nearly double the rate he had inherited from Ford.

The increase in inflation created a myriad of other problems. Spending for entitlement programs soared because they were indexed to inflation. The trade deficit increased, the value of the dollar on foreign money markets declined, and foreign currency holders began to sell off their American dollars. A giant run on the dollar soon developed. To make matters worse, the president appointed Paul Volcker, a conservative Republican "monetarist," to be the new chairman of the Federal Reserve in the early fall of 1979. Volcker's solution for inflation was to increase interest rates and tighten the money supply. However, the tight money strategy only made matters worse, bringing on a recession and aggravating unemployment without making a dent in inflation. As the economy declined, revenues decreased and the budget deficit began to move even higher. With inflation reaching 20 percent, the president again announced his determination to hold the line on the budget deficit, promising a balanced budget for 1981. He also announced higher taxes on gasoline and a $14 billion spending cut. Again, the Democrats were furious that the president seemed willing to abandon his party's long-standing tradition of supporting programs that helped people without regard for budget deficits, while the Republicans complained that the deficit was too high.

In the end, the recession pushed up government spending for such things as unemployment insurance and reduced government tax receipts, undermining the balanced budget that the president had worked so hard for. Thus, all of the fiscal austerity and budget cutting for which Carter had angered Congress and the Democratic groups failed to bring the expected rewards.

Energy Conservation and a President Who Could Not Manage Government

When Jimmy Carter took office, he inherited an energy shortage that neither Nixon nor Ford had been able to solve and which was becoming increasingly severe. Even so, most Americans were acting as though there was no crisis. The Arab oil embargo had produced fear and even panic when it occurred, but once it was over, toward the end of 1974, Americans went right back to their wasteful ways. They seemed to believe that there could be no energy problem as long as gasoline was available to fill up their cars. By the time Carter took office, the country was importing more than half of the oil it consumed, and the new president soon decided that solving the energy crisis was at the top of his agenda. Jimmy Carter typically considered issues from the view of the long term, according to Burton Kaufman (1993), and from that vantage point, the energy problem was indeed a crisis that needed immediate attention. He believed that until the United States had a comprehensive energy program that would cut consumption and develop new energy sources at home, new and more serious shortages lay ahead, with catastrophic consequences for the American economy.

To address this, Carter's first task was to convince the American public that there was a problem. On April 8, 1977, he opened his energy campaign with a nationally televised address in which he sought to shock the nation with the seriousness of the energy problem, saying that it was the moral equivalent of war, "the greatest challenge that our country will face during our lifetime." Two days later he went before a joint session of Congress to present his energy proposal: a full-scale conservation program that also called for switching to other fuels such as coal when possible, and for producing more oil and gas from domestic sources. The specifics of the program, Garland Haas (1992) reports, included a tax on gas-guzzling cars, an increase in the price of all domestic oil to the level of foreign oil to encourage domestic production, and a standby gasoline tax that would go into effect if total gasoline consumption exceeded annual targets.

Although some pundits later pointed out that the acronym for "moral equivalent of war" was "meow," Burton Kaufman (1993) reports that the public response to the president's program was favorable. Congress's response, on the other hand, was not; members were particularly upset that the program had been developed almost completely in secret and without consulting or informing them beforehand. By midsummer of 1977, then, Congress had approved one of Carter's energy goals—the creation of the Department of Energy—but his energy bill was stalled in the Senate, where it had encountered fierce opposition. To make matters worse, says Garland Haas (1992), much of the public did not seem to care; polls showed that half the nation still refused to believe that an energy problem existed at all. Meanwhile, as a result of the nation's increasing dependence on high-priced foreign oil, double-digit inflation had hit the nation and the trade deficit soared to an unprecedented $26 billion.

Without strong public support, Carter's energy bill remained bogged down in Congress, and it was not until October 15, 1978 (the last day of the ninety-fifth Congress), that a compromise bill was finally passed. That bill was nothing like Carter's original proposal: Congress refused to discourage energy consumption through a tax on domestic crude oil, refused to tax businesses and utilities that did not convert to alternative fuels, and refused to tax domestic producers on the windfall profits that would result from decontrol of oil prices. Although several members of Congress urged Carter to veto the bill, claiming that the oil companies would merely gouge the public, he was anxious for an energy bill and signed it.

Once again, however, the president had been damaged. He had burned up much of his political capital in getting the package through Congress because of his failure to consult key members in advance. Carter could have undercut the opposition to his program by bringing congressional leaders into the preparation process and by seeking allies within the energy industry itself. But instead, viewing himself as a trustee of the nation's welfare who had to conduct his administration above the political fray and according to his perceptions of the national interest, Burton Kaufman (1993) argues, he refused to engage in the type of power-brokering employed by successful presidents since at least Woodrow Wilson. In addition, Democratic liberals would never forgive Carter for the ultimate decontrol of oil and gas, while environmentalists resented the emphasis on coal and the encouragement of nuclear power development. Indeed, according to Erwin Hargrove (1998), many of Carter's political advisers wondered whether the effort had been worth the cost. Even the president himself later likened the experience to "chewing on a rock" (Carter 1982, 91). As one White House staffer said, "The energy bill was the single greatest mistake we made in our first six months. When we couldn't pass it, people got the impression that the president just couldn't manage the government. We never recovered from that impression" (Haas 1992, 71).

Welfare Reform

As had happened with the energy bill, Carter's heavy-handed tactics with Congress ultimately sabotaged his goals for large-scale welfare reform. His experience as governor of Georgia had convinced him that the national welfare system was highly destructive of family values in America and that it was corrupting people by preventing them from working. Sensing that public opinion was favorable, the president decided to push hard to reform the welfare system. In August 1977 he sent to Congress a comprehensive reform package that would shift the financial burden from the cities to the states and Washington and would establish a single uniform payment across the nation. When an assistant told the president that he ought to go for an incremental rather than a comprehensive welfare reform package because the latter would be too expensive, Carter replied, "You know it's people like you that I've been sent to Washington to shape up" (in Hargrove 1988, 18). The president then submitted his comprehensive plan to Congress, and happily, it was applauded by both the press and the public. However, the bill floundered in Congress: the high cost of the program ($20 billion) was cited as the reason.

The president was not to be deterred, however, and in May 1979 he tried again with two bills that were less ambitious than the initial proposal. Although the House passed this version in November 1979, it was opposed by the Senate Finance Committee (recall the irritation of Chairman Long at having his prized water projects summarily axed by the president). The Senate took no action on the bill in 1979, and ultimately it was abandoned. Carter had botched an opportunity to reform the troubled and expensive welfare program.

The Energy Crisis and "National Malaise"

Carter had been able to pass an energy bill in late 1978, although it barely resembled his initial proposal to Congress. Nonetheless, momentous legislation had been proposed by the president and been passed by the Congress in an attempt to deal with the energy problem. Unfortunately, however, the president had "caved" on the bill, and the United States was still not mobilized in the face of threats to its energy security. Instead of taking action to reduce American dependence on foreign aid, the country was in fact becoming more vulnerable. That vulnerability was fully exposed—became an open wound, in fact—in January and February 1979. At that time, a revolution in Iran forced the country's shah, who was friendly to the United States, to flee his country and brought Iranian oil production nearly to a halt. Once again, the United States was faced with serious gasoline shortages. In short order, prices soared while motorists were forced to wait for hours in line to fill their gas tanks. By March and April, "Sorry, out of Gas" signs had become commonplace throughout the nation.

Congress, however, was in no mood to cooperate with Jimmy Carter, according to Garland Haas (1992). In response to the crisis, the president asked Congress for standby power to impose national gasoline rationing, but it turned him down—the House vote of 246 to 159 was a humiliating defeat—and the states were forced to find their own solutions. Congress also refused to support the president in early April, when he decided to go forward with the gradual phase-out of price controls on domestic oil. As expected, this move resulted in even higher prices for gasoline and heating oil. At the same time that Carter announced the price decontrol on oil, he had also proposed a modest windfall tax on the huge profits that American oil companies would reap from decontrol. However, once again Congress refused to cooperate, and the proposal became mired in congressional debate.

By early July, Haas argues, most Americans were apprehensive, angry, and contemptuous of Carter's efforts to deal with the crisis, and many suspected that the oil companies had engineered the shortage to raise prices. In Levittown, Pennsylvania, truckers barricaded highways and began the nation's first energy riot, resulting in two nights of violence that left one hundred people injured. As gasoline supplies dwindled, so did Carter's approval rating—from 50 percent in early January to 28 percent in June. Finally, on July 5, 1979, the president announced a nationwide address that would reveal to the nation his plans for dealing with the energy crisis. However, the speech was abruptly canceled the day before it was scheduled. Amidst the ensuing confusion—both at home and abroad—Jimmy Carter instead summoned his top aides and more than 130 national figures to a "national retreat" at the presidential lodge at Camp David to discuss the energy crisis, the mood of the nation, and his own political future.

Finally, on Sunday, July 15, a somber president addressed the nation, delivering what has become known as the "Malaise Speech." In his address, the president tied the energy crisis to his oft-repeated idea that the fundamental issue was the spiritual health of the people. He warned that Americans were suffering a "crisis of confidence" that posed a "fundamental threat to American democracy," a national malaise. The answer, Carter continued, was for Americans to "snap out of it" and to meet the challenges to the nation, the greatest of which was the energy problem (in Haas 1992, 84). After the speech, Carter dramatically reorganized his cabinet, even though he had promised at the beginning of his administration to keep the cabinet intact for four years to promote stability (he did keep it in place longer than any president in the twentieth century). Joseph Califano of Health, Energy & Welfare, Michael Blumenthal of Treasury, and Brock Adams of Transportation were all fired, while James Schlesinger of Energy and Attorney General Griffin Bell resigned. Unfortunately for Carter, Garland Haas (1992) argues, the shake up produced great concern in Washington and abroad, with many concluding that the president valued loyalty above competence.

After the speech, the percentage of Americans who believed that the energy shortage was a hoax fell from 74 percent to 65 percent. However, the speech accomplished little else, and during the remainder of 1979, gasoline supplies continued to dwindle and prices continued to rise, even though in the real world of oil production things were back to normal by July. In the world of fear—a world where President Carter kept warning of growing shortages—panic and hoarding quickly reopened the gap that higher levels of production were beginning to close. According to Anderson & Boyd (1983), by the middle of 1980, so much excess oil had been bought and hoarded that the amount held was twice that lost by the Iranian shutdown a year before. By then, however, OPEC knew that the West would tolerate oil priced at $40 per barrel, and its members quickly hoisted their contract prices into the mid-thirties to low forties, which then became the new norm.

While the second oil shock was driving prices up, Carter was still finding it difficult to get Congress to cooperate with his plans for saving the nation from the energy crisis. Finally, on October 23, 1979, Congress approved a standby plan to ration gasoline, if necessary. However, Congress still would not grant the president power to force electric utilities to switch from oil and natural gas to coal, and it was not until March 1980 that Congress finally enacted the windfall profits tax on domestic oil companies that Carter had asked for, although the bill that finally passed was watered down dramatically, creating considerably less revenue than the president wanted. Nonetheless, he hailed it as a victory.

Despite such bravado, the president had been badly damaged by his fights with Congress over energy, and as Garland Haas points out, he had given up his original approach to the energy problem—controlling demand—and instead had been forced to switch to the position of expanding supply. This shift caused critics to charge, rightfully, that Carter had backed away from his loudly proclaimed values of conservation and social equity.

The Carter Record with Congress

Indeed, President Carter repeatedly found himself backing away from his promises because of his troubles with Congress. He had assumed, for example, that he would have no problem establishing a consumer protection agency, an agency he had called one of his highest priorities in the heat of campaigning. However, the proposal was soundly rejected by the House and never even made it to the Senate, and consumer organizations complained that the president had done almost no lobbying on its behalf. Likewise, Carter failed to win passage of the AFL-CIO-backed common-site picketing bill. The bill was intended to make union organizing easier and of course was quickly overcome by the opposition of business. After the bill's defeat, according to Garland Haas (1992), Carter was again criticized for his halfhearted support of his proposal in Congress, but this time the criticism came from organized labor—a key constituency for a Democratic president who hoped to be reelected in 1980. Indeed, at the Democratic Midterm Conference in 1978, a "dissident budget" maintaining the current levels of social expenditures was proposed by the president of the United Auto Workers, clearly demonstrating the concerns of organized labor about Carter's conservative economic policies. By then, members of organized labor had had enough—they were in open rebellion against the administration.

Other legislative priorities also fell victim to the Carter administration's inability and unwillingness to work with the legislative branch. These included hospital cost controls aimed at reducing inflation, national health insurance, and tax reform. Of course, it would be a mistake to see the Carter administration as nothing but a series of legislative defeats. Charles Jones argues, for example, in his 1988 book, *The Trustee Presidency,* that Jimmy Carter did have more success with Congress as his administration improved its methods for formulating programs and building coalitions. Some of the most impressive accomplishments of the Carter administration include deregulation of the airline and trucking industries, civil service reform, Social Security reform (although it included an increase in payroll taxes of $227 billion over ten years), an increase in the minimum wage (although organized labor was furious with the president for the small size of the increase), and the creation of the Department of Education.

As impressive as these accomplishments are, one cannot help but wonder what more could have been accomplished if the Carter administration had had a better relationship with Congress. With Democrats controlling both branches of government, certainly great things were expected. However, much of Carter's agenda seemed decidedly conservative—an attack on interest group liberalism itself—and many in the liberal wing of the Democratic Party felt betrayed by the president according to Erwin Hargrove (1988). Carter himself later recognized and took responsibility for his relatively limited success with Congress, saying "There is not doubt that I could have done some things better . . . it would have been advisable to have introduced our legislation in much more careful phases—not in such a rush . . . now I can also see more clearly the problems we created for the legislators. In looking over the list of our proposals that were approved, it was hard to find many goodies for the members to take home" (in Hargrove 1988, 67).

Of course, the Carter years were also the product and the victim of the post-Vietnam, post-Watergate era. It was the time in America that gave birth to a fiercely independent and rebellious Congress, one determined to limit the powers of the presidency. It was also the time that brought a consummate outsider to power as president—the kind of man least able and willing to understand and work with a renegade legislative branch.

Foreign Policy

Considering his troubles with Congress, it is no wonder that the great successes of the Carter administration cited by most historians occurred mostly in foreign policy. As we will learn in chapter 4, President Carter did have several grand successes in the international arena, particularly on problems that were universally viewed as incredibly difficult. Because Jimmy Carter believed that it was his mission to take on these hard problems, he forged spectacular results, including the Panama Canal treaties, peace between Egypt and Israel, and formal recognition of the People's Republic of China. In addition, Jimmy Carter ushered in a new era in American foreign policy—an era in which idealism would provide the basis for American power in the world.

Thus, according to Friedbert Pfluger (1989), American foreign policy in the Carter era was founded upon a "Wilsonian" world view that valued peace, cooperation, and human rights as paramount. Jimmy Carter quickly acted on this new emphasis in foreign policy, protesting publicly against the persecutions of the Charter 77 human rights group in Czechoslovakia only six days after his inauguration. One day later, the State Department published another declaration in which the administration openly took the side of the Soviet dissident Andrei Sakharov. And this was only the beginning; throughout his administration, Jimmy Carter continued to emphasize human rights in his foreign policy. Although this new tack in American foreign policy was to have its ups and downs during Carter's presidency, there is no question that he helped to usher in a new era in American foreign policy and in the way the world conducts its business. Carter's human rights philosophy is now widely endorsed by Republicans as well as Democrats, and to this day, the topic occupies a primary location on the world agenda of international politics.

Carter and the Failure of Détente

Once again, however, Carter's arrogant moralizing about what was best not only for the nation but also for the world and his refusal to consider com-

promising on what he saw as a fundamental principle led to foreign policy failures that were as disappointing as those in the domestic arena, and even more
dangerous. The greatest of these failures was Carter's hand in bringing about
the final downfall of détente with the Soviet Union. The new president clearly
hoped to carry on the policy of détente with the Soviet Union; he said as
much in a letter to Soviet leader Leonid Brezhnev just six days after moving
into the White House. In fact, Carter wanted to use détente not only to maintain the arms control legacy of the SALT I agreement but also to convince the
Soviets to go even further and agree to massive cuts in the size of both countries' nuclear arsenals.

However, Carter and his advisers believed that the president could speak
out against Soviet infringements of human rights without jeopardizing relations between the two superpowers. They were clearly wrong; the first clash
over human rights between Washington and Moscow occurred only a week
after Carter took office. The administration's public protest about the treatment of the Czechoslovakian intellectuals, as well as its statement calling Soviet dissident Andrei Sakharov an outspoken champion of human rights,
infuriated the Soviets. How could they not be angry at the administration's
public warning that any effort to intimidate Sakharov would conflict with accepted international standards of human rights? In their view, the Carter administration had broken a long-standing though unwritten rule between the
two superpowers not to comment on each other's internal affairs.

As Anatoli Dobrynin, the Soviet ambassador to the United States, met
with Secretary of State Cyrus Vance to protest the administration's actions,
the Soviets intensified their repression of political dissidents at home. Meanwhile, according to Burton Kaufman (1993), the Carter administration, ignoring the growing strain in Soviet-American relations, was attempting to
mount its diplomatic effort to win a new arms reduction agreement with the
Soviets. Of course the Soviets responded bitterly to these initiatives, even
though they badly wanted a new SALT agreement. Kaufman reports that
Brezhnev rejected the American proposals without offering any counterpro-
posals and canceled the rest of the negotiating sessions that had been scheduled. Just a few short weeks after taking office, the Carter administration had
made a mess of U.S.-Soviet relations.

The United States's allies in Western Europe were quick to express their
dismay. European leaders found Carter's approach to the human rights issue
preachy, and many believed that the president was unnecessarily provoking

Moscow. In fact, French President Valery Giscard d'Estaing gave a magazine interview in which he accused Carter of having "compromised the process of détente" (Kaufman 1993, 49) by his clumsiness in dealing with Brezhnev. By July of 1977, things had gotten so bad that West German chancellor Helmut Schmidt traveled to Washington, carrying a message from the leaders of the Common Market countries urging Carter to moderate his campaign on human rights. As if to confirm such urgings, former Undersecretary of State George Ball observed in *Time* magazine that the human rights campaign "had become a stuck needle, getting in the way of things which might be more important in the long run" (1977, 8–23).

It did indeed get in the way. Although Carter did moderate his stance a bit on human rights in response to the dip in relations between the Soviet Union and the United States, he predictably refused to back away from his stance on human rights completely. While the president finally achieved a SALT II agreement with the Soviets after several more delays, it was, as Gaddis Smith has described it, "a mere instant of good feeling, evanescent as a soap bubble, the slightest of pauses in a deteriorating relationship" (1986, 208). Quite simply, the American relationship with the Soviets was crumbling. What the president wanted was a reasoned and measured policy toward the Soviet Union, one that balanced outrage at Soviet misconduct with the imperatives of ending the cold war. What he achieved, however, was a policy "strewn with contradictions and inconsistencies," according to Burton Kaufman in his 1993 book on the Carter presidency (94).

The last bricks in the wall holding up the pretense of détente finally came down when on Christmas day of 1979, the Soviet Union invaded Afghanistan to provide support for a weak pro-Communist regime there. This action appeared to indicate a renewed Soviet expansionism and the reopening of the cold war, and the president finally admitted that it was no longer possible "to do business as usual with the Soviet Union" (in Haas 1992, 112). In fact, Jimmy Carter felt personally betrayed in his efforts to win ratification of SALT II, so much so that, according to Erwin Hargrove (1988), some of his closest aides felt that the invasion changed Carter—that it steeled and toughened him. Many in Congress and across the nation believed that this change had come too little and too late, however, and that the invasion was a result of the impression of American weakness abroad, a weakness that had emboldened the Soviets to take aggressive action. For Carter, it was a lesson. He abandoned the goal of cooperation with the Soviets, and confrontation became the name of the game. Bent upon punishing the Soviets, argues Burton Kaufman (1993), the president ignored the counsel of his foreign policy advisers and adopted every punitive measure suggested to him, regardless of its immediate or long-term consequences. As a result, U.S.-Soviet relations became mortgaged to the Soviets' withdrawal from Afghanistan, dealings between Moscow and Washington became even more tense, and ratification of the SALT II agreement (one of Carter's highest priorities since taking office) was indefinitely postponed.

Congress and Carter's Defense Policy

Equally disappointing and dangerous was the series of problems arising between Carter and Congress over his defense policy. The first battle came over the president's pledge to withdraw U.S. troops from South Korea. Because he saw no useful military purpose for American troops in Korea and because he considered the politically repressive government of South Korea to be morally repugnant, he announced shortly after taking office that he would withdraw the troops. At home and abroad, the news was not greeted with enthusiasm: the Japanese were afraid of instability in the region and were upset that the president had made his decision without even consulting them. At home, foreign policy hard-liners and military officials feared that the pullout might encourage the North to launch another invasion. In fact, several influential Democratic senators—including John Glenn, Sam Nunn, Henry Jackson, and Hubert Humphrey—joined Republicans in opposing the president, and even Carter's senior advisers (with the exception of National Security Adviser Zbigniew Brzezinski) were against the plan. With opposition to troop removal so great, says Burton Kaufman (1993), the president wisely deferred implementation and ultimately withdrew the request for troop withdrawal. However, he had started out on the wrong foot with key members of Congress on defense.

Things only got worse when Carter decided to scrap the development of a new class of B-1 bombers. For more than a decade, the fight had raged in Washington over whether to build this new bomber as a replacement for the United States's aging fleet of B-52s. Over a period of five months, Carter met with defense experts to assess the military value of the B-1 bomber, and Burton Kaufman (1993) argues that most in Washington expected the president to approve at least some. But at the end of June, the president shocked reporters at a news conference by announcing that he was discontinuing production of the new weapons system. Never before had a president killed so large a program so close to production.

If the president had only done something to soften the impact of his announcement on congressional and public attitudes, the troubles and criticism he received probably would not have been so great. Kaufman (1993) argues that he could have sought some Soviet concessions in return for elimination of the B-1 program, or he could simply have delayed any action until the SALT II talks had been concluded. As it was, Carter's timing could not have been worse in cutting the program just two days after the House had voted down a measure canceling production of the bomber. Many accused him of purposely trying to embarrass Congress, and they also charged the president with again failing to provide for national security. As the fall of 1977 approached, there was a growing perception, even among Democrats, that the administration's foreign policy was seriously flawed. By the end of 1977, more than 51 percent of Americans disapproved of the way Carter was handling foreign policy, according to a Harris poll.

The charge of not being firm enough on national defense was one that would haunt Jimmy Carter throughout his administration and well into the 1980 elections. When he announced in April 1978 that he was deferring production of the neutron bomb (against the unanimous recommendations of his chief advisers), a new political storm broke out, both in the United States and abroad. On Capitol Hill, Senator Sam Nunn warned that cancellation of the program would "place in the minds of the Soviets an image of a timid and hesitant America which lacks the courage to confront the difficult choices ahead," and the Senate minority leader told reporters that cancellation would be "another in a long line of national defense mistakes" (Kaufman 1993, 95) on the part of the president. In Europe, according to Burton Kaufman (1993), West Germany's chancellor, Helmut Schmidt, charged the president with betrayal while other NATO leaders began privately to question American leadership. Moreover, by the spring of 1979, 54 percent of the people questioned by the president's own pollster thought that the position of the United States in the world was "fair" or "poor," while only 13 percent of the interviewees thought the nation's position in the world was "growing stronger." Sixty-two percent believed that it was "becoming weaker" (Kaufman 1993, 151).

Meanwhile, things did not look good in the Senate for the SALT II treaty that the Carter administration had worked so hard and so long to attain. Once again, the president was bashed for "giving away the store" to the Soviets. Defense hard-liners such as Senator Henry Jackson kept attacking SALT on the grounds that it weakened the United States's defense posture, while liberal Democrats on the other side argued that it did not go nearly far enough. As hearings on the treaty continued into August, the debate over SALT turned from the details of the agreement to the size of the military budget. Kaufman (1993) reports that this occurred when Georgia senator Sam Nunn, widely respected on Capitol Hill as an expert on arms control, declared that he would not vote for the SALT treaty without a commitment by the president to increase the defense budget by 5 percent after inflation. In the end, the weakened president had to accede to the increased spending, which jeopardized his efforts to keep inflation under control. The Soviet invasion of Afghanistan in December prompted the president to remove the treaty from Senate consideration, but it is doubtful that it would have passed anyway.

When Cyrus Vance, Carter's secretary of state, resigned in the spring of 1980, the news media seized upon it as evidence that the president's foreign policy was in a quagmire. "As things now stand," *Newsweek* reported, "the president's uncertain diplomatic strategy has left allies perplexed, enemies unimpressed, and the nation as vulnerable as ever in an increasingly dangerous world" (1980, 42–53). More and more, it seemed that President Carter was becoming a prisoner of events that he could not control.

The Iranian Hostage Crisis

This impression of a weak president who was led by events that he could not control came to a head with the actions of November 4, 1979. On that day, a group of Iranian militants seized the American embassy in Tehran and took sixty Americans hostage. The militants had been pushed to action by a seventy-nine-year-old Moslem fundamentalist, the Ayatollah Ruhallah Khomeini, who was in Western Europe fomenting opposition to the shah. While the mob surrounding the embassy chanted hatred for America, the bound and blindfolded hostages were forced to parade around the embassy compound. Then the captors demanded that the American authorities send the exiled shah—who had arrived in the United States for medical treatment just two weeks before—back to Iran to face trial for "crimes against the Iranian people" (Haas 1992, 109–10).

At first, the American public rallied around their president, who made the hostage crisis his own personal responsibility—refusing to hit the campaign trail until the hostages were safely home, as well as refusing to light the Christmas lights on the White House Christmas tree until he knew that they were free. However, as the months passed without a resolution to the crisis, the tide of public opinion began to turn against the president. He had made the hostage crisis a front-and-center issue, and he had staked his own personal reputation on bringing the hostages home. His failure to bring them home confirmed the impression of Carter as inept, incompetent, and weak. As one campaign aide to Carter later recalled, this approach "got to be a real trap" as the hostage crisis wore on (Jones 1988, 190).

Indeed, Gaddis Smith (1986) argues that the fifty-two hostages still held captive in Tehran symbolized the ineffectiveness of the president and of the United States under his leadership. In addition, the perception set in with the American public that Carter was using Iran for political purposes. Then came the botched rescue mission, and that was the end for Jimmy Carter. He was attacked from all sides over the United States's lack of military preparedness and over his unilateral decision to proceed with the operation. At the same time, the president was scoured for not acting more forcefully to end the conflict. The hostage crisis had clearly revealed to Khomeini, other radical militants around the world, U.S. enemies and allies, and the American people alike that there was a real element of vulnerability in the United States. Americans became convinced that President Carter was weak, and that the president's weakness had brought down America.

The 1980 Elections

As the fall of 1979 and the presidential election season approached, Jimmy Carter found himself dogged by charges that he had permitted the nation to drift because of his weakness, ineffectiveness, and incompetence. By the summer of 1979 an Associated Press-NBC Poll showed that only 19 percent of those interviewed rated Carter's performance favorably—the lowest job approval rating given a president since Harry Truman in the midst of the Korean War and Richard Nixon in the depths of Watergate. According to Garland Haas, Carter, "like Lewis Carroll's Cheshire Cat, was fading away, leaving only a smile behind" (1992, 116). That weakness made the president a sitting duck for challenges within his own party for the Democratic presidential nomination. In no time at all, Governor Jerry Brown of California and

Senator Edward "Ted" Kennedy had jumped into the race. Kennedy was clearly the most serious challenger for Carter. Although he had fairly consistently supported Carter on Capitol Hill, the senator decided to run against the president after his "Malaise Speech." According to Garland Haas, that speech had deeply upset Kennedy, who believed it violated the spirit of America—the things Kennedy believed the American people wanted to do and feel about themselves. Immediately following his entry into the race, polls showed him strongly favored over the president.

Ironically, Kennedy's popularity declined after he had become a candidate. Once he had officially announced, he was open to the usual intense scrutiny that presidential candidates must endure, and there was plenty to be found in his past for people to be concerned about. The "character issue" became a major stumbling block for Kennedy, mostly as a result of the famous 1969 incident at Chappaquiddick Island in Massachusetts. In addition, Garland Haas argues that Kennedy was significantly behind Carter in terms of preparedness for the campaign: when he announced his intention to run he had no organization in place and little money raised. Also, after the crisis in Iran exploded, the president had become a rallying point for Americans, and his ratings shot up. Carter's strategy of refusing to campaign until the hostages came home—in essence campaigning by staying in Washington and being presidential—was quite effective initially, and it soon seemed that Kennedy would not be able to overcome Carter's lead in delegates.

Then came the abysmal failure of Carter's rescue attempt of the Iranian hostages in April, and the tables began to turn for Kennedy. Although by that point it was mathematically impossible for Kennedy to catch up in the delegate count, he believed that a mood could develop in the Democratic Party to take the nomination away from Carter. After winning five of the eight primaries on Super Tuesday, June 3, Kennedy announced that he would pursue the nomination right into the convention. Although he removed his name from nomination shortly after the convention opened (when it became clear that he could not win), the divisiveness within the party was not healed by the end of the party gathering in New York. Not only did Kennedy forces believe that Carter could not win the general election, they also forced the addition of controversial planks that Carter did not like to the platform. To the last moment of the convention, most of the Kennedy delegates continued to chant, "We want Ted." To add insult to injury, Kennedy did not use the opportunity presented by his platform speech to endorse Jimmy Carter.

On the Republican side, a wide field of contenders emerged, including former Treasury Secretary John Connally, former CIA Director George Bush, Tennessee senator Howard Baker, former vice presidential candidate Robert Dole, and—of course—former California governor Ronald Reagan. Even with this rather large group of contenders, however, Reagan was the clear favorite, and by early summer he had the nomination all sewn up: he had moved steadily through the largest number of Republican primaries in history, and he had won twenty-nine and lost only six (all to George Bush). In addition, between the time of Bush's concession to Reagan in May until the Republican Convention in July, Reagan wisely worked hard to heal party wounds. Most significant, he agreed to help the losers pay off nearly $3 million in campaign debts at a series of Republican unity dinners. Thus, as Garland Haas describes it, the Republican Convention was to be more like a coronation than a convention, and it was. Reagan selected George Bush as his running mate, mended fences with former President Ford, and became the nominee of a united party.

Meanwhile, Jimmy Carter entered the fight still trying to bring his party together. The president had been badly damaged by the Kennedy challenge, and fighting Kennedy for the nomination had been very costly for his own personal campaign and for the party generally. Both Carter and the party lost many opportunities to raise money and to prepare for the general election. Not only was Carter weakened by the Kennedy challenge and a divided party, he was also damaged by his own record in office. Inflation was still in the double digits and by January 1980 had reached a record high of 20 percent. Unemployment had risen to almost 8 percent nationwide and reached as high as 20 percent in some areas. Interest rates were at their highest level since the Civil War. In addition, the public was now growing impatient with the Iranian hostage crisis as it reached its tenth month without resolution. Unsurprisingly, Carter received the lowest approval rating ever recorded for an incumbent president during the summer of 1980 (Haas 1992, 153).

Carter's campaign advisers decided that they could not allow the election to become a referendum on the Carter administration. So the president abandoned the "Rose Garden" strategy, went on the road, and began to campaign actively, hitting hard at Reagan's extremely conservative and ideological issue positions, his inexperience in national affairs, and his tendency to shoot from the hip. On the defense issue, particularly, Carter pounded away at Reagan, warning that if Reagan were elected president, he would set off a massive nuclear arms race that could lead to war with the Soviet Union. Reagan himself helped Carter's cause with a series of gaffes that made him look inept and inexperienced, including proclaiming that he was in favor of reestablishing "official" diplomatic relations with Taiwan (which sent the Chinese into fits), attributing 80 percent of air pollution to trees, and calling unemployment insurance a prepaid vacation plan for freeloaders.

According to Garland Haas, the criticism that followed each of Reagan's gaffes never seemed to make a dent in his popularity with the public, at least in part because of his ability to laugh at himself and to appear optimistic and decisive. Further, Carter had his own scandals to contend with. First was the "BillyGate" affair, in which questions were raised regarding the relationship between the president's brother and the government of Libya. Then came the "Stealth Disclosure," wherein Reagan charged that the Defense Department had breached national security in leaking details about the secret warplane in order to benefit Carter politically. Finally, Carter began to make personal attacks on Reagan, implying that he was a racist who would split the nation apart. These personal attacks, says Haas, undermined one of Carter's strongest assets—his reputation for compassion and fair play—and made him look nasty and petty.

To make matters worse, the Reagan campaign attacked Jimmy Carter where he was weakest, faulting the president for timid foreign policy and failed leadership. Reagan charged that the Carter administration had allowed U.S. military capabilities to become dangerously weak, and that Carter was "totally oblivious" to the Soviet Union's drive toward world domination. He raked the president and the Democrat-controlled Congress for the state of the economy and pledged to deal with inflation through supply-side economics (specifically, an incredibly popular three-year, 30 percent tax cut for individuals as well as businesses). Finally he asked, "Are you better off than you were four years ago?" In the end, very few could say yes. Add to this the fact that John Anderson's campaign as an Independent was stealing support away from Carter, and the fact that traditional Democratic allies (for example, the Teamsters' Union, which endorsed Reagan) had become increasingly cool to Carter, and it appeared that the president had little chance of being reelected. In yet another blow, interest rates went up and the stock market went down in the week before the election.

Nonetheless, going into that final week of the campaign, the election was widely viewed as too close to call. In fact, most polls indicated that Americans generally were unenthusiastic about both candidates. Then on Sunday, November 2, just two days before the election, the Iranian parliament voted to release the hostages if the United States met several specific conditions. Carter, believing that it might still be possible to have the hostages released before Election Day, cut short his campaign to return to the White House. However, some of the conditions posed by the Iranians were so legally complicated that they required further negotiations, and the hostages were not freed. Meanwhile, Reagan was quoted in the press as saying, "I believe that this administration's foreign policy helped create the entire situation that made their kidnap possible. And I think the fact that they've been there that long is a humiliation and a disgrace to this country" (Drew 1981, 324).

So, in a landslide that astonished even his most optimistic supporters, according to Garland Haas, Ronald Reagan soundly defeated Jimmy Carter with a plurality of nearly nine million popular votes. Indeed, Reagan carried forty-four states, winning 489 electoral votes to just 49 for Carter. It was the second straight election—but only the fourth in the twentieth century—in which an incumbent president was defeated for reelection, but in this case it was the defeat of the first elected president following Watergate.

Even in the end, Carter the outsider managed to obliquely alienate his party; he formally conceded to Reagan early in the evening while almost half of the states were still going to the polls. West Coast Democrats reported that after the president conceded, thousands of voters left the voting lines and countless others never showed up, and several Democratic candidates in the region suffered defeat (or believed that they did) because of it. Once again, Jimmy Carter had shown his disdain and disinterest in the welfare of his party and other Democratic candidates; he was a true outsider to the end.

The Failure of the Politician Who Was above Politics

Jimmy Carter was elected president of the United States because he was an outsider. He promised honesty, integrity, and competency in government, and he told the American people that he would never lie to them. This was what America thought it wanted and needed: a president who was above politics. As one of the president's closest aides later recalled,

We used to joke that the worst way to convince the president to go along with your position was to say this would help you politically, because . . . he wanted to be a different type of president. He was elected somehow to be a different kind of president. He was running against the sort of system of in- side deals and so forth. He saw himself as above that system . . . he liked to make a decision on the merits and check the decision box that seemed to him the best direction for the nation to go . . . that was an enormous strength and has an enormous amount of intellectual integrity. It was also however a liability at times because you can't always simply check the right box. (Har- grove 1988, 17)

Indeed, Jimmy Carter paid the price for being a politician who was above politics. As an outsider who believed his role was to promote the public good over private interests, he refused to barter with members of Congress. As a man who could not wait to tackle all the nation's problems, he failed to set clear priorities and to develop political strategies to achieve them. Thus he sent too much to Congress in the first year, and he did not calculate what to initiate and when. He launched major domestic initiatives without realizing how controversial those issues were, and he did not develop the extensive leg- islative campaigns necessary for success. As an outsider who was above politics as usual, Carter did not like politicians and he made no effort to cultivate them. In fact, he acted as though he did not need them, when in fact he did. Finally, Jimmy Carter was a political neophyte who believed that if he always chose what he believed to be the "right" course, then he would be politically rewarded for it. He was therefore a man, according to Erwin Hargrove, who did not take care to safeguard his professional image in Washington or with the public.

For all of these reasons, Carter's presidency was much less than it should have been. In the end, his inability—or refusal—to exercise strategic leader- ship by joining his good ideas and good intentions to thoughtful calculations about political strategies and feasibility quite simply led the American people to believe that Jimmy Carter was not a leader at all. Elected by the slimmest of margins in the first place, he did not have the political mandate from the peo- ple to be a "trustee" president or to force Congress to do his bidding. He had come to power promising to solve all of America's problems, and he clearly set himself up for a fall, since such a thing was not possible. The final irony was that he became the scapegoat for all unresolved national and international problems. According to Erwin Hargrove, everybody—from politicians to in- terest groups, the media, and the public—piled the blame on him. Indeed,

Garland Haas reports that after the election, two of every five people who voted for Reagan explained their choice as a dislike of Carter.

Not only did Carter pay personally for his perceived weakness and lack of leadership, so did his party. As the nominal head of his party, Carter weakened the overall image of the Democrats. Carter's perceived weakness also prompted a strong challenge against him from within his own party, dividing the party and destroying Democratic unity. Jimmy Carter's very nature as an outsider caused great friction between the president and the legislators in Congress—a Congress that was controlled by Democrats and which received public scorn for its apparent inability to deal with the problems pressing on the nation. Being an outsider within his own party meant that the president did little and thought little about helping his party or its candidates (as demonstrated by his early concession in 1980). As Erwin Hargrove argues, Carter was a policy politician, "an elected politician who concentrates on policy work and who makes the achievement of good policy his main goal. His metier is issue politics more than party or institutional politics, and his forte is issue leadership rather than the leadership of institutions or organizations" (1988a, xix).

So the party that selected Jimmy Carter as its presidential nominee in 1976 paid the price for that selection, starting in 1980. The Republicans won control of the Senate for the first time since 1954—something that not even the GOP had dreamed possible. With Republicans winning control of the White House and the Senate, picking up thirty-three seats in the House and finishing with a net gain of four governorships at the state level, it was widely assumed that at long last the nation was witnessing the demise of the party system dominated by the New Deal coalition. As Garland Haas has written, "It seemed that a party realignment was about to occur and that a Republican Party majority was about to emerge" (1992, 171). "For the first time in a generation," wrote David Broder in the *Washington Post*, "it is sensible to ask whether we might be entering a new political era—an era of Republican dominance" (1980).

But the damage of Carter's weakness—the price that had to be paid for a president who was an outsider, a president who would not play the game— was not limited to the damage done to Carter himself and to his party. The nation also had to pay the price—in opportunities lost to make dramatic changes at home, in the loss of American stature in the world, and in the nation's inability to fully restore its confidence in a time of great crises. Thus, what the nation thought it wanted—a moralizing outsider who promised never to tell a lie—was not what the nation needed. Jimmy Carter's notion of his role as trustee suited the post-Watergate public mood, but what went with that role proved that an outsider could not govern: he put himself above the fray instead of working with the other institutions of government; he arrogantly assumed that he knew what was best for the nation; and he insisted upon doing things his way or not at all— and usually it was not at all. When it became clear that a moralizing outsider could not govern, the people turned away from him, claiming him incompetent and weak. He was not really what the nation needed because, ultimately, he could not get the job done.

In many ways, the Carter presidency was a tragedy. There is no doubt that Jimmy Carter came to power in a difficult time and faced a Herculean task: he had to deal with the wounds of Vietnam and Watergate, a breakdown of the historically strong party system, and dramatic changes in Congress and its role in American government. All of these things had worked to compromise the power of the presidency and made governing much more difficult. Yet Jimmy Carter did have his successes even with these limitations—the Panama Canal treaties, energy legislation, and the historic peace accord between Israel and Egypt that was brokered at Camp David. He had successfully continued Ford's work of healing the wounds that remained from Vietnam and Watergate. In addition, Carter must be given credit for his attempt to focus the nation's attention on pressing problems that it would rather—to its detriment—have ignored. All of these accomplishments should have been heralded by Americans. Instead, the events of Jimmy Carter's presidency projected an image to the American people, according to Burton Kaufman, of "a hapless administration in disarray and of a presidency that was increasingly divided, lacking in leadership, ineffective in dealing with Congress, incapable of defending America's honor abroad, and uncertain about its purpose, priorities, and sense of direction" (1993, 3). Jimmy Carter was seen as weak, and so America was feared to be weak. This weakness invited insecurity from allies and aggression from enemies. This weakness paved the way for Ronald Reagan. This weakness continued to undermine the crumbling confidence of a nation facing its limits for the very first time. In the end, Jimmy Carter's service as a trustee, outsider president was a disservice to the nation: it was a failed presidency.

4

American Foreign Policy in the Seventies

Coming to Terms with the Limits of American Power

IN AN INTERVIEW shortly after his election in 1968, Richard Nixon told Theodore White that although the American public was obsessed with the problems of Vietnam, the war would end there someday and the world would still be waiting for attention. What did the president-elect mean by this statement? Well, he said that the first problem was the relationship between the Soviet Union and the United States—not just the hard issues of missile systems, nuclear disarmament, or tensions in the Middle East—but simply setting up a carefully designed system for continuing dialogue. He said that America had been neglecting Europe, and that the Middle East cried out for a solution, as did Latin America. Then, he said, there was the China problem. The new president promised that he was looking forward to starting a dialogue with the Chinese.

As these early statements demonstrate, Richard Nixon ascended to the presidency with foreign policy at the forefront of his mind, and not only because of the ongoing war in Vietnam. As every modern president has understood, Nixon knew that foreign policy would be the one area where he could really command and control. Thus, it is no surprise that Richard Nixon's greatest successes as president (or perhaps those best remembered) came in the area of foreign policy. This is in part the result of his own personal interest in and command of the details of international affairs, and in part because Nixon came to power in a transitional period both in the world and at home. Times of transition often offer a unique opportunity for foreign policy innovations, and according to Joan Hoff (1994), Nixon took advantage of those opportunities. Indeed, his administration ushered in an era of dramatic changes and innovative approaches in foreign policy, including détente with the Soviet Union and an opening of relations with China.

To truly understand the new thinking that Richard Nixon and Henry Kissinger, Nixon's primary partner in foreign affairs, created in foreign policy, we must first explore the world in which Nixon came to power. Immediately following World War II, the United States was the dominant power in the world, and many said that this period was the beginning of an "American century." But the time of American hegemony was not to last even thirty years; by the 1960s, America's role was proving to be too costly, in terms of both lives and resources. When Nixon came to power in 1969 the era of American dominance was already in the early stages of decline, and according to John Robert Greene (1992), the nation had to face that it could no longer do everything in the world that it wanted to do. The economies of the members of the Western Alliance had rebounded (with American assistance) faster than any thought possible after the war. Not only did they thus begin to challenge American economic control, but they also began to show signs of political independence, as did developing nations, which were becoming more nationalistic and demanding. In addition, while the Soviet Union was fast approaching military parity with the United States after a six-year crash program of missile building, the oil-producing nations were banding together in a threatening way. In the end, the limits on American power and resources were becoming more and more obvious, argues Michael Genovese (1990), as was brought home most pointedly and painfully by the inability to win the war in Vietnam.

Nixon attempted to deal with what was fast becoming an overextension of American power by an orderly and controlled readjustment of American foreign policy. As Tad Szulc has said, "during the Nixon years the United States went a long distance to adjust its position to the global realities of the 1970s" (1978, 7–8). President Nixon had a vision of a "structure of world peace" (Szulc 1978) that was bold and innovative and was based essentially upon the notion of a balance of power in the world (as opposed to American hegemony). According to Greene, the president recognized and accepted that over the preceding decade the world had changed from a bipolar to a multipolar one, with several seats of power. With this acceptance of the limits of American power, and with his new structure of world affairs, Michael Genovese argues that Richard Nixon worked to reshape the world and America's place in it.

What were the elements of Nixon's new foreign policy? In 1969, the president unveiled the "Nixon Doctrine" of foreign policy—something that he called "Peace through Partnership." The central thesis of this doctrine was that the United States would participate in the defense and development of allies and friends, but that America could not—would not!—be responsible for all of the defense of the free nations of the world. The president pledged that America would help where that assistance could make a real difference and where it was considered to be in its best interest. The United States would not abdicate its leadership, but others would have to bear more of the costs—"hegemony on the cheap," as David Calleo (1982) has called it. The Nixon Doctrine therefore envisioned a reduced role for the United States in the affairs of the world, and the president took concrete action in implementing this new doctrine: according to Michael Genovese, the defense budget was stabilized, the draft was eliminated, and an all-volunteer army was instituted.

In addition to this approach of "partnership" (as opposed to the old roles of leader and follower), Nixon's new strategy for peace emphasized the elements of strength and negotiation. Strength required that the United States maintain its place and its credibility in the world even as it moved from leader to partner. Negotiation meant an acceptance of the power of Communist nations in international relations and, thus, the beginnings of détente with the Soviet Union and improved relations with China. United States foreign policy from President Truman to Johnson had been conducted with an amazing amount of continuity: the waging of a cold war that embraced the strategy of global containment of the Soviet Union based upon a realpolitik (power politics) approach and an emphasis on anti-Communism. Specifically, Western Europe was revived and rearmed, a string of anti-Soviet alliances was to be organized around the world, a hostile face toward China would of course be maintained, and the United States must forever strive to maintain superiority in nuclear weapons over the Soviet Union. Ultimately, argues Jerel Rosati (1993), this foreign policy approach led to such concepts as the "domino theory" and the continuing escalation of American intervention in the Vietnam War.

Vietnam, however, had ripped apart the national consensus on containment as America's primary foreign policy goal. The United States's apparent inability to repel the Communists in Vietnam brought into question its ability to contain the much more powerful and aggressive Communist threats from China and the Soviet Union. Meanwhile, at home, the nation was deeply torn over American activities in Indochina, and those divisions were becoming increasingly bitter and violent. Not only was there little confidence in the United States that the country could conduct an effective foreign policy, states William Hyland (1987), but America's international position in the world was deteriorating badly.

President Nixon therefore diverged from the long-standing American foreign policy tradition of complete and total containment. Instead, he promised a willingness to negotiate American points of difference in a fair and businesslike manner with Communist countries. To this end, Nixon promised that the U.S. would "continue to probe every available opening that offers a prospect for better East-West relations" (1970). Thus, power rather than anti-Communist ideology would guide American actions and responses in order to secure stability in the world. This meant that the United States could negotiate with the Soviet Union in areas that could lead to mutual benefit. It meant that some Communist nations could even be befriended (China) in order to contain the threat of other Communist countries. And it meant that American interests, not morality or ideological fervor, would now take precedence in foreign affairs.

Dubya shd read this

The Soviet Union and Détente

Nixon's ambitious new plan for peace and stability in the world was a complex and complicated program that required victory on both short-term and long-term goals. As American dominance declined and the Soviets approached parity in strategic arms with the United States, argues Michael Genovese, one of the most pressing long-term goals was a new relationship with the Soviet Union. Although he had long been a dedicated anti-Communist, Richard Nixon approached this new relationship with the Soviets by acknowledging that the old confrontational approach to the Communist power could never ensure world peace. So he opened the door to a new relationship with the Soviet Union through his announcement that negotiation was to be a primary component of the new structure for peace; it was through negotiations and the agreements that they produced that Nixon was able to move toward a system of détente with the Soviets. What is détente? Webster's *Ninth New Collegiate Dictionary* defines "détente" as a relaxation of strained relations or tensions. This is exactly what Nixon hoped to accomplish: a relaxation of superpower tensions through a change from confrontation to negotiation. Détente was a means of maintaining the balance of power in a way that would be consistent with the resources that the United States had available. According to John Gaddis (1983), détente did not define friendship; rather, it was a strategy for a relationship among adversaries.

Ironically, it was the Soviets who took the first steps toward détente by indicating their interest to the Nixon administration in moving ahead on Strategic Arms Limitations Talks (SALT). In mid-1970, Henry Kissinger was then able to propose the idea of a summit to Soviet Ambassador Anatoly Dobrynin. Over the next year, the idea encountered several obstacles, but then President Nixon announced his trip to China, which raised great concern in the Soviet Union. Thus, in September 1971 both sides finally agreed to a May 1972 summit.

The 1972 summit in Moscow was truly one of the high points of the Nixon presidency. Of course, it was a highly choreographed event; Henry Kissinger had secretly spent four days in Moscow the month before to decide on an agenda and to work on a declaration of principles to be signed at the summit. Nonetheless, a variety of important agreements were produced by the summit, with the two most important being the Basic Principles of United States-Soviet Relations and the SALT treaty. The Basic Principles agreement provided the basis for détente: it stated that the two countries recognized that in the nuclear age there was no real alternative to attempting to peacefully coexist and to avoiding confrontations that could lead to direct conflict between them. The agreement also renounced the use of force between the United States and the Soviet Union, and the two countries pledged to pursue "normal relations based on the principles of sovereignty, equality, non-interference in internal affairs and mutual advantage" (in Genovese 1990, 141–42). In addition, the document articulated an agreement between the two superpowers to actively promote commercial and economic ties.

The second major agreement signed at the 1972 summit was the Strategic Arms Limitation Talk compact, which was the culmination of a process that began under Lyndon Johnson. SALT produced two major agreements: the Antiballistic Missile Treaty (ABM) and the Interim Agreement on the Limitation of Strategic Arms. The first agreement prohibited testing and deployment of ABM systems and limited each nation to no more than two ABM sites, and the second set a maximum on intercontinental ballistic missiles, submarine-launched ballistic missiles, and missile-carrying submarines. These agreements were possible because Nixon believed that it was time for the United States to seek sufficiency in its arms control goals rather than superiority. Thus, the United States moved from a defense strategy based on nuclear superiority to an acceptance of "mutually assured destruction" (MAD) (Genovese 1990, 142).

The Moscow summit was to be the first of many meetings of the U.S. and Soviet heads of state. However, none of the following summits were to have the drama or the results of 1972. When the 1973 summit commenced on June 18, the SALT II talks were going slowly and Watergate was in the air. Even so, President Nixon and Leonid Brezhnev did sign several significant agreements and had lengthy discussions on a variety of issues, including Jewish emigration from the Soviet Union. Perhaps most important, the 1973 summit was a step toward institutionalizing yearly summits between the superpowers. By the time of the 1974 summit, however, Watergate was a full-blown crisis for Richard Nixon. The 1974 summit did produce the Protocol to the Treaty on the Limitation of Antiballistic Missile Systems and the Treaty and Protocol on the Limitation of Underground Nuclear Weapons Test, along with several lesser agreements. But the Watergate crisis had injured Richard Nixon. Despite all the hard sell tactics used to promote détente, according to Michael Genovese, public support for it had declined enough to allow opponents of détente in Congress to limit what could really be accomplished at the summit.

Changing the World Balance in China

Nixon's rapprochement (establishment of or state of having cordial relations) with China is often cited as the greatest success of his presidency. It was certainly a bold and risky move, and one that changed the international balance of power. Nixon was able to use improved relations with China to press the Soviet Union into the service of détente, and the president certainly hoped that reduced tensions with China would simultaneously reduce the military pressure on the United States in Asia (and thus the overseas deployment of American troops). Perhaps more than that, however, the president was working to build his new structure for global peace, and a warming of relations with China was needed to ensure the integrity of that structure. This dramatic reversal of policy toward China, argues Doak Barnett (1971), accepted that a Chinese Communist regime was no passing phenomenon and recognized the need to ease tensions in the world so long as Communist China remained estranged from the international community. In addition, John Gaddis points out that warming relations with the Chinese would also quickly and dramatically reduce the number of enemies that the United States believed that it had to keep "contained."

How did Nixon manage this spectacular feat? For nearly thirty years the United States had refused to recognize the Communist government of the People's Republic of China, instead insisting that the Republic of China on Taiwan should be viewed as the legitimate government of all China. For two decades the basic relationship between the two countries had been one of mutual fear and hostile interaction, as in the Korean War. With so much at stake, Nixon began and accomplished rapprochement in secrecy. According to Joan Hoff (1994), in the early 1970s the U.S. government began to reverse its standard cold war policy of nonrecognition by way of a number of unilateral gestures of reconciliation: toning down American anti-Chinese rhetoric, removing some trade and visa restrictions, and reducing the number of U.S. troops at bases surrounding China and in Vietnam.

In fact, only a week after his inauguration as president, Nixon had instructed Henry Kissinger to seek "unofficial contacts with China" (White 1973, xii). Then on March 15, 1971, the U.S. government announced its decision to end all special restrictions on travel by Americans to the People's Republic of China. Three weeks later, an American Ping-Pong team participating in an international tournament in Japan announced that it had been invited to visit mainland China. In what was later to become known as Ping-Pong Diplomacy, the team embarked on a whirlwind tour of China. Their visit climaxed on April 14 when Premier Chou En-lai received the Americans and declared that the visit "opened a new page in relations between the Chinese and American peoples" (in Barnett 1971, xiv).

These early, tentative moves on both sides were just the beginning of a new dance between the United States and the People's Republic of China. Only a few months later, in July of that same year, Henry Kissinger pretended to be sick with a stomach problem in Pakistan and made a secret visit to China. There he met with Premier Chou En-lai to arrange a Chinese-American summit. As with the Soviet summits, this visit was carefully orchestrated, and so

Richard Nixon made dramatic history in February 1972 as the first American president to visit China. Upon meeting Mao Tse-tung, Nixon said, "What brings us together is a recognition of a new situation in the world and recognition on our part that what is important is not a nation's internal philosophy. What is important is its policy toward the rest of the world and toward us."

Again, Nixon's new foreign policy doctrine, which was concerned more with power than with ideology, brought a change in international relations: by the end of the week-long summit in Beijing, the United States and China took their first steps toward normalizing relations, issuing the Shanghai Communiqué. While the communiqué did admit to differences between the two nations over matters such as the status of Taiwan and ideology, Michael Genovese argues that it also indicated a commitment by both China and the United States to harmony in Pacific relations. This was in addition to a move made by Nixon just six days before arriving in Beijing on February 20: he ordered that U.S. trade with Beijing be on the same basis as trade with Moscow and Soviet-bloc nations. Altogether, the president's initiatives toward China and his visit there amounted to a stunning triumph to couple with his summit in Moscow in May, particularly with the 1972 elections right around the corner.

It would be a mistake, however, to see rapprochement with China as a great victory without its own costs. The price the United States paid in this case was the sacrificing of Taiwan as an ally. Some in the Nixon administration, such as Secretary of State William Rogers, had deep reservations about an opening of relations with China. They feared that the United Nations would be unwilling to admit China and still recognize Chiang Kai-shek's government in Taiwan as the legitimate representative of the Chinese people. Those fears were, of course, realized. Although Nixon attempted to pursue a "two-China" policy, hoping that the United Nations would recognize both governments, Joan Hoff reports that the United Nations expelled Taiwan and admitted the People's Republic of China in late 1971. One of America's oldest friends and allies was gone.

Vietnam and Betrayal at Home and Abroad: My Lai, the Pentagon Papers, and America's Bums

As mentioned above, Nixon's new plan for peace in the world required victory on both short-term and long-term goals. Premier among the short-term goals was ending the long war in Vietnam that was causing so much trouble at home. In fact, some scholars, such as Joan Hoff (1994), have argued that the original purpose behind improved relations with both the Soviet Union and China was to bring pressure to bear on both nations to improve the situation for the United States in Vietnam. As Nixon's foreign policy plan detailed in its unveiling, strength was a primary component of America's new role in the world, and so the first concern was extricating the United States from Vietnam with honor. It would never do to accept defeat and thus undermine Nixon's long-term goals for America's place in the world: American power had to remain a credible force in world politics. Unfortunately, getting out of Vietnam ended up being far more difficult than either Nixon or Kissinger expected, and "peace with honor" proved elusive (Genovese 1990, 115).

As we know from chapter 1, America was ready for peace in Vietnam when Richard Nixon sought the presidency in the late 1960s. Indeed, in every poll taken during the campaign, Vietnam was always the number one concern of the American public. The United States had approximately 520,000 troops there when Nixon took office, and the failure of Lyndon Johnson to bring an end to the war allowed Nixon to talk of his plan for ending the conflict. Unfortunately, it turned out that the Nixon plan was not much of a plan at all. His early efforts at a negotiated compromise—a secret conciliatory letter to President Ho Chi Min of North Vietnam and equally secret negotiations between Henry Kissinger and North Vietnamese officials—did not work. The president then decided that if talking would not accomplish "peace with honor," then increased military pressure might do the job.

Thus, in an effort to get the Paris negotiations going, Nixon decided in 1969 to play the old "carrot-and-stick" game with the North Vietnamese. The carrot was a phased withdrawal of American combat troops from Vietnam; by early 1970, Washington had reduced U.S. troop strength in Vietnam to below 400,000, and by 1971 the total had been reduced to about 200,000. The troop pullout was part of what was called "Vietnamization," a plan promoted by Secretary of Defense Melvin Laird that called for turning the war over to the South Vietnamese (see Hoff 1994). In turn, Vietnamization was an outgrowth of the Nixon Doctrine, by which the United States would maintain its commitments abroad while at the same time reducing its direct military involvement. Of course, Nixon also hoped and believed that the troop withdrawal would calm the antiwar unrest that was plaguing him at home.

The other side of his strategy, the stick, according to Michael Genovese, was the simultaneous stepping-up of military pressure in Vietnam and neighboring countries, as well as intensified pressure on North Vietnam's allies (China and the Soviet Union) to pressure them into ending the war. So while American combat troops were being withdrawn from Vietnam, B-52s began massive bombings of the North. Between 1969 and early 1973, the United States dropped on Vietnam an average of a ton of bombs each minute. Even as the president knew that the pressure would have to be further increased to get the Vietnamese talking, however, he feared the reaction at home of the antiwar protesters. His solution was to expand the war effort by bombing the North Vietnamese based inside the neutral nation of Cambodia, but to do it in secret! On March 18, 1969, the first B-52 raids against Cambodia took place. The first phase of the bombing, called Operation Menu, lasted over fourteen months. In that period, B-52s flew 3,875 sorties into Cambodia and dropped 108,823 tons of bombs.

This secret war in Cambodia was truly a presidential war, as Michael Genovese argues. It was conducted by the executive branch on its own, with no congressional approval or oversight, no public scrutiny, and no democratic controls. In fact, to keep Nixon's private war secret, the military had to set up improvised chains of command outside of normal military channels, to file false reports, and to create a dual reporting system, otherwise known as double-bookkeeping. Henry Kissinger also repeatedly lied to the Senate Foreign Relations Committee about American activities in Cambodia in order to keep the B-52 raids a secret. Thus, the bombings were "illegal and criminally concealed," according to Joan Hoff in her 1994 book on Nixon's presidency. Although Bill Beecher reported the bombings (thanks to one of those leaks that so drove Nixon and Kissinger crazy) in May 1969 in the *New York Times,* the public did not become fully aware of these covert strikes until almost a year later, on April 30, 1970.

On that day, the president went on national television and shocked the nation with his announcement that he had ordered American troops into Cambodia to destroy North Vietnamese headquarters and sanctuaries based there. He said that the action was intended to save lives and insisted that it was essential to his plan for "Vietnamizing" the war. The president also said that he was outraged that the enemy had violated the neutrality of Cambodia by setting up sanctuaries there. Then he claimed, "neither the United States nor South Vietnam [had] moved against these enemy sanctuaries, because we did not wish to violate the territory of a neutral nation" (Hoff 1994, 217–18).

Even as Nixon made this statement to the public, however, bombing missions continued into Cambodia. In fact, they continued until August 1973, when Congress forbade them. (The administration did not officially acknowledge this violation of Cambodia's sovereignty until the spring of 1972.) The total tonnage of bombs dropped on Cambodia in approximately four years was 540,000 tons.

In the end, it was not enough. According to Michael Genovese, Nixon's strategy of troop withdrawal, bombing escalation, and negotiation did not work. First, there was no way the South could assume fighting responsibility for the war. Second, Nixon misunderstood and underestimated the will of the North Vietnamese, who had no interest in compromise and so were not interested in negotiating either. In addition, the president badly overestimated the influence of the Soviets and the Chinese on their North Vietnamese allies; his attempts to use warming relationships with both of the Communist powers failed to change the North's position. Last, the American troop withdrawal did not have the intended effect; it was taken as a sign of weakness by the North Vietnamese, says Genovese, who became even more convinced that they could outlast Nixon and win total victory. Thus the Paris negotiations got nowhere as the North refused to move from its position: no end to the war until the United States withdrew all of its troops as well as its support for the Thieu government of the South.

While the bombings did not hurt the Communists enough to change anything at the negotiating table, they did do real damage to President Nixon as the war at home heated up beyond anything he expected. College campuses erupted in the anger born of betrayal after the president's announcement regarding the expansion of the war. They were angered further when President Nixon said on May 1 that campus radicals who opposed his policies in Vietnam were "bums." The tragedy at Kent State followed on May 4, in turn provoking the student strike and the closing of campuses across the country a few days later, a massive antiwar rally in Washington on May 9, and the killing of two more students at Jackson State College in Mississippi a week later. By then the president was nearing the end of his rope; his efforts to end the war in Vietnam were only meeting with frustration at the negotiating table and were creating more chaos at home.

In February 1971 came a major testing of Nixon's program of Vietnamizing the war: South Vietnamese troops with American air and artillery support invaded Laos (thus violating the neutrality of a second nation). The goal of the invasion was to defeat the North Vietnamese army in the Laotian panhandle at the Ho Chi Min Trail, but according to Michael Genovese, the U.S.-backed forces were trapped inside the Laotian jungle and suffered enormous casualties. They were driven out within six weeks, and the campaign ended in complete catastrophe. Nixon's popularity took a steep dive in the polls, and the tempers of those opposed to the war at home flared. Senator Fulbright even proposed a resolution in March that challenged Nixon's authority to commit U.S. troops to combat in or over Laos, saying, "The Senate must not remain silent now while the president uses the armed forces of the United States to fight an undeclared and undisclosed war in Laos" (Trager 1992, 1025).

Sen. Byrd said same thing re: W & Iraq

Vietnam and Betrayals at Home

Obviously, things at home were going badly: the antiwar movement seemed to grow larger and angrier with each passing day, and congressional doves were working effectively to undermine the president's position. Early in his term, Nixon had faced a public that was frustrated by the continuing war in Vietnam and impatient to see it brought to a close. As we know, Nixon ended the draft and brought a large number of troops home from Vietnam, but this did not soften either the public's or Congress's opposition to American policy in Asia. With the expansion of the war into Cambodia and Laos, whatever trust or support Nixon had with the public and with the Democrat-controlled Congress was shattered.

However, this was only the beginning of the betrayals that were hitting the American people because of Vietnam. There were also the painful revelations that came when Captain Ernest L. Medina, Lieutenant William L. Calley, and four other soldiers were charged with premeditated murder and rape at the South Vietnamese village of My Lai (Songmy) in 1968. According to Theodore White, the "national conscience vomited" when the details came out: Calley's platoon was ordered to purge My Lai of Viet Cong, but when it arrived there the Viet Cong had fled. Nonetheless, platoon members rounded up the remaining old men, women, and children and killed them. Women with babes in arms were killed by single shots while old men were clubbed to death (1973, 58).

Shortly after these revelations had produced shock and disbelief for many Americans, the bad news was compounded when General Samuel W. Koster was forced to resign as superintendent of the U.S. Military Academy at West Point. His resignation came following accusations that he and thirteen other officers had suppressed information regarding the My Lai incident. Perhaps the biggest betrayal of My Lai occurred, however, after William Calley was found guilty of murder by a military tribunal on March 31, 1971. Although Calley was convicted of murdering twenty civilians at My Lai, President Nixon considered bolstering his flagging Southern Strategy by intervening on behalf of Calley, someone he called a Southern war hero. According to Joan Hoff, Nixon personally took the case under review and placed Calley under house arrest instead of stockade confinement until his sentencing. Appeals resulted in several reductions of Calley's sentence (reduced to twenty years in 1971, ten years in 1974). After an acquittal was overturned, Calley was paroled in November 1975 and was dishonorably discharged, having served almost no jail time for his actions.

But My Lai and all of its associated subterfuge was not the end of the betrayals at home caused by Vietnam. On June 13, 1971, the *New York Times* published the first installment of the Pentagon Papers, bringing about the Nixon Justice Department's attempt to censure the American press (out of concern for its own war effort). Ultimately the American public was to discover that the publication of the Pentagon Papers led to even further betrayals, such as the White House "Plumbers" and their break-in of Daniel Ellsberg's doctor's office. Indeed, the intractable nature of the situation in Vietnam, its unpopularity at home, and the pressure of public dissent that arose from that unpopularity gave birth to some of the greatest betrayals of the seventies.

Raising the Stakes in Vietnam: Is This Really Peace with Honor?

Meanwhile, Henry Kissinger came home from Paris with the bad news that Le Duc Tho (of North Vietnam) would not compromise. His position was not a surprise, considering the rout in Laos and the unrest at home in the United States. At this point, the president had to either surrender or to escalate further. Considering his intent to achieve "peace with honor" and to maintain America's credibility in the world, he could not choose surrender. So U.S. planes began to bomb Haiphong and Hanoi on April 16, and rail and roadways were bombed as well—further dragging out the war that was to last several times longer than any previous war in American history.

Under the grueling pressure of round-the-clock bombing, the North finally agreed to return to the negotiating table. In the summer of 1972, with the presidential election approaching, the two sides met in Paris. But the North wanted a victory, and it was driving a hard bargain in Paris. So the bombings continued in the hope of forcing the North into an agreement more amenable to American interests. Then North Vietnam's politburo made a breakthrough concession: it would drop its demand for coalition government in the South and the South's current president, Nguyen Van Thieu, could stay in office. From that point on the negotiations moved ahead, and by the fall of 1972 an agreement was in sight, despite the fact that South Vietnam was not a party to this agreement. Nonetheless, on October 26—less than two weeks before the presidential election—Henry Kissinger shocked the world (and the White House) when he announced at a press conference that "peace [was] at hand" in Vietnam. Nixon was furious with Kissinger, according to John Robert Greene, and quickly released what amounted to a retraction, saying that there were still differences to be resolved.

Those differences were substantial: President Thieu of South Vietnam refused to accept the deal. Kissinger and North Vietnam's Le Duc Tho met in mid-November to try once again to iron out an agreement, but when the South's demands were included in the bargain, the North Vietnamese raised objections. At this point, a desperate President Nixon decided to step up the pressure on both the North and the South. On December 18, 1972, American B-52s began a twelve-day, round-the-clock bombing of North Vietnam in which the United States dropped more tons of bombs than had been dropped in the entire 1969–71 period. According to Michael Gneovese, the "Christmas bombing" shocked the nation and the world with its brutal show of force. As the bombs showered the North, Nixon sweetened the pot for the South, giving it an additional billion dollars in military aid while promising that if the North violated the agreement, the United States would "save" the South from a Communist takeover.

In the end, neither side could resist Nixon's pressure. The North returned to the bargaining table, Nixon ordered a halt to the bombings, and South Vietnam's Thieu acquiesced to American pressures and promises. On January 23, 1973, the Agreement on Ending the War and Restoring Peace in Vietnam was initialed by Henry Kissinger and Le Duc Tho in Paris (for which they shared the Nobel Peace Prize). Even though the Paris Peace Accords were never submitted to the Senate for approval, Richard Nixon claimed his "peace with honor."

Twenty-seven months after the signing of the Paris Accords, the Saigon government fell to the Communists, despite Nixon's secret promise to Thieu that the United States would "respond with full force" if the North violated the agreements. The night before the South surrendered, horrific scenes were broadcast on America's television news programs of the evacuation of the American embassy in Saigon. With the Communists advancing on the city, thousands of Vietnamese stormed the embassy, screaming to be taken along. As Americans watched from their living rooms, embassy personnel used clubs and fists to beat away people from the helicopters. By that time, however, Nixon had been forced from office, and America had no more stomach for a return to Vietnam. Indeed, by May 1973, the House of Representatives had outlawed more bombings in Indochina.

When all was said and done, the Vietnamese had lost 1.3 million people to the conflict, and America's combat death toll had reached 56,000. After the loss of these lives, along with $141 billion in U.S. aid, the North had ultimately conquered the South by force. The Communist Khmer Rouge controlled Cambodia (where it began a wholesale slaughter of intellectuals, political enemies, dissidents, and peasants guilty of "mistakes"), and Laos fell to the Communist Pathet Lao after nearly twenty-five years of U.S. efforts to block such a takeover. Yes, when all was said and done, Vietnam had finally extracted the ultimate betrayal of the American people and the American spirit: it was the first war America ever lost.

The Middle East

In Kansas City on July 6, 1971, Richard Nixon announced a second foreign policy strategy that was almost as important as the Nixon Doctrine: the pentagonal strategy. This five-power strategy was to replace the bipolar, confrontational mode of the cold war by bringing the five great economic regions of the world (the United States, the Soviet Union, mainland China, Japan, and Western Europe) into constructive negotiation. The president thus outlined a "pentagonal strategy" for promoting peace and economic progress by linking the interests of the major regional powers. This meant that from the beginning of the Nixon administration, entire areas of the Developing World,

including the Middle East, occupied a clearly secondary place in the administration's view of foreign policy. Nixon and Kissinger would therefore often ignore many foreign policy considerations in dealing with the Developing
World, according to Joan Hoff, instead linking events in those countries to relations among the major powers. When it came to the Middle East, this approach created an erratic and problematic structure for American foreign
policy.

Indeed, when Richard Nixon came to power in 1969 the Middle East was
a ticking time bomb, needing only a lighted match to explode again into violence. This time bomb could be traced back, most recently, to the Six-Day
War of June 1967. The short war easily demonstrated that the Israeli military
had overwhelming superiority in the region: the Arab countries were routed,
and Israel occupied the entire Sinai Peninsula and the Gaza Strip in Egypt, the
Golan Heights in Syria, and the city of Jerusalem and the West Bank in Jordan. Although the United Nations called for a cease-fire and asked Israel to
withdrawal to its previous borders, it refused to comply. Added to this was the
fact that the West Bank and the Gaza Strip were full of refugee settlements,
most of them Palestinian. Tensions were thus high in the region in early 1969,
with Nixon saying at a press conference on January 27 that he considered it "a
powder keg, very explosive. It needs to be defused" (in Hoff 1994, 253).

Nonetheless, the Middle East was clearly a secondary foreign policy concern for the Nixon administration, and instead of having Henry Kissinger deal
with this troubled area, Nixon assigned it to Secretary of State William
Rogers. Through the first months of Nixon's administration, according to
John Robert Greene (1992), Rogers and Joseph Sisco (the State Department's expert on the Middle East) struggled to come up with an approach
that would defuse the situation and be acceptable to Nixon. They knew that
they needed to proceed with caution. The United States was of course prepared to defend Israel, its ally, and the president believed that he also needed
to be responsive to the power that American Jews held in the United States
(euphemistically referred to by Nixon and his staffers as "domestic political
considerations"). At the same time, however, the United States could not appear to be disregarding the concerns of the Arab states. In particular, the president did not want to alienate the oil-producing nations in the region,
especially when the Soviet Union was clearly attempting to strengthen its relationships with the Arab states.

What Rogers and Sisco came up with was the "Rogers Plan," so named because it never had the full support of President Nixon. The essential components of this plan called for an American-Soviet agreement on a comprehensive peace settlement to bring an end to the conflict, since according to George Lenczowski (1990), Nixon accepted the thesis that the Soviets were the main cause of Middle East tensions. The Rogers Plan broadly followed UN Security Council Resolution 242 and upheld the principle that Israel should return the occupied Arab territories in exchange for Arab pledges to end the state of war and to respect Israel's territorial integrity. However, with all parties to the negotiation promptly rejecting it, the Rogers Plan was a failure, and the time bomb continued to tick.

Then on September 6, 1970, two armed men hijacked a Pan Am Boeing 747 en route from Amsterdam to New York. They rerouted the plane to Beirut where they took dynamite aboard, flew on to Cairo, evacuated all passengers via emergency exits, and blew up the aircraft two minutes later. Other members of the Popular Front for the Liberation of Palestine (PFLP) hijacked two other planes and forced them to land in Jordan, and the next day a fourth jet was taken (Trager 1992). By that time, the PFLP had 478 hostages—many of them Americans—in Jordan. On September 12, they moved the hostages to their camp and blew up the three remaining planes.

Within days, Jordan found itself responding to the crisis by breaking out in a civil war, and Syria decided to take advantage of the unrest to advance its agenda and invade Jordan near the Golan Heights. President Nixon, whom George Lenczowski claims was "obsessed" with the danger of a possible Soviet-American confrontation in the Middle East, immediately viewed the Syrian invasion as a crisis between the United States and the Soviet Union and began to threaten intercession. Although it looked as though events were leading to an all-out superpower confrontation—at least in part because of Nixon and Kissinger's policy of linking Middle East politics to relations among the superpowers rather than attending to them directly—the crisis was averted. It was not averted because of reasoned negotiation and communication between the superpowers however; war was avoided, according to Michael Genovese, because Israel was able to give Jordan the support needed to drive the Syrian forces back into Syria.

After the crisis in Jordan, the region was left as volatile as ever, while the Nixon administration virtually ignored it in favor of détente and rapprochement: the time bomb continued to tick. And the fuse was lit in October 1973—on the Jewish holy day of atonement, the most holy of the Jewish holidays—when Egypt and Syria simultaneously attacked Israel's northern and southern borders. Known as the Yom Kippur War, it was the fourth and fiercest Arab-Israeli war since 1948.

Within four days, reports George Lenczowski, Nixon had ordered Defense Secretary James Schlesinger to carry out a massive airlift of American arms to Israel, and soon the United States was providing Israel with a thousand tons of war material a day. Then Soviet planes began to airlift equipment to Arab forces on both fronts, and Moscow announced on October 15 that it would "assist in every way" the Arab effort to regain the territory taken by Israel in 1967. To make matters worse, the Arab oil-producing nations cut oil supplies to America, Western Europe, and Japan in retaliation for their support of Israel.

Finally, after a superpower game of nuclear "chicken" in which Brezhnev threatened unilateral action against the Israelis and all U.S. forces were put on worldwide alert, the crisis passed. But in only eighteen days of fighting, much damage was done: Israel had 4,100 men killed or wounded, Egypt had lost 7,500, and Syria, 7,300. In addition, the sense of vulnerability in the United States intensified, as it came to understand that Israeli military superiority in the region would not be enough to promise peace. The United States also awoke to the reality that its dependence on foreign oil could be used to blackmail American interests abroad.

Nixon's Foreign Policy Limitations and Legacy

As mentioned above, the successes that Richard Nixon had in foreign policy—usually described by the exemplars of détente with the Soviet Union and rapprochement with China—are often the most positive aspects remembered about his presidency. However, just as it is inappropriate to belittle Nixon's successes in the domestic arena, it is equally wrong to lionize everything that his administration did in foreign policy. There were plenty of problems with the Nixon policy in Vietnam, as we know, as well as with the actions that his administration took in other areas of foreign policy.

Because the developing countries played little role in Nixon's grand design for world peace and stability, many areas of the world went virtually unattended to by the Nixon White House. As is clear from the discussion of events in the Middle East, the Nixon administration policy of linking events in developing nations to superpower relations rather than viewing them as areas deserving of attention in their own right was problematic. In other cases, Nixon's foreign policy decisions were problematic because they were morally wrong or discounted the human element, or because they were damaging to other U.S. interests in the area, particularly economic interests (such as U.S. dependence on oil from the Middle East). There are many examples of such problematic foreign policy actions, including the administration's handling of the India-Pakistan War (in which it was caught in a damaging lie about professed public neutrality), the "tar-baby" policy in Africa (abandoning black revolutionary movements in favor of cooperation with white minorities in countries like Angola, Rhodesia, and South Africa), and the covert undermining of the democratically elected government of Chile.

There were still other difficulties with the Nixon administration's foreign policy. In 1973, for example, Robert Art called Nixon's rapprochement with China one of the best examples of "presidentially imposed, presidentially initiated policy," but this was the problem with most of Nixon's foreign policy—it was overly personalized. In fact, it depended heavily on the personal relationships between Nixon and Kissinger on the one side and their counterparts in foreign countries on the other, particularly Leonid Brezhnev and Ambassador Dobrynin of the Soviet Union. What this means is that the successes of Nixon's foreign policy could not and, in most cases, did not last; Nixon's successors simply could not keep his initiatives going after he had been destroyed by Watergate. Nixon's détente, for example, did not really change the conflicting cold war strategies of the United States and the Soviet Union; according to Joan Hoff, it only provided a temporary blurring of hostilities that Ronald Reagan revived to a fever pitch in the early 1980s.

In addition, most of Nixon's foreign policy was conducted in secret, at least initially: détente, rapprochement, the bombings of Cambodia, and so on. This secrecy suited the paranoid tendencies of both Nixon and Kissinger but caused problems for the long-term health of the nation. By conducting foreign policy in secret and withholding important information from the American public and Congress, Richard Nixon again circumvented the democratic process that Americans hold so dear, resulting in foreign policy initiatives that lacked legitimacy. Although this approach brought him great success in foreign policy in the short term, it was not good for the country in the long term. Not only could those successes not be maintained, but this approach also engendered the feeling among Americans that they had been betrayed when the facts were finally revealed later.

Can America get as outraged now as it was then?

The Vietnam War and the accompanying protest movement are good examples of the crisis in confidence caused by Nixon's approach to foreign policy. Not only did the war in Vietnam and at home create a crisis in the public's confidence in American foreign policy, it also contributed to a rising isolationist sentiment in the United States, a sentiment barely kept at bay in the years preceding the mess in Vietnam. In addition, one of the major outcomes of the Vietnam disaster and the Nixon years more generally was a change in attitude regarding American foreign policy. Prior to Vietnam, most Americans believed that foreign policy was a field best left to experts in the executive branch of government. However, as a result of the overly personalized and secret excesses of the Nixon years, the nearly absolute authority of the president in foreign policy began to be questioned (consider, for example, the War Powers Resolution). At this point, there began to be a demand for broader participation by the Congress and the public in the formulation of foreign policy, and a new criterion was employed for judging successful foreign policy: could it attract wide-based popular support? The problem with this approach, of course, is that the best policies, the right policies, are not always those that are the most popular.

Foreign Policy and the Ford Administration: Fighting the Legacy of Richard Nixon

In every area of governing, Gerald Ford was left with the unhappy job of attempting to overcome the Nixon legacy. Because of that legacy in foreign policy, the early 1970s saw a resurgence of congressional will to be a participant in foreign policy decision making, and so Gerald Ford faced an especially vocal and, in his view, obstructionist Congress when it came to foreign affairs. As Michael Genovese has written: "If the presidency under Nixon had become "imperial," the Congress saw to it that under Ford, it was imperiled, shackled, and restrained" (1990, 162). One of the best examples of this fact came, ironically, with the foreign policy highlight of Ford's tenure: the attack on a U.S. merchant ship called the *Mayaguez*. In the incident, the Cambodian navy fired on and then boarded the ship and captured the crew. In response, the president and his advisers decided not to attempt to negotiate with the Khmer Rouge (recalling the harsh lesson of the *Pueblo* crisis, according to

John Robert Greene) and instead quickly assembled an amphibious task force to attempt a rescue operation. Although the mission cost nearly as many lives as it saved, Ford was applauded by the public, the Congress, and the press for his decisive action in the crisis.

However, the Nixon legacy and its effects can be seen even with this undisputed success. Although the president acted boldly in immediately ordering the heroic rescue mission, argues John Robert Greene, he was painfully aware of the high level of scrutiny that his actions would receive. Even as he planned his strategy for saving the crew of the captured ship, the president was careful to term the capture of the merchant ship an act of "piracy" rather than an act of war. He did so in order to be able to treat the crisis as one that allowed his immediate action under his emergency powers; otherwise he knew that he would be fighting for his life and the lives of *Mayaguez*'s crew against a recalcitrant Congress.

On the other hand, Ford's foreign policy failure with Nixon's legacy of détente was twofold. First, he could not keep it going for reasons that we have already stated. Second, he should not have tried to, as it ultimately aided in his loss to Jimmy Carter in 1976. Indeed, after the nearly disastrous confrontation with the Soviets during the Yom Kippur War, public support for détente was on the wane and the antidétente forces in Congress were geared up for a full assault on a policy that they saw as dangerous and unproductive. According to John Robert Greene, the assault started in October 1973 when these forces, led by Senator Henry "Scoop" Jackson, a conservative Democrat from Washington State, helped to scuttle a trade bill with the Soviets. Ford was furious at them for meddling in the foreign policy prerogatives of the president and for destroying a trade agreement that could help the hurting U.S. economy. Then Jackson's criticism of the grain deal between the Soviets and the United States forced Ford to place an embargo on all overseas shipments of wheat and corn in October 1974, showing Ford bending to the will of a Democratic senator and angering Brezhnev in the process. Even Ford's successful summit with Brezhnev at Vladivostok was attacked widely, as Jackson criticized the agreement for failing to reduce Soviet forces, neatly setting the stage for the vitriol that was to accompany the Helsinki Accords.

According to Warren Zimmermann (1986), when President Ford, General Secretary Leonid Brezhnev, and thirty-three other leaders gathered in the great Finnish architect Alvar Aalto's Finlandia House, they constituted the most important collection of statesmen to meet on pan-European themes since the Congress of Vienna in 1815. As well, they signed an agreement that was the closest thing the global community will ever have to a post-World War II peace settlement. The Helsinki Accords essentially formalized détente between East and West and established a forum in which key East-West issues could be discussed by all of the European states, the United States, and Canada. Even though the Soviet Union signed an agreement to follow a more liberal human rights policy—an agreement that provided an opportunity for the United States to subject the Soviet Union to rigorous human rights criteria—there was a problem.

The problem was that the final terms of the Helsinki agreement seemed to be an endorsement of the Soviet position in Eastern Europe: the Final Act made permanent the Soviet postwar frontiers and those of their Eastern satellites. Back at home in the United States, it seemed as though détente had allowed President Ford to give away the store once again, having gained little in return. The president was attacked in the press, and the White House was flooded with angry letters. The Helsinki Accords thus damaged Gerald Ford badly as he went into the 1976 presidential election, forcing him ultimately to publicly repudiate détente in favor of a "policy of strength." In fact, the accords and the antidétente frenzy they engendered very nearly sounded the final death knell of détente as the primary foreign policy goal of the United States in relation to the Soviet Union.

Thus, within a rapid time period, Nixon's "peace with honor" in Vietnam had been destroyed, Cambodia had fallen to the Communists, and U.S. relations with the Russians had gone back to being nearly as chilly and dangerous as ever. Indeed, Ford also had difficulty in bringing a resolution to the precarious situation in the Middle East, even with the aid of Henry Kissinger's shuttle diplomacy. Shortly after Ford took office, all hopes of a Jordanian-Israeli compact were dashed when the new Israeli government stalled on coming to the negotiating table. Soon after that, according to John Robert Greene (1995), Ford botched an effort to bring the intransigent Israelis around on negotiations with Egypt on the Sinai II Accord: he sent a strongly worded letter to the prime minister, threatening to reassess American relations with Israel. Instead of encouraging the Israelis to negotiate, the letter stiffened their resolve. Reacting in kind, Sadat rejected all Israeli demands and the Sinai II talks disintegrated.

When they did, Ford kept his promise to reassess American policy toward Israel, but this also proved to be less than profitable for the president and his struggling administration. For three bitter months, Ford's anger at Israeli intransigence played itself out: negotiations on Israel's request for F-15 fighter planes were suspended, a shipment of missiles was indefinitely delayed, and scheduled visits by Israeli diplomats were canceled. However, the Israelis still refused to budge. In the meantime, the American Jewish community was offended by Ford's new policy, and it began to lobby Congress with ferocity. In short order the legislative branch was again interfering in the presidential arena of foreign policy: in May 1975, seventy-five senators sent Ford a letter urging him to be responsive to Israel's request for several billion dollars in aid and to support Israel's demand for "defensible" frontiers.

In June, Kissinger began yet another round of shuttle diplomacy to negotiate the possibility of resolving Sinai II through the creation of a buffer zone that would be monitored by American civilians. However, in private negotiations, Rabin pressed the United States for more arms than the $1.5 billion that Ford had previously promised. Greene (1995) argues that, desperate for a foreign policy victory and pressured by Congress, Ford agreed, and on September 4, Egypt and Israel signed the Sinai II Accord. In a secret side agreement with Israel, Ford also promised not to negotiate with the PLO as long as it refused to accept Israel's right to exist, and he guaranteed weapons supplies and oil for Israel if necessary.

Ford bought a tenuous peace in the Middle East but at an extremely high price—an analogy for the conduct of foreign policy throughout the Ford administration. The pledge concerning the PLO, for example, was a novelty. It constituted self-limitation of the United States's sovereign right to recognize or negotiate with any individual or organization it might wish, and politically, it conveyed the idea of subordinating an important sector of America's foreign policy to Israeli guidance. Gerald Ford was forced to take peace on Israeli terms. He was forced to do this because he was hobbled by the Nixon legacy in every area of the world: he was restrained by a public and a Congress that were determined to take power away from the president in foreign policy. Further, Ford seemed completely unable to strike out on his own and to make his own mark on the international scene. Thus, in the one area where Ford might have been willing to be the caretaker president of the Nixon legacy, he proved unable to do so.

The Carter Years: Morality and Foreign Policy

Unlike Gerald Ford, when Jimmy Carter came to office he had no interest in being the caretaker of his predecessor's foreign policy. According to
Burton Kaufman (1993), he came to office instead with the pronounced conviction that the time had come to strike out in new directions in foreign policy, and he intended to take charge of that new foreign policy himself: he alone
would establish priorities, set direction, and make the final decisions. Also like
Nixon, Carter believed that the time for American intervention in all of the
problems of the world was over, and he accepted that limitation. However,
Carter believed that idealism was more practical than realpolitik in foreign
policy, that idealism could provide the strongest basis for American power in
the world. He wanted human rights to be "a central theme for American foreign policy"; as he stated: "it was time for us to capture the imagination of the
world again. As president I hoped and believed that the expansion of human
rights might be the wave of the future throughout the world" (1982, 144).

On May 22, 1977, the president articulated the specifics of this vision for
U.S. foreign policy, describing what Garland Haas (1992) calls the five cardi-
nal premises on which American foreign policy should be based: improved relationships with the Soviet Union and the People's Republic of China; a
commitment to advance the cause of human rights; close cooperation with
the other industrialized democracies; an effort to reduce the divide between
rich and poor nations; and cooperation with all nations to solve the problems
of the threat of nuclear war, racial hatred, the arms race, environmental damage, hunger, and disease. Through it all, he firmly believed that American foreign policy had to be grounded in a confident, positive, and moral basis. As
one senior aide explained it, Carter was "fundamentally the Christian warrior"
who was "terribly innocent and naïve," with a "do-good view of the world"
(Hargrove 1988, 112).

This "do-good" view and Carter's new moral emphasis in foreign policy
produced many positive outcomes for the Carter presidency, the United
States, and the world. Because Carter saw it as his mission to "do good" in the
world, he did not shy away from the hard problems. In fact, Jimmy Carter believed that if the most difficult issues were not addressed and resolved quickly
that they would later erupt and even more severely damage American interests. His deliberate pursuit of intractable international problems produced a
string of foreign policy successes that some consider the highlights of his pres-

idency: the Panama Canal treaties, a Middle East summit, and the recognition of the People's Republic of China.

The Panama Canal Treaties

According to Robert Strong (1991), the Panama Canal was one of the United States's favorite success stories. Succeeding where the French and British had failed, Americans had built the canal, had discovered the cause of yellow fever, and had given the American public a lasting source of national pride. The Panama Canal was thus a powerful symbol of American strength in the world for the American people. Over the years, however, the Panama Canal had become an irritating thorn in the side of the Panamanian people; according to Garland Haas (1992), they had become increasingly resentful over American control of the canal. After a bloody riot in 1964 in which four American soldiers and twenty Panamanians were killed, the Panamanian government demanded and the United States agreed that the canal treaties had to be renegotiated. Despite support by both Presidents Nixon and Ford for three renegotiated treaties, however, they had never been submitted for ratification because of intense opposition in the Congress.

But this was not to deter Jimmy Carter, who believed that the issue needed to be resolved or further violence would ensue. According to Gaddis Smith (1986), Carter and his advisers also saw the Panamanian settlement as the foundation for a new day in the hemisphere; it would demonstrate that the United States had fully abandoned colonialism and would perhaps help earn enough goodwill in the region to help solve other problems. Thus, before he even assumed office, the president-elect had decided that the canal negotiations should be an immediate priority, and American negotiators quickly proposed two new treaties soon after Carter took office. One set forth new arrangements for the joint operation of the canal for the rest of the century, at the end of which Panama would assume total control. The other guaranteed the permanent neutrality of the canal and the right of the United States to defend it. After many breakthroughs and setbacks in the negotiations with the Panamanians, reports Garland Haas, the treaties were finally signed on September 7, 1977, at an elaborate, televised Washington ceremony that was attended by the heads of eighteen different nations of the hemisphere.

The happy moment was not to last, however, for signing the treaties was the easy part—now the Senate had to ratify them. Carter knew well that Congress and the public would be opposed, but he believed that he could win their support by presenting the facts. Unfortunately, Jimmy Carter had woefully underestimated the difficulty of the task! According to Robert Strong, the opposition to ratification was ferocious. Indeed, public opinion polls in the summer of 1977 showed that 78 percent of Americans were against the treaties, and a coalition of conservative organizations and members of Congress of both parties immediately began to charge that the treaties were a "giveaway" of the canal and that they endangered American security.

Meanwhile, the president put everything he had into getting support for ratification; he gave numerous personal White House briefings on the matter to key players, as well as two "fireside chats" on national television to appeal directly to the American people. Cabinet officials and their staffs made hundreds of appearances throughout the nation to explain the treaty directly to the public, and endorsements for the agreements were sought and won from Gerald Ford, Henry Kissinger, Dean Rusk, John Wayne, and William F. Buckley. Trips were also arranged for senators who wished to visit Panama, and according to Robert Strong, before the ratification process had ended, almost half of the Senate had gone to see the canal and to meet with Panamanian leaders for themselves. Finally, in mid-January 1978, the tide finally turned Carter's way when the Senate's majority and minority leaders both endorsed the treaties.

When all the votes were counted, sixteen Republicans supported the president and provided the margin of victory for the treaties. It was an important victory for Carter in foreign affairs—perhaps the most important of his young presidency to that point. He had lobbied hard for the treaties and had contacted every senator at least once, some as many as eight times. He had won over undecided lawmakers, argues Burton Kaufman, by putting the prestige of the presidency on the line and by making support of the treaties a test of Democratic loyalty to his administration. Unfortunately, this was not a performance that Jimmy Carter would be able to repeat again.

Another Great Victory? A Settlement in the Middle East

Probably the most significant success in foreign policy for President Carter is seen as the negotiation of a settlement in the Middle East crisis. For when Carter ascended to the presidency in 1977, there still was a crisis in the Middle East: in spite of the Egyptian-Israeli and Syrian-Israeli disengagement agreements concluded during the Ford administration, the situation in the area remained tense and no formal peace treaty had been signed. Thus, the search for peace and stability in the region was a foreign policy priority for Carter from the start.

The president began by engaging personally each of the leaders of the nations involved in the dispute: President Anwar Sadat of Egypt, Prime Minister Menachem Begin of Israel, King Hussein of Jordan, Crown Prince Fahd of Saudi Arabia, and President Hafez al-Assad of Syria. In a stroke of good fortune, according to Erwin Hargrove (1988), Jimmy Carter and Anwar Sadat discovered at their first meeting in April 1977 that they liked and trusted each other. This deep, personal friendship was the key to all of the later steps on the path to peace, as at crucial moments in the next years Sadat believed that Carter would support him in the risks he took to win peace.

Sadat took his first risk—the first whisper of the possibility of peace—in November 1977 when he announced to his country's parliament that he would be willing to go to Jerusalem and talk peace with Menachem Begin, Israel's prime minister. This was indeed a risky move on the part of Egypt's leader: he would be the first president of an Arab country to go to Israel at a time when it was not politically popular to visit the Jewish state. Israel responded with an invitation to Sadat to speak to the Israeli Knesset (that country's parliament), and so he visited Jerusalem between November 19 and 21 of that year. During the visit, the Egyptian president offered Israel recognition and permanent peace (again, a courageous and risky offer). However, negotiations soon broke down, and Garland Haas reports that by the summer of 1978 relations between Egypt and Israel had gotten so bad that an explosion seemed imminent. In fact, after a meeting of the three foreign ministers in England in July of that year, Secretary of State Cyrus Vance and his aides concluded that the two parties would not be able to develop a peace plan by themselves: the United States would have to do it.

President Carter boldly and courageously reached out to both sides—risking nearly certain failure—and invited Sadat and Begin to meet at Camp David (the presidential retreat located in the Catoctin Mountains of Maryland). For nearly two weeks, Carter served as the active mediator between the two leaders who did not like each other, conducting patient and masterful negotiations. Finally all the risks and personal presidential involvement paid off: on September 17, in a prime-time televised ceremony, Begin and Sadat signed the accords that promised a "framework for peace" between Israel and

Egypt—a prize that had eluded peacemakers for more than thirty years. There can be no doubt of the importance of this event: for the first time since 1948 Israel was formally recognized by an Arab country, one with which it had fought four wars. Of course, in response to his role in bringing about this historic feat, President Carter's popularity ratings rose seventeen points in two weeks.

However, when the bright lights of cameras and the loud noise of applause had faded, the implementation of the accords proved difficult. Both Begin and Sadat were under heavy pressure at home, argues Garland Haas, and Begin gave in to some of that pressure from old allies now turned against him. He announced plans to expand the West Bank settlements and revealed that he was thinking of moving his office to East Jerusalem. When the December 17 deadline for the accords passed without a treaty, President Carter personally visited the Middle East to restore the agreement. Again, the personal effort paid off when Egypt and Israel signed the historic peace treaty at a ceremony at the White House on March 26, 1979, finally and formally ending a state of war between the two countries that had existed for nearly thirty-one years.

The signing of the treaty officially ended the hostilities between the two main antagonists in the Arab-Israeli conflict, and it was a great foreign policy triumph for the Carter administration—at least initially. In the long run, however, this historic moment accomplished surprisingly little for any of the key players. The Arab world reacted quickly and negatively to the signing of the treaty: the Algerian government called it "An act of treason," and Syria's state-run Damascus radio broadcast it as "humiliating concessions" (Kaufman 1993, 123) because agreement was reached without resolving anything with regard to the fate of the Arab Palestinians. At the end of March, representatives of eighteen Arab League states and the Palestine Liberation Organization voted to sever diplomatic and economic ties with Egypt. High officials in the Syrian, Libyan, and Iraqi governments called for Sadat's assassination. Thus, the historic peace treaty had only served to alienate Egypt from its Arab neighbors, crippling chances for a more comprehensive peace.

Carter himself got little credit for his pivotal role in producing the agreement once the hoopla had died down, and his approval ratings at home plummeted shortly afterward. In fact, according to Haas, Jody Powell concluded that the entire effort in the Middle East as a whole was decidedly a net minus for Jimmy Carter. The Arab world blamed the United States as an evil spirit, one which pretended to play peacemaker while actually becoming the great divider of the Arab world. Carter had feared that the collapse of negotiations would cause the Arabs to welcome the Soviets back into the area, but ironically, the opposite proved to be true. It gave the Soviets greater opportunity to pose as a friend and protector of Arab rights and national dignity, argues George Lenczowski, even among the more moderate Arab states.

In addition, relations between Israel and the United States experienced a chill. American Jews were angry and resentful about Carter's apparent attempts to pressure Israel into making concessions to the Arabs to establish the peace. Israel itself accused the United States of a tilt in its relations toward the Palestinians when President Carter expressed displeasure over "preemptive" raids by Israel into southern Lebanon (the location of several PLO strongholds) (Haas 1992, 102).

Although the Carter administration could rightly point to the conclusion of the Egyptian-Israeli peace as a major achievement, it is debatable whether such a separate peace warranted the investment of such tremendous amounts of presidential energy, particularly when other pressing international problems (such as the coming of revolution in Iran) were calling for the president's attention. According to George Lenczowski, Carter's original ideas about the need for a comprehensive settlement in the Middle East, his hopes for promoting human rights by ensuring a Palestinian homeland, and his plan for a more evenhanded policy in the conflict were in fact crushed by the accords of Camp David. Rather, Israel was strengthened at the expense of the Arabs by isolating Egypt from the Arab community and by leaving the issue of Palestine vague and in suspension. Thus, in the end, the success at Camp David was less than many think and almost all hoped.

Recognition of the People's Republic of China

As was clear from his earliest foreign policy statements, Jimmy Carter was very interested in normalizing relations between the United States and China. He saw cooperation with China as a way to promote peace in the world, and an improved relationship with China could also better the understanding between the United States and the other nations of the Pacific Rim. Shortly after taking office, according to Erwin Hargrove (1988), Carter instructed Secretary of State Vance to continue the discussions with Beijing that had been begun by President Nixon in 1972. By June 1977, a working group of the National Security Council and the State Department had produced a paper on normalization of relations with China that called for full diplomatic recognition. Although Secretary of State Cyrus Vance wanted to slow down on China so as not to risk problems with the SALT negotiations (fearing that improving relations between the United States and China would anger the Soviets), it was agreed that Vance would visit China in August and pursue normalization. He did travel to China that summer, but the visit was inconclusive.

Throughout the winter of 1977–78, Zbigniew Brezezinski, director of the National Security Council and assistant to the president on national security affairs, worked to persuade Carter to renew the initiative to normalization. Garland Haas asserts that he cultivated relations with Chinese officials in Washington, solicited an official invitation for his own visit China, and lobbied the president to support the trip. However, the State Department and Cyrus Vance were still much opposed to such a visit, focusing on SALT as the priority and fearing that improving relations with China would alienate the Soviets. Nonetheless, the president allowed Brezezinski to go on the trip in order to test the waters for further progress (while Vance went to Moscow to work on SALT). Brezezinski did an excellent job of laying the groundwork for later negotiations, which occurred during the summer and fall of 1978. These negotiations were so successful that on December 15, 1978, President Carter was able to announce that he planned to formally recognize the People's Republic of China and to end American ties with the nationalist regime on Taiwan.

Carter's announcement caught many members of Congress by surprise and angered them as well. First, conservatives charged that the United States was abandoning an old ally in leaving Taiwan out in the cold. In the Senate, Barry Goldwater of Arizona termed the president's decision on China "one of the most cowardly acts ever performed by a president of the United States" (Kaufman 1993, 129). Beyond concerns about abandoning Taiwan, members of Congress also objected strenuously that the president had once again failed to consult them before severing the treaty relationship with Taiwan—an unconstitutional act. Despite these objections, however, and despite attempts in both the House and the Senate to incorporate language that would have been unacceptable to Beijing, Congress did approve the legislation formalizing relations between the two nations. So Jimmy Carter won another historic foreign policy moment on January 1, 1979, when full diplomatic relations were established. A few weeks later, Chinese vice premier Deng Xiaoping visited the

United States, meeting with congressional leaders and seeing the sights around the nation's capital. He even made the cover of *Time* magazine as "Man of the Year." At the conclusion of the visit, Deng and Carter signed agreements concerning consular exchanges, trade, science, technology, and cultural exchanges.

Normalization of relations with China was another positive foreign policy outcome for Jimmy Carter, although its success was blunted quickly by China's invasion of Vietnam shortly after Deng's visit. Nonetheless, normalization did change the nature of strategic alignments in the world. In particular, as Cyrus Vance had so greatly feared, normalization put a heavy strain on relations between the United States and China's old ally, the Soviet Union.

The Soviet Union, SALT, and the Fate of Détente

As mentioned above, President Carter was determined to improve relations with the Soviet Union and to downplay the dangerous rivalry between the superpowers. In fact, in two major foreign policy speeches in 1977, Carter stressed cooperation between the United States and the Soviets as a major policy goal of his administration. As well, President Carter was committed to using arms control negotiations with the Soviets to win extensive arms reductions, even pledging in his inaugural address that his highest priority in foreign policy would be the immediate reduction of nuclear arsenals and the ultimate elimination of all nuclear weapons from the earth.

On January 26, 1977, President Carter attempted to open discussion on the issue with the Soviets by sending the first of a series of personal letters to the Soviet president, Leonid Brezhnev, suggesting that the two nations proceed on arms control. Brezhnev's reply to Carter's first letter made it clear that the Soviets wanted a quick SALT agreement based on Vladivostok. Carter in turn suggested that it might also be possible to move toward agreement with deep reductions in existing forces. When he received no encouraging response from Brezhnev, Carter decided to mobilize world opinion for nuclear disarmament. In February of that year, he went public with his proposals to reduce greatly Soviet and American long-range missiles and bombers.

Unfortunately, this move backfired. The Soviets, preferring to work in secret, rejected such a forthright approach, according to Erwin Hargrove (1988). They were also uneasy about Carter's desire for sharp reductions in nuclear weapons, and they were upset by the president's outspoken criticism of human rights violations in their country. In mid-March, when Secretary of State Vance visited the Soviet Union with a range of new proposals, he received a cool reception. Brezhnev indicated that unless the United States accepted the principal of noninterference in internal affairs, efforts to improve relations between the two countries would be impossible.

As expected, President Carter refused to modify his commitment on human rights, but by the time the two countries met again in May in Geneva, the pressure was mounting in both the United States and the Soviet Union to reach a new agreement (the first SALT agreement would expire in October 1977). Both sides agreed to resume the SALT negotiations, and by October the elements of a second SALT agreement had been worked out. However, when Vance met again with foreign Minister Andre Gromyko in Geneva in December, Gromyko held up the agreement: the Soviets were now upset with the American normalization of relations with the Chinese. It took another six months to reach agreement on SALT.

Of course, there was strong opposition to the treaty at home and abroad. Critics recited the failures of détente yet again, pointing out that despite the SALT negotiations, thousands of Cuban troops that were being assisted by Soviet advisers had appeared in Angola and Ethiopia. The Soviets were also in the process of supplying arms to terrorists and client states in the Middle East and Central America. Further, Soviet naval bases near the Horn of Africa could be used to cut off shipments of Arab oil to the United States and its allies in the event of a Soviet-American war. Quite simply, says Garland Haas, the critics charged that the United States was being out-bargained and out-maneuvered with the SALT II treaty.

The SALT II agreement was finally signed in Vienna, Austria, on June 18, 1979. It was signed by Carter and Brezhnev, who kissed each other on both cheeks to seal the bargain. But the deal was far from done yet: the treaty needed to be approved by the Senate, where opposition was strong. In fact, that longtime opponent of détente, Senator Jackson, sharply attacked the treaty as appeasement—one more in a long line of concessions made to Moscow by an administration he felt was all too eager to maintain the appearance of United States-Soviet accord. According to Garland Haas, he promised a fight to amend the treaty. Despite that attempt, and despite revelations that the Soviets had stationed a combat brigade of three thousand troops in Cuba (which had been there since 1962 and which they asserted was for training only), the Senate Foreign Relations Committee voted in November to send the treaty to the full Senate.

Then without warning on Christmas day, 1979, the Soviet Union invaded Afghanistan to provide support for a weak pro-Communist regime there. On January 7, the UN Security Council voted to condemn the Soviet invasion, but the resolution was nullified by a Soviet veto. A week later, the Soviets vetoed another resolution sponsored by the United States. These actions appeared to indicate a renewed Soviet expansionism and the reopening of the cold war, and the president finally admitted that it was no longer possible "to do business as usual with the Soviet Union" (Haas 1992, 112). Carter abandoned the goal of cooperation with the Soviets, and confrontation—and the old approach of containment—became the name of the game.

On January 4, Carter responded to the invasion of Afghanistan by ordering an embargo on sales to the Soviet Union of American grain, over the strong objections of his own vice president, who was deeply concerned about the impact on grain-belt farmers. Then in his State of the Union Address the president delivered his toughest attack on the Soviet Union since taking office, enunciating what came to be known as the "Carter Doctrine." According to the Carter Doctrine, any attempt by an outside force to gain control of the Persian Gulf region would be regarded as "an assault on the vital interests of the United States of America, and such an assault will be repelled by any means necessary, including military force" (in Kaufman 1993, 164). The president justified this statement by invoking the threat of the Soviet invasion in Afghanistan to the rest of the region.

To show that he meant business, reports Burton Kaufman, the president proposed that all men between the ages of eighteen and twenty-six be required to register for a future draft. He also asked for five annual increases of 5 percent in real military spending rather than the 3 percent that had been his goal since 1977, and he requested $400 million in military and economic aid to Pakistan, which bordered Afghanistan. The president also indicated that he believed that the United States should boycott the Moscow Summer Olympics. Only after much debate, and even then very reluctantly, did the United States Olympic Committee vote in April 1980 to boycott. The Soviets responded by denouncing the boycott as a "flagrant violation" of the United States's commitment to détente (Haas 1992, 113).

Then on January 3, 1980, President Carter asked the Senate majority leader to delay Senate floor debate on the ratification of the SALT II treaty; he recognized that the Soviet invasion of Afghanistan made ratification impossible. He still believed SALT II was in the national interest, and he left open the possibility that it could be taken up later. He need not have bothered, however, for he was never to have the chance to convince the Senate of its necessity: Carter lost in 1980 to Ronald Reagan, a man who had campaigned by attacking Carter's weakness with the Soviets and by promising to rebuild America's defenses. Détente was finally and completely dead.

The Crisis in Iran

Carter's perceived weakness in foreign policy—both in supporting détente with the Soviet Union and in deciding not to go forward with several defense systems—was nothing compared to the criticism that was ultimately to follow the Iranian hostage crisis. Trouble had been coming in Iran for some time, since 1950 in fact, when the United States government had put the young shah back on the throne of Iran with the help of the CIA. Since that time, the shah had remained an important strategic friend to the United States. Even Jimmy Carter, who was concerned about human rights violations in Iran, had continued to support the shah as a strong and essential ally to the United States, calling Iran "an island of stability" in a troubled area of the world (Carter 1982, 438). Even so, pressure was coming to bear inside Iran against the monarch for a variety of complex and long-standing reasons, and by August 1978, Iran was experiencing what Burton Kaufman calls "revolutionary convulsions." Over the next several months the situation deteriorated from bad to worse.

However, when the revolution began in Iran in mid-1978, the Carter administration was already overloaded with the Panama Canal treaties in the Senate, the post-Camp David negotiations between Egypt and Israel, the negotiations with China, and the continuing SALT talks. The top Carter people just could not give the Iran issue the attention it deserved. In fact, according to Burton Kaufman, the Carter administration seemed paralyzed and unable to respond to the events that were sweeping Iran. Internally, members of the administration could not decide what the best course of action would be, and so they neither made serious efforts to support the shah, nor did they ever seek to open lines of communication to the shah's political opponents, particularly to the Ayatollah Khomeini. By the time the revolutionaries had captured their

American hostages in November, argues Erwin Hargrove (1988), any opportunity the president might have had to influence the situation on behalf of U.S. interests was long past.

Americans were taken hostage in Tehran in November 1979. President Carter refused the captors' demands to return the shah and denounced the hostage taking as a flagrant violation of international law. According to Garland Haas, he also moved quickly with an intensive campaign of pressure and diplomacy that he hoped would free the hostages, including pushing for economic sanctions against Iran among NATO countries and even imposing an expensive oil embargo on imports from Iran. This approach failed, however, which served only to undermine the initial public support Carter had experienced on the hostage issue. The public instead began to complain that the president had not taken strong action against Iran after the hostages were seized, and it wondered why Carter had not supported the shah more firmly while the revolution was unfolding. Meanwhile, the nightly television news programs showed frightening scenes from Iran displaying rabid anti-American fervor and relentlessly counted out the days that the hostages had been held. Americans felt outraged, betrayed, frustrated, and impotent. They tied yellow ribbons around trees in honor of the captives, flew giant-sized American flags, and rang church bells every day at noon.

By April 1980, the mood in Washington over the holding of the hostages turned aggressive, with Carter announcing a ban on all exports to Iran, severing diplomatic relations with it, and imposing strict economic sanctions. The president even began to openly suggest that military steps might have to be taken to free the hostages. Even though both Democrats and Republicans on the Senate Foreign Relations Committee sent the president a letter reminding him that he would need to consult with Congress before taking such an action, the president authorized a military rescue operation— code named Operation Blue Light—on the night of April 24. According to Haas, the president believed that a successful rescue mission would prove to the press, to the public, and to his political opponents that he was not the indecisive president who was afraid to act that they all seemed to think he was. He also believed that a successful action would bolster the opinion of the world community, which was increasingly skeptical about American power.

Jimmy Carter might have been right about the positive impacts of a successful rescue mission, but we will never know for sure because Operation Blue Light was an unmitigated disaster. After multiple equipment failures, in fact, the mission was aborted in the Iranian desert. More devastating was the fact that eight commandos had been killed when a transport plane and a helicopter collided. Then, several days after the fiasco, Cyrus Vance resigned as secretary of state as a result of the rescue operation, which he had opposed from the beginning.

The failure of the rescue mission was the end for Jimmy Carter. He was attacked from all sides over United States military preparedness and over his unilateral decision to proceed with the operation. To the end, Carter hoped that the hostages would be freed while he was still president in order to justify the decisions that he had made from the start of the crisis. Several times, Iran indicated that it was ready to discuss the resolution of the hostage situation, and each time Carter was unable to see his hopes fulfilled. In fact, Carter held out that hope all the way up to the last moment; on January 19 it appeared that the freedom of the hostages was imminent, and Carter arranged (again) to fly to Wiesbaden, Germany, to greet them as his last major official act. At the last moment, however, the Iranians delayed the signing of the formal agreement until the morning of January 20—Inauguration Day. The disappointed president instead joined Ronald Reagan for the traditional ride to the inauguration in the presidential limousine (Haas 1992, 172).

Jimmy Carter's Foreign Policy Legacy

There was much success for Jimmy Carter in foreign policy during his four years as president. The triumphs of the Panama Canal treaties and the Camp David Accords, for example, were striking moments for Carter, and those accomplishments brought some healing to a wounded nation. In addition, Carter's emphasis on human rights in the conduct of American foreign policy did restore a sense of domestic self-confidence and foreign credibility to an America shaken by Vietnam, Watergate, and the CIA scandals. Indeed, more than thirty countries were punished for human rights infringements during Carter's time in office, and by 1978 the International League of Human Rights had indicated in its annual report that interest in questions of human rights had increased worldwide. This positive feeling was attributed to Jimmy Carter, and all across the world, according to Friedbert Pfluger, the United States of America was no longer identified with Vietnam and Watergate, but once again with freedom and human rights. In turn, Jimmy Carter's advocacy of human rights in American foreign policy unleashed the topic on the world agenda of international politics.

However, the healing of Carter's human rights emphasis and his indisputable successes in foreign policy must be juxtaposed with his failures. First was the death of détente. The president and his advisors believed that the United States could maintain a productive and friendly relationship with the Soviet Union on the one hand, while they criticized the Russians for their record on human rights on the other. Unfortunately, they were wrong, and this mistake served only to undermine an already crumbling relationship. In fact, by the end, much of the American public had come to believe that détente was really nothing but a scam that had only emboldened the Soviets to further aggression in Africa and Afghanistan. Jimmy Carter was associated both with the weakness détente seemed to represent and with its failure. He carried the blame for this loss, and for the sense that America had made a bad bargain.

Ultimately, the legacy of the death of détente enabled the fall of Carter and the rise of the era of Reagan. During the Reagan era, The United States returned to the dangerous and sometimes reckless stance of confrontation with the Soviet Union, which threatened nuclear war and the destruction of the planet. The nation again assumed that virtually unlimited resources were necessary for defense, but those resources were available only through deficit spending, providing another kind of danger to American well-being and security. John Lewis Gaddis claims that with little real confidence in the prospect of settling differences with the Soviets through negotiation, Americans believed that "situations of strength" had to be created, and they were willing to pay a high price for them.

The death of détente and the sense of weakness that it engendered were only one aspect of Carter's foreign policy failures. Carter also failed to fulfill his own expressed aim: the creation—by means of his human rights policy—of the basis of a new and durable foreign policy consensus in the United States. It seemed at first that the president might realize this dream, but when he proved unable after months on end to solve the crisis in Iran and to bring the hostages home, America's self-confidence was deeply damaged and the president suddenly found himself standing alone. His attempts to emphasize human rights, disarmament, and honesty in dealing with other nations no longer fit the political climate at home. According to Friedbert Pfluger, Americans no longer wanted to be constantly "suffering from a bad conscience." Instead, they wanted power to take privilege over morality so that the rest of the world could not be given the chance to "push America around" again (1989, 710).

Thus the hostage crisis and Carter's inability to bring it to an end quickly and successfully became a national wound, and the impression of weakness that it represented became the foreign policy legacy that Jimmy Carter left behind. It was truly a symbol of American weakness, and like the Vietnam War, it was a great American betrayal, forcing America to come to terms with the limits of its power in the world. In the end, the sense of weakness and the feelings of betrayal washed away Carter's triumphs. In the end, what was left for America was only this: the feeling that the nation was isolated and vulnerable in the world.

5

Social Movements in the Seventies

BY THE LATE 1960s, the nation was afire with protest movements that demanded racial justice, that violently demonstrated opposition to the war in Vietnam, and that took swipes at the predominant structures in American society and challenged all forms of authority in that society. Once the activism, violence, and excesses of this time had played themselves out, however, they brought forth a legacy of quieter, more mature, and more sophisticated social movements seeking change. Thus, argues Frederick Siegel in his 1984 book *Troubled Journey*, the massive antiwar and civil rights crusades of the 1960s gave birth to a whole new range of movements of inclusion and social protest. These new movements, of which feminism and environmentalism were the most important, were organized by the people who were shaped by both Kennedy-like appeals to national greatness and by the traditions of social criticism born in the 1960s.

Thus, while the struggle for racial equality continued in America, argues Robert Hargreaves (1973), several new social movements seemed to guide the nation's destiny by the early 1970s: new concern with the environment, worries about the effects of pollution and of unlimited economic growth, and radical changes in the perceptions of the role of women and of the young.

Environmentalism and the Age of Awakening:
From Earth Day to Three Mile Island

The hopes and promises of the 1940s and early 1950s in America were tied to the high-tech, high-energy methods of production developed during World War II. These methods had succeeded in raising the American standard of living dramatically in those years, and Americans saw only prosperity and endless possibilities in their future. Then the dream was shattered in the 1960s, as so many American dreams were, by a new realization. Beginning with the 1962 publication of Rachel Carson's *Silent Spring,* the nation became increasingly aware of the negative side of high-technology productivity. Carson's book exposed the terrible effects of the wonder pesticide DDT, which had greatly increased crop yields: DDT killed off not only harmful insects but birds and wildlife as well, while petrochemical fertilizers "created vast nitrogenous wastes that drained into rivers and lakes," virtually killing them, according to Frederick Siegel in his 1984 book (210–11). At the same time, the oil and strip-mined coal that the nation depended on for energy left the soil barren and the air filled with a smog so poisonous that in many major cities it became a real threat to public health.

Thus, high-tech mass production had raised living standards and vastly increased the number and quality of the goods available to Americans, but it had also wreaked havoc on the nation's air, water, and soil. And so the popular movement for a better environment began in the 1960s. It was during the seventies, however, that the issue of the environment really began to solidify with the American public and to become an issue of political interest. In less than a decade, according to Joan Hoff (1994), the nation experienced a surging concern among its citizens about the environmental consequences of a growing population and expanding technology. For example, from the time in 1965 that Gallup and other pollsters began to include the environment as an issue in their questionnaires until 1970, a leap from a little over one-third to almost two-thirds of the public had become concerned about water pollution. In May 1971, fully a quarter of the public thought the issues of pollution and ecology were important, up from just 1 percent that had thought so two years earlier.

This relatively new concern about the environment was symbolic of a broader preoccupation with the quality of American life, particularly for a generation that was freed for the first time from a constant concern with just making a living. Since few communities were spared the effects of air and water pollution and the misuse and abuse of the land, a truly new consciousness was born. Indeed, once Americans realized in the early 1970s that it was in fact possible to "run out of" clean air and water, concerns about pollution, the loss of open space, and the decimation of wildlife took root. Those concerns led to the kind of passionate opposition that proved capable of fueling a new generation of reform politics, state Vig and Kraft (1990),and the environmental movement that was sweeping the country catapulted environmental policy onto the national political agenda. This was perhaps best symbolized on April 22, 1970, when the nation celebrated the first Earth Day with a massive outpouring of support for environmental protection. By that date, environmentalism was so popular with the public that Congress adjourned for the day and ten million schoolchildren took part in events to mark the occasion. Nationwide "teach-ins" about environmental problems symbolized the new place of ecology on the nation's political agenda, while some ten thousand people flocked to the Washington Monument for twelve hours of partying. The celebration was a prophetic symbol of what could come.

Indeed, 1970 marked a watershed year for new environmental organizations, according to Switzer and Bryner (1988), with the founding of the Center for Science in the Public Interest, Citizens for a Better Environment, Environmental Action, Friends of the Earth, the League of Conservation Voters, the Natural Resources Defense Council, and Save the Bay. Thus, by the time of the 1972 presidential election, no issue other than that of peace in Vietnam received wider attention than environmental quality. The public very quickly grasped the importance of environmental hazards and overwhelmingly supported increased protections and greater federal spending on the issue. As Theodore White has argued, by the time of the 1972 elections, the cause of the environment had swollen into the favorite sacred issue of all politicians, all TV networks, all writers, all goodwilled people of any party. Therefore every legislator and every presidential candidate had to have a position on the issue.

This awakening to the environmental problem and to concerted action to protect the planet is the story of the ecology movement during the decade of the seventies.

Environmental Legislation

Although the popular movement for the environment really had its birth in the 1960s, it reached fruition in a series of federal and state laws passed in the early 1970s. Responding to the popular outcry represented by the first Earth Day celebration (California Democrat Jesse Unruh claimed that "Ecology ha[d] become the political substitute for the word 'mother' "), Congress passed clear air, clean water, and safe waste disposal legislation. The legislative cornerstone of all of this environmental protection legislation was the Na-

tional Environmental Policy Act (NEPA) of 1969, which served as a foundation for the policy initiatives that were to follow throughout the next twenty
years. The act was groundbreaking in requiring that major projects undergo
detailed assessments of their environmental impacts, giving birth to a new
strategy that would be used more and more extensively by policy makers in the
next decades to justify controls on various toxic substances in the air, in the
water, and on the land. When Richard Nixon signed the bill in 1970, he said:
"The 1970s absolutely must be the years when America pays its debt to the
past by reclaiming the purity of its air, its waters, and our living environment.
It is literally now or never" (Trager 1992, 1030).

Other important pieces of federal legislation followed the NEPA in the
1970s. The Clean Air Act of 1970, for example, was the toughest measure of
its kind to date. It was strict even though major compromises had been made
with automakers, who were given six years to develop engines that were 90
percent emission-free. In 1972, Congress passed the Water Pollution Control
Act, setting a 1977 deadline for the installation of the "best practicable" pollution control equipment for treating fluid waste discharges, and setting a
1983 limit for the installation of the "best available" equipment. The Toxic
Substances Control Act, passed by Congress and signed by President Ford in
1975, was also important in requiring the phasing out of all production and
sale of PCBs, which had been linked to cancer and birth defects, within three
years. The Surface Mining and Reclamation Act passed in July 1977 required
that companies restore stripped coal lands to approximate original contours.
It also forced the companies to obtain a permit before they could strip-mine
coal from farmland and to demonstrate that they were technologically capable
of restoring the land to productivity afterward.

In 1977, Congress even went so far as to amend the far-reaching Clean
Air Act of 1970 with new restrictions on air pollution while allowing California to set even stricter limits in an effort to reduce that state's mounting smog
problem. The result was that the manufacturers of automobiles in the United
States began to install catalytic converters, which reduced tailpipe emissions
by 90 percent. These examples are just several of the many victories claimed by
the environmental movement during the 1970s. Other important legislation
passed by environmentally activist Congresses during the decade included the
Marine Mammal Protection Act (1972), the Federal Environmental Pesti-
cides Control Act (1972), the Endangered Species Act (1973), and the Re-

source Conservation and Recovery Act (1976). In all, Congress enacted more than twenty major pieces of legislation during this period.

While Congress was thus firmly on the environmental protection bandwagon, President Nixon's position seemed much less stable. He had refused to issue a proclamation in support of Earth Day, but when he signed the NEPA that same year he used the occasion to declare the next ten years the "environmental decade." With his creation of the Council of Environmental Quality and of the Environmental Protection Agency (EPA) by executive order in 1970, Joan Hoff argues, Nixon moved ahead of Congress in the race to be the quickest to take advantage of the public's newfound passion for the issue. Further, his administration did support other important environmental legislation, including federal regulation of oil spill cleanup, noise pollution, and state coastal zone management. But by the summer of 1971, the president was attaching a message to the Council of Environmental Quality's second annual report that stated, "it is simplistic to seek ecological perfection at the cost of bankrupting the very tax-paying enterprises which must pay for the social advances the nation seeks" (Hoff 1994, 24). Later, he vetoed the Federal Water Pollution Control Act Amendments of 1972, and by the end of his presidency was actively working against environmental laws by impounding money set aside for environmental protection.

Quite simply, President Nixon was in a bind that only clearly came to light with the environmental activism of the 1970s. Everyone recognized that it would not be easy to modify the historic freedoms associated with America's laissez-faire economy. Indeed the American way of life has always been embodied by an essential belief in growth. So by the early 1970s, industry—always a backer of Nixon and the Republican Party—was urging restraint. Indeed, it was during the seventies that the nation witnessed a turnaround in leverage, argues Michael Genovese (1988), as business and industry mobilized to slow the pace of environmental legislation. Industry spokespersons, for example, began to portray environmentalists as hysterical radicals who wanted to bring the nation to its knees. American business downplayed environmental risks and suggested that business be allowed to clean things up on its own, without more government regulations. Richard Nixon was caught in the middle. He knew the problem of the environment was real, but the solutions were costly—both financially and politically. So after early efforts to deal with environmental issues, the Nixon administration backed into a pattern of bold rhetoric and mild action. As the public, Congress, and environmental groups became activated, says Genovese, Nixon attempted to talk tough but to water down congressional efforts to impose stricter, costlier restrictions on industry. When it came down to "a flat choice between smoke and jobs," Nixon privately and publicly made it clear that he favored jobs and a strong economy (Hoff 1994, 23).

This environmental dilemma continued, and continues, to be a vexing problem for the public, for presidents, and for other public officials alike. As environmental protection has come into direct conflict with widespread economic problems and the needs of business, the horns of the dilemma have never seemed sharper. One good example of this dilemma is represented by the plight of the tiny snail darter at a time when the inflation rate topped 10 percent. In the late 1970s, the three-inch-long snail darter fish, whose only known habitat was the Little Tennessee River, was threatened with extinction. Under the provisions of the 1973 Endangered Species Act, a federal court of appeals ordered the Tennessee Valley Authority to stop construction of a dam on the Little Tennessee River in 1977 in order to preserve the snail darter's habitat. Although $116 million had already been spent on constructing the dam and although it was nearing completion, the Supreme Court affirmed the decision the following year. The victory of the snail darter and environmentalists was short-lived, however. In 1979, over angry objections, President Carter, "with regret," signed legislation exempting the dam from any laws that might prevent its completion (Marty 1997, 200).

Environmental Crises Focus Public Attention

Several unexpected events during the 1970s periodically refocused national attention on the environment and kept the environmental movement energized and activated. Just as the 1969 Santa Barbara oil spill had galvanized public opinion at the beginning of the decade—it covered a thirty-mile stretch of California shoreline with 235,000 gallons of crude oil, killing fish and wildlife, and continued to leak oil for years afterward—so too did the 1979 blowout of a Mexican offshore oil well. The accident in 1979 contaminated fisheries and beaches in the Gulf of Mexico with millions of gallons of oil in the largest spill ever recorded to that date. In fact, after three months of uncontrolled spillage, the oil had traveled six hundred miles from the hole drilled by explorers, shaking confidence in the ability of so-called blowout preventers and backup systems to protect the environment.

Meanwhile, the 1973 Arab oil embargo had pushed energy to the top of the policy agenda, although a succession of presidents had sought to make the United States "energy independent." The 1969 testimony of Sierra Club executive vice president David Brower before the House Merchant Marine and Fisheries Committee had aided in bringing about the EPA's ban on nearly all uses of DDT in 1972. Brower testified that mother's milk contained four times the amount of DDT permitted in cow's milk, saying, "Some wit suggested that if [mother's milk] were packaged in some other container we wouldn't allow it across state lines" (Trager 1992, 1024). Of course, these examples are just a few of the many environmental tragedies that came to light during the decade, and not all of them received public attention or proved capable of motivating action on behalf of environmental protection. However, three particular incidents gained wide public attention during the decade, and they did serve to heighten public fear about the quality of the environment as well as to invigorate the movement toward continued activism: the discovery of the role of fluorocarbons in destroying the ozone, the tragedy at Love Canal, and the accident at Three Mile Island.

Hair Spray and the Ozone Hole. Events in the 1970s provided dramatic evidence of the fragility of the environment, but sometimes the evidence was subtle or unseen. For example, it hardly occurred to Americans who sprayed on their deodorant and hair spray each morning that the propellant used in their sprays contained ingredients that were harmful to the environment. In the mid-1970s, however, scientists fixed part of the blame for the gradual destruction of the ozone shield covering the earth on the molecules of fluorocarbons in aerosol propellants. Since the ozone shield prevents the most harmful ultraviolet radiation from reaching the earth's surface, experts feared that its destruction would cause increases in skin cancer and cataracts and possibly genetic damage to plant and animal life.

The result, according to Myron Marty (1997), was that environmentalists called for a ban on fluorocarbon gases. Producers opposed a ban, claiming it would hurt their industry, which added $8 billion to the gross national product and employed nearly one million workers. As concerned consumers began to turn away from the environmentally unsound products, however, producers gradually switched to another propellant. By 1979, when the FDA began to prohibit shipment of products with fluorocarbon propellants, most manufacturers had already replaced them with other substances.

Love Canal and Toxic Wastes. A dramatic example of the environment's fragility attracted national attention in 1978. In a residential neighborhood known as Love Canal, located east of Niagara Falls, New York, a chemical dump that had been buried there more than twenty years before began to bubble up in lawns and basements. Given the toxic nature of the bubbling chemicals, the state of New York bought the property bordering the Love Canal and evacuated scores of residents to new homes. However, not only did the toxic chemicals migrate beyond the evacuation line, but nearby residents also reported a high incidence of birth defects and illnesses believed to have been caused by the chemicals. Indeed, by 1980, studies seemed to show that the chemicals were responsible, although the studies' adequacy and accuracy were disputed.

The press gave the Love Canal story extensive coverage, and the sad experiences of the Love Canal families reawakened America's concerns over toxic waste. Finally, in 1980, a new federal law (which had passed four years earlier) went into effect that provided for strict controls on toxic waste disposal. Myron Marty claims that the new law provided little comfort, however, to the families living near Love Canal who could not move out of their homes until someone bought them (and who would want to do that?). It was also cold comfort to the thousands of families across the country that lived near sites similar to that at Love Canal. Indeed, incidents painfully similar to the Love Canal story occurred in Kentucky in 1979, where seventeen thousand drums of leaking chemicals were discovered, and again in 1983 in Times Beach, Missouri, where high levels of dioxin were thought to have contaminated the entire town.

Nuclear Power and Three Mile Island. Following World War II, the general sentiment of the nation favored finding new and innovative uses for nuclear energy. Some nuclear experts were highly optimistic about the prospects of harnessing the recently discovered source of energy for generating electricity. They believed that nuclear power could replace fossil fuels in meeting the energy needs of the nation. But this optimistic view of using nuclear energy for the betterment of the human condition, says Arthur Neal (1998), soon collided with pessimistic views about the dire consequences of producing a highly radioactive environment.

Opposition to nuclear power plants began to increase with the growing concern in the nation for the environment, and many people expressed fears about the potential for accidental leakage of radioactive materials into the atmosphere. As time passed, many Americans became doubtful about claims of the safety of nuclear power. These anxieties were intensified by the popular movie *The China Syndrome,* starring Jane Fonda as an investigative reporter for a television news program. The movie conveyed the image that nuclear power plants were unsafe, and that attempts had been made to cover up defects in their design and construction. The movie also suggested that employees who attempted to talk to the press about such problems met with violent and mysterious deaths (an allusion to the case of Karen Silkwood, a nuclear fuel facility laboratory technician who died in a mysterious automobile crash near Oklahoma City in 1974 while on her way to meet a reporter). In short, the movie made it seem that nuclear power plants were catastrophes waiting to happen; the idea of "the China syndrome" was, according to Arthur Neal, that a nuclear meltdown would start a chain reaction that would continue until it burned a hole through the entire earth.

Thus, the tide of public opinion about nuclear power was moving in a negative direction even before the nuclear accident at Three Mile Island near Harrisburg, Pennsylvania, in March 1979. A malfunction in the cooling system at Unit II of the nuclear reactor raised alarms that the year-old reactor might explode and release radioactive cesium. Although the overheated reactor shut down automatically, Metropolitan Edison Company operators were misled by ambiguous indicators and believed that water pressure was building in the reactor. So they shut down the pumps that were still operating. This caused the reactor to heat up even further, while tons of water poured out and overflowed into an auxiliary building through a valve that should have been shut.

The media coverage of the Three Mile Island accident was dramatic, and for an extended period of time the episode remained the lead item in the news. As events played out, people began to believe that a nuclear explosion might occur. From the heat that continued to build in the reactor, there was the risk of a nuclear meltdown. Deep public fears grew out of uncertainty over what was happening and over what was going to happen next, reports Arthur Neal, and despite pronouncements by the utility company that everything was under control, the governor of Pennsylvania advised pregnant women and those with preschool children to evacuate the area. Confusion mounted as police went door-to-door, instructing people to remain inside, to close all windows, and to turn off their air conditioners. Some 144,000 people, mostly pregnant women and small children, were evacuated from the area. Unbelievably, the reactor core did not melt down despite exposure and damage, and little radiation was released into the air.

Nonetheless, the accident set off an intense national controversy over the risks and benefits of nuclear power. According to some estimates, the nuclear reactor at Three Mile Island came within thirty to forty-five seconds of a complete meltdown before it was brought under control. In addition, the problems of the aftermath were of a kind and of a magnitude that neither the utility company nor governmental regulatory agencies were prepared to handle. So, despite assurances from the company and government officials that the crisis was over, Arthur Neal argues that many people remained doubtful. Millions of Americans watched on television as radiation detectors were used to check people and food supplies for possible contamination. Many remained convinced that nuclear power could never be safe.

Thus, Three Mile Island became the major symbol of the controversy over nuclear power in the United States during the mid- and late-1970s. Following the Three Mile Island episode, concerns were registered in public demonstrations throughout the country, and a hastily organized rally in Washington, D.C., drew a crowd of about one hundred thousand. Nuclear plants throughout the country were surrounded by picket lines, and a new era of protest against the use of nuclear power was born. Nine new U.S. nuclear reactors did begin commercial production in 1979, and France, Japan, Soviet Russia, and other nations continued to expand nuclear energy capabilities and to reduce dependence on petroleum. However, the malfunction at Three Mile Island and the public's activist reaction did discourage the creation of new atomic energy facilities. United States utility companies canceled eleven reactor orders in 1979 alone, and they canceled several more the following year. Further, the installation of several other reactors was indefinitely delayed.

Concerns of the Movement for the Eighties

In 1977, President Carter launched a study that resulted in *The Global 2000 Report to the President*. The report identified environmental, resource, and population stresses that were intensifying and would increasingly determine the quality of human life on the planet. According to Myron Marty, it projected deterioration and loss of resources essential for agriculture at an accelerating rate, and it forecast the extinction of five hundred thousand plant and animal species over the next twenty years. Despite the overwhelming evidence and thorough documentation in the report, however, its concerns attracted little attention.

Events such as that at Love Canal and at Three Mile Island made the concerns reported in the *Global 2000* report less than startling. Even so, those who opposed environmental regulations continued in their efforts to reverse what had been accomplished, and legislators seemed unwilling to believe the report's conclusions. Meanwhile, the late 1970s was a time of energy shortages, high unemployment, and even higher inflation, causing the Carter administration to pull back from some of its environmental commitments. Quite simply, the environmental decade was coming to an end. Meanwhile, those that were still active in the ecology movement grew concerned and fearful about the possible election of Ronald Reagan in 1980, says Myron Marty. They feared that his election would lead to a reversal of the gains they had made in enacting and enforcing environmental protection laws.

They were right to be afraid, for Reagan was highly critical of the movement and had already stated that he would do such things as invite coal and steel industries to propose revisions to clean-air laws. Thus, while the seventies were an age of environmental awakening and activism, the future did not look terribly promising for the environment or the environmental movement. The seventies had seen the United States adopting dozens of major environmental and resource policies, creating new institutions such as the EPA to manage environmental programs, and greatly increasing its spending on such programs. The eighties, however, were the years of the Reagan administration, which curtailed these programs and the enforcement of environmental protection severely.

Civil Rights and Race Relations in the Seventies: Backlash

The civil rights movement grew out of the struggle of black Americans to regain constitutional rights long denied them. Using the nation's courts, political pressure, and active protest, blacks brought an end to decades of legal discrimination during the triumphant and violent years of the 1960s. But the blind rage that had led to the riots of the sixties in Watts, Detroit, Newark, and scores of other cities began to subside with the advent of the 1970s. The mood of helpless violence that swept through the black community after the assassination of Dr. Martin Luther King Jr. in 1968 had evaporated by the early 1970s. Even the revolutionary Black Panthers had turned away from confrontation and to the ballot box. The death of Martin Luther King, the riots, and exhaustion, argues Robert Hargreaves (1973), took much of the impetus out of the movement, and the election of Richard Nixon in November 1968 dealt it an additional blow. The civil rights movement that had led to the major reforms of the sixties had finally petered out, while Johnson's Great Society programs were slowly but surely being discredited and dismantled by Nixon, a president who had seemingly abandoned integration as a national policy.

Indeed, the radical and violent element of the civil rights movement that came to predominance in the 1960s caused a white backlash, a lessening of white sympathy for the black movement, in the 1970s. This could be seen in opposition to civil rights demonstrations and in increasing resistance to civil rights legislation in Congress. The election in 1968 of Richard Nixon, no friend of civil rights, signaled the end of the most active phase of the civil rights movement, according to Findling and Thackeray (1996). The notion of establishing race-conscious policies and preferential treatment for blacks to remedy past injustices (affirmative action) also intensified the backlash by those who thought the movement had already gone too far, too fast. Pursuit of civil rights goals in the courts encouraged the backlash further, particularly on the matter of busing to achieve school desegregation. Indeed, polls taken in the early seventies indicated that two-thirds of Americans felt that blacks were asking for more than they were ready to assume. Furthermore, about half of Americans felt that African Americans sought to live off handouts, and a majority then felt that minorities had the same or better opportunities than white Americans in getting jobs, education, housing, and other advantages.

Richard Nixon took advantage of this backlash, says Myron Marty, playing on the resentments of whites. He opposed busing as a means to desegregate schools and called for "law and order" during the 1968 campaign. In office, Nixon attempted to weaken the enforcement provisions of the Voting Rights Act and continued to oppose busing. He nominated several conservative Southerners to serve on the Supreme Court, and as we shall see, while Congress, the courts, and the federal bureaucracy often frustrated Nixon's attempts to slow the civil rights struggle, the era of federal activism had clearly ended.

Even so, African Americans had made some gains with the 1960s movement, winning legal protections and an end to de jure (legal) segregation. In addition, black leaders had sought to increase their representation in politics at all levels, and by 1971, twelve African Americans held seats in the House of Representatives and a number of cities had African-American mayors. The congressional Black Caucus was formed in 1971, and it cooperated in planning a National Black Political Assembly for March 1972 that aimed at moving the black masses from the politics of desegregation to the politics of "real empowerment" (Marty 1997, 89). Black Americans had also had some economic success. By the early seventies, for example, one-third of them had become members of the middle class. Even among those middle-class blacks, however, the gains were uneven. Few were able to move to the suburbs, and the unemployment rate for blacks was twice that of whites.

Even worse, poor blacks in urban areas really suffered. According to Findling and Thackeray (1996), the inner cities had become battlegrounds, avoided by both whites and politicians, while gangs and drug dealers controlled the streets. Indeed, the one fact that dominated the 1970 census figures was the decline of the American city. The numbers revealed what Theodore White called the "most important political story in America": white people, by the millions, were leaving the big cities of the North and the East while black and Spanish-speaking people were replacing them. White explained it this way in 1973: "The civil rights programs of the 60s had delivered much of honor and vast achievement, but they had placed the burden of progress on the people of the big cities, and wherever white people could find their way out, they were fleeing the solutions imposed on them" (141).

The minorities who were left behind were left to their ghettos, as they could do nothing to stop the process of ghettoization of the inner city and white flight to the suburbs. As the more affluent populations fled the inner cities, the tax base declined sharply. Urban areas thus grew more and more impoverished and the services and amenities of urban life degenerated. What became clear in 1970, says Myron Marty, was that the two races lived in an America of greater and greater separation, mutual hostility, and dread. While the United Nations spent the years of the 1970s attacking the racist government of South Africa, America had given birth to its own version of apartheid. Indeed, much of the "urban renewal" that exported blacks out of unwanted areas and condensed them into ghettos was accomplished with the assistance of substantial federal moneys. Meanwhile, except in southwestern regions of the United States, Miami, and New York City, it was easy for Americans to ignore the presence of persons of Hispanic descent. Although Spanish-speaking Americans tried to organize for more effective political clout during the 1960s and 1970s, they had to struggle to overcome their diverse interests and backgrounds. In addition, Native Americans faced conditions that were in many ways even more distressing than those of African Americans and Hispanics.

Thus, black Americans and other minority groups did not feel in any way that they had achieved their objectives. To the contrary, despite all of the progress made in the decade of the 1960s, these groups, particularly black Americans, still had not seen the majority of their goals met and were still angry. The United States was very much in danger of becoming a society split wholly in two, separate and unequal. Segregation of the races by law had vanished in the United States during the last decade, but de jure segregation had merely been replaced by de facto segregation. As Robert Hargreaves argues, segregation remained as strong as ever in housing patterns, schools, and social interactions. The issue simply remained one of the most explosive in American society, with feelings on both sides running deeply and intensely. Unfortunately, the politics of the 1970s and the white backlash against the struggle did nothing to alleviate those tensions.

Richard Nixon Sets the Stage for Race Relations in the Seventies

We already know that Richard Nixon took control of the White House in a time of social and political unrest. We know, too, that one of the largest elements of that unrest was reflected in the civil rights movement, which had gained momentum in the late 1950s and had emerged as a powerful force in American politics in the 1960s. What was most frightening for those involved in the struggle, according to Michael Genovese, was the fact that Nixon owed his nomination and election to the same forces in the Deep South that had stubbornly blocked the evolution of civil rights for black people for so many years. In fact, Richard Nixon received less than 10 percent of the black vote in the 1968 election, so he owed them nothing. Since there was little likelihood that he would be able to win over black voters, it is not surprising that his administration was at best lukewarm to the promotion of civil rights. On the other hand, he had a debt to repay to the white South, and it was paid in what became known as the "Southern Strategy." That strategy meant playing up to white Southern voters in an effort to woo them away from the Democratic Party (and George Wallace). It also meant retreating on black civil rights and giving special favors to Southern segregationists, particularly in terms of taking off the federal pressures forcing school desegregation.

At the start, however, Richard Nixon presented himself as a president who was ready to aid the black community in its struggle. For example, he met with six black leaders after his election to discuss general civil rights and racial problems. During that meeting, Nixon was quoted by those present as pledging "to do more for the underprivileged and more for the Negro than any president has ever done" (Evans and Novak 1971, 134). But in short order, Nixon was on his way to being the president most disliked and distrusted by blacks since the rise of black political power following World War II. At a meeting with the thirty-five highest-ranking black officials in the federal government in April 1970, James Farmer informed the president of "a growing spirit of [African-American] hopelessness that the Administration [was] not on their side" (Evans and Novak 1971, 135).

In March 1970, for example, a January memorandum from Daniel Patrick Moynihan, Nixon's top adviser on race issues, was leaked to the press. In it, Moynihan suggested to the president that "the time may have come when the issue of race could benefit from a period of 'benign neglect,'" to which Nixon responded, "I agree" (Hoff 1994, 83). A major public relations explosion followed, with a group of civil rights leaders attacking the policy as a "calculated, aggressive, and systematic" effort by the administration to "wipe out" gains made by the civil rights movement (Genovese 1990, 82–83). Although the administration responded by insisting that "benign neglect" was merely an effort to deflate the hot rhetoric of the race issue, the damage was done. Indeed, scholars such as Hugh Davis Graham note that Nixon's civil rights policy was characterized chiefly by neglect and inattention. Although his administration did take several steps to promote civil rights, according to Michael Genovese (1990), overall the Nixon approach to civil rights was to withdraw and retreat. By late 1970, the anti-civil rights side of the Nixon administration had come to dominate the policy and political agenda.

School Desegregation and Busing

When the famous *Brown v. Board of Education* decision was handed down in 1954, it sparked a movement that would profoundly change the face of the American nation. At the time of the decision, the Supreme Court had refused to describe a definite timeline for the completion of school desegregation. Instead, in *Brown*'s reargument, the Court called for school systems to desegregate with "all deliberate speed." According to John Robert Greene (1995), this vague description of timing for desegregation suited the presidents, including Nixon, who came to power following the *Brown* decision—until 1969, that is, when the Burger Court demanded immediate desegregation in *Alexander v. Homes County*. In that decision, the Court made it clear that separate but equal schools were no longer permissible under the Constitution.

Although Nixon was opposed to segregation, he believed that speedy, federally forced integration was worse than no integration at all, as it would alienate most white Southerners and increase racial tensions throughout the country. To Nixon, "no panacea of speedy integration was more undesirable than forced busing," according to John Robert Greene in his 1992 book on the Nixon and Ford administrations (41). To avoid busing, Nixon took the early position of supporting the cutoff of funds to any school district that refused to comply with integration guidelines. However, Attorney General John Mitchell later convinced the president that this approach would merely engender the rage of Southern whites against the administration. He counseled that instead of the fund cutoffs, the Justice Department should push for enforcement of integration guidelines through the judicial process. This approach would ensure a slower, more cautious procedure for integration and would place the ugly burden of enforcement on the courts, rather than on the Nixon White House. Thus, according to Greene (1992), on July 2 the president announced that the administration was shifting its strategy to the courts and would ignore other desegregation deadlines—particularly those regarding the cutoff of funds—set by the previous administration. The result? Black leaders were infuriated, white Southerners were mollified, and the press attacked Nixon for his flip-flop on civil rights. In fact, the U.S. Commission on Civil Rights called the policy statement on school integration inadequate, overcautious, and possibly the signal for a major retreat.

Nonetheless, the president was forced to deal with a situation that he would have preferred to ignore, and so John Robert Greene (1995) argues that he chose to make a public distinction between de jure segregation in the South (segregation by law) and de facto segregation in other areas of the country (social segregation). In doing so, Richard Nixon made it clear that, as president, he could attack only de jure segregation, not de facto. This moderate approach was far more acceptable to white Southerners than the more aggressive tactics of previous administrations and resulted in a positive outcome: the percentage of African-American children attending segregated schools fell from 68 percent to 8 percent during the Nixon administration. Although the president was forced to move ahead on desegregation by court decisions, he had nonetheless been able to use the issue to pursue his Southern Strategy and ingratiate himself to the white segregationists of the South. The administration's early indecision on school desegregation gave direct encouragement to those opposed to it, state Evans and Novak (1971). Even though nothing had changed—not the court decisions nor the laws—Nixon allowed many white Southerners to believe that it had.

The problem of segregated schools in the North (de facto segregation) was obviously ignored by the Nixon administration, however. Until the 1970s, it had been widely assumed that school segregation was only a problem of the South. But as the seventies commenced, the fact slowly dawned that the most segregated schools were generally to be found in the North and the West, the result of housing patterns. In many cities, there was no hope of achieving any semblance of racial balance, mostly because there were not enough white children to make it possible. In other cities where integration might be possible, the federal courts were intervening in an attempt to bring it about. The tool they had employed in many cases was busing, and the ubiquitous yellow school bus became a symbol of great conflict in the 1970s. Exaggerated stories of young children spending hours on buses stirred up strong emotions during this time, although in the vast number of cases, states Robert Hargreaves, the distance to be traveled was no more than four or five miles! Those few children who were bused long distances—in cities such as Los Angeles, for example—were already traveling long distances by bus to get to school.

Even after the Supreme Court ruled on April 20, 1971, in *Swann v. Charlotte-Mecklenburg Board of Education,* that busing to achieve racial integration was legal, President Nixon continued to employ delaying tactics and refused to endorse busing to enforce school desegregation in the North. In March 1972 the president proposed two bills to Congress: one to provide more funds for improving poor-quality schools, and the other to "stop excessive busing" and to establish "uniform national standards for school desegregation, in which busing would be a remedy of last resort" (Hoff 1994, 89). Thus, Nixon's belief that the federal government should not make itself an instrument of integration led him to denounce busing at every opportunity and to effectively turn his back on de facto segregation. In so doing, argues Greene (1992), he left racial tensions in the cities essentially as he had inherited them from Johnson: a powder keg, waiting for the next opportunity to detonate.

Busing Turns Even Uglier

That detonation occurred in Boston in 1974, when the U.S. District Court found the city guilty of unconstitutional segregation of its schools and ordered the immediate development of a busing plan. When the School Committee refused to comply, the Court worked out a plan itself with the State Department of Education that called for integrating only those schools that were near each other, thus requiring a minimal amount of busing. Nonetheless, violence broke out on the opening day of school, with black students being attacked by screaming white parents and flying rocks. The ensuing riot injured nine children, damaged eighteen buses, and began an organized white boycott of the city schools.

President Gerald Ford took the same approach to busing that Nixon had, arguing that it should be employed only for the purposes of correcting the effects of intentional segregation—again ignoring the problems of de facto segregation. It is no surprise then that Ford publicly stated that he disagreed with the Court's order in the Boston case. Nor is it a surprise that his Justice Department under Edward Levi refused to intervene and to initiate proceedings that would force the Boston school board to obey the order. The president even decided not to send in the National Guard when violence again erupted in Boston in December 1974. In that incident, an angry white mob smashed police cars and refused to allow black students to leave one of the integrated schools after a fight had resulted in the stabbing of a white student.

The tensions that had led to such incidents in Boston were finally resolved, not because of any leadership on the part of the president or his administration, but because three members of the Boston School Committee were held in contempt for refusing to comply with the desegregation order. Late in January 1975, reports John Robert Greene (1995),the committee finally submitted a desegregation plan. But controversies over school policies, court decisions, and legislative and executive actions aimed at desegregation continued throughout the 1970s. Several of them became violent. In addition, the various Supreme Court decisions regarding the integration of schools, and busing in particular, had a larger and more profound effect in another way. Myron Marty argues that color consciousness and sensitivity to group identities came to permeate virtually all decisions in schools, particularly in urban districts.

The Civil Rights Act

Richard Nixon wanted to pursue his Southern Strategy and to back away from blacks and their struggle, but his administration was often blocked by law from doing so. This meant that the only tactics that were really open to it, according to Michael Genovese, included delaying implementation of the law (as it did in the school desegregation cases) and limiting or controlling the level of civil rights enforcement. The best example of the latter came in June 1969 when John Mitchell, Nixon's attorney general, testified in Congress against renewal of the Voting Rights Act. The act had been one of the most effective civil rights bills ever passed, increasing voter registration among blacks in the South and giving the black community some hope for gaining political power. Soon after the administration took office, however, Attorney General Mitchell suggested replacing the act with a much weaker bill.

What he suggested in its place was a bill that would "nationalize" voting rights by providing for uniform residence requirements and by banning literacy tests all over the country, not simply in the South. As such, argues Joan Hoff, Mitchell's replacement seemed reasonable enough: it would no longer stigmatize the South as being the only area of the country where African Americans were denied the right to vote. However, Mitchell's bill would also have brought an end to the requirement that Southern states submit any changes in their voting laws to the Justice Department for approval. Evans and Novak (1971) argue that this would also have weakened the potent enforcement features of the original bill and ended special sanctions against the South—elements that had added almost one million black voters to the rolls.

Ultimately, Congress voted to renew the vital provisions of the Voting Rights Act and even expanded its guarantees to Spanish-speaking Americans and other "language minorities" in one of the few legislative victories for civil rights in the seventies. Similarly, the Supreme Court later upheld (in March 1977) the racial quotas used in reapportioning legislative districts in order to comply with the Voting Rights Act.

Affirmative Action Adds to the Backlash

The extension of the Voting Rights Act was a legislative victory for the civil rights movement in the 1970s, but an even bigger advance for the movement—one that ultimately only added to the backlash against minority rights, however—was the birth and institutionalization of affirmative action. In the late 1960s and early 1970s, a new approach to advancing the position of minorities in America began to take root. It began with the consciousness, first articulated by President Lyndon Johnson in 1965, that the fabulous legislative and legal gains of the 1960s had not really been enough. Those gains provided for legal equality, but they provided only equality. The problem with simple equality, according to this new consciousness, was that it did not make up for decades of segregation and exploitation. In Johnson's words, one could not take a person who for years had been hobbled by chains and liberate him, bring him up to the starting line of a race, and expect him to be able to compete with all the others fairly. To overcome the legacy of slavery and segregation, then, blacks would have to be treated not equally but differently, by taking their race into account when allocating opportunity. The notion behind affirmative action was born.

The birth and institutionalization of this new notion thus began during the Johnson years. His administration pursued affirmative action in the private economy first by reinterpreting and using Title VII of the Civil Rights Act of 1964, which forbids discrimination in employment on account of race, color, religion, sex, or national origin. The Equal Employment Opportunity Commission (EEOC), which is charged with enforcing Title VII, began to use the statute to attack discrimination caused not by the "bad motives" of employers (which would be hard to prove), but to attack discrimination more broadly defined—based on unequal group outcomes, or "disparate impact." Thus, employers could be held responsible for disparate group outcomes regardless of their motives. The Supreme Court upheld this more extensive reading of the discrimination outlawed by Title VII in 1971. In *Griggs v. Duke Power Company*, the Court ruled that Title VII proscribes not just overt discrimination, but also employer practices that are fair in form but that have adverse effects on minorities. Only if an employer could demonstrate "business necessity" for such practices could he or she avoid liability under Title VII (Eastland 1996, 54). In this particular case, that meant that Duke Power

Company could no longer require a high school diploma or its equivalent—which many fewer blacks had than whites—for certain jobs at its power plant.

The first steps on the path to numerical affirmative action—an extension of this new reasoning that discrimination could be broadly defined based upon unequal outcomes—came in 1966, according to Terry Eastland (1996). That year, the first director of the Office of Federal Contract Compliance (OFCC) announced that contractors who wanted to bid on several large projects in the Cleveland area would have to devise affirmative action plans. Those plans would have to have the result of assuring that there was minority group representation in all trades on the job in all phases of the work. Later that year, the OFCC sought to integrate the construction trades' unions in Philadelphia by demanding manning tables that embodied the same idea.

During the Nixon administration, this "Philadelphia Plan" was revived by requiring that a target range of minorities be hired, expressed as a percentage that the contractor would try to meet. The Philadelphia Plan was also extended during the Nixon administration when Nixon's secretary of labor, George Shultz, required the same compliance from nine other cities. The new and revised plan required a meeting with low bidders before awarding contracts to review their affirmative action plans and to obtain agreements for on-the-job compliance reviews. Nixon later expanded it even further with an order to include all government contracts of $50,000 or more in all areas of employment. In December 1971, the order was further extended to include women. Finally, in May 1974, the administration went all the way by stating specifically that a potential contractor's affirmative action programs had to have as their goal "prompt and full utilization of minorities and women at all levels and in all segments of its work force" (Hoff 1994, 92–93). Ultimately, these affirmative action requirements were extended not just to construction contractors in other cities, Eastland reports, but also to nonconstruction contractors everywhere, reaching one-third of the nation's workforce at the time.

During the remainder of the 1970s, affirmative action continued to expand and to gain ground. Indeed, the Labor Department swept banks, utilities, insurance and real estate companies, manufacturers, producers, and universities all in under the requirements of affirmative action. For example, from 1974 through the end of the decade, the department under both Ford and Carter increased the regulatory pressure upon government contractors to hire minorities and women according to a model of proportional representation. This meant that a contractor had to compare his utilization of minorities or women in each job group with their availability in the area work force. If there were deficiencies, the contractor had to make up for them through affirmative action goals for hiring and promoting minorities and women, as well as with timetables to meet those goals. In 1977, Congress got on the bandwagon by passing the Public Works Employment Act, which set aside at least 10 percent of the $4 billion appropriated under it for minority business enterprises (Eastland 1996, 61–62).

Then in 1978, the Supreme Court heard the case of Alan Bakke, a case that attracted national attention. Bakke claimed that he had been denied admission to a California medical school because he was white and was, therefore, a victim of reverse discrimination. His suit was an attack on affirmative action programs since he argued that a quota plan employed by the university allowed the admission of less-qualified blacks and Hispanics, resulting in his own unconstitutional exclusion. Since many observers believed the case to be the Court's most important civil rights case since *Brown v. Board of Education,* the Court's ruling in Bakke's favor, argue Findling and Thackeray, seemed to be a serious blow to affirmative action. However, even though the Court concluded that the particular plan that Bakke challenged was invalid, five of the justices did hold that race and ethnicity could be taken into account in making admission decisions, as long as strict quotas were not imposed. So while the Bakke decision had clearly forbidden racial quotas and noncompetitive evaluations of minority candidates, it did not bar schools from considering race and ethnic origin in their efforts to obtain diversity within student bodies.

Later, in 1979, the Court decided another closely watched case: *United Steelworkers v. Weber.* In this reverse discrimination suit, the Court ruled that it was legal for private employers to give special preference to black workers to achieve "manifest racial balance" (Marty 1997, 188) in jobs that were traditionally limited to whites. Thus, the Court rebuffed Kaiser Aluminum and Chemical lab technician Brian F. Weber, who had sued his union and employer over a job-training program that gave preference to blacks. The decision gave blacks some measure of assurance, but it also inflamed many whites further. They charged that they were victims of reverse discrimination and were being made to pay for century-old offenses in which they had played no part. In fact, as the seventies progressed and affirmative action programs took root and found judicial sanction, more and more whites became incensed.

More and more of them began to resent the advances of blacks and minorities that they saw as unfair, particularly in an economy that was struggling, and the backlash grew. The divide between white and nonwhite America grew too.

Hispanics Begin Their Struggle

Mexican Americans were the largest subgroup of persons classified as Hispanic living in the United States during the seventies. They were concentrated primarily in five southwestern states from Texas to California, and between 1970 and 1980, this population group nearly doubled in size—from 4.5 million to 8.7 million. There was also a considerable influx of Central Americans during this period, as economic and political instability in their home countries forced them to look for opportunities in the United States. Of the more than 330,000 persons residing in the United States in 1980 who had been born in a Central-American nation, more than one-third had arrived in the previous five years.

No matter their country of origin, however, Hispanics were also affected by the backlash that slowed the progress of blacks, according to Myron Marty. Although the 1965 Voting Rights Act was extended in 1975 to include Spanish-speaking Americans, the law had little real effect on the daily lives of most Hispanics. Their wages were nearly one-third below the average of white males' earnings, and the unemployment rate for Spanish-speaking Americans was well above the national average. Thus, the feeling that Hispanics were highly unwelcome competitors in a very tight job market—particularly in the later years of the seventies—made it even more difficult for them to work toward improvements.

Nonetheless, many of the Hispanic community's most active leaders continued to try to organize and activate their constituencies. Cesar Chavez, for example, worked throughout the decade toward improving the lot of Spanish speakers in American life. In one event that actually received a fair amount of press attention, Chavez led the United Farm Workers through a bitterly contested eight-month strike against California lettuce growers in 1979. His successes, however, were limited. Indeed, the strike was marred by violent confrontations between the strikers and non-union harvest crews, and the lettuce growers found ways around the nationwide boycott of lettuce that grew up in support of the strike.

Native American Activism in the 1970s

Native Americans faced conditions that were often more distressing than those of blacks and Hispanics during the seventies. In 1973, the Census Bureau reported an Indian population of nearly eight hundred thousand, an increase of more than 50 percent since 1960. Nearly half of them lived in urban areas, and the other half lived on reservations or in similar rural areas. Most who lived on the reservations suffered from abject poverty, while those in the cities fared only somewhat better. Wherever they lived, however, Native Americans had much to learn from the struggles of other minority groups. Of course, their situation made organizing extremely difficult, but they did organize and become more confrontational in the late 1960s.

By the early 1970s, there was a concerted movement among Native Americans for increased autonomy, including the activation of groups that were more militant and radical. Thus, between the occupation of Alcatraz Island in 1969 and Nixon's resignation in August 1974, there were forty-five occupations of territory or buildings by Native Americans across the country. In 1972, for example, about five hundred Indians organized by the American Indian Movement (AIM) seized control of the Bureau of Indian Affairs (BIA) building in Washington and demanded changes in the agency. They agreed to leave off their occupation a week later, but they took with them artifacts, paintings, and thousands of government documents. A shake-up of the BIA followed, says Myron Marty, and policy changes and other actions seemed to commit the government to responding to the AIM's grievances.

By far the most inflammatory incident of this kind took place during a bloody confrontation at Wounded Knee. Wounded Knee was a small Indian settlement on the remote Pine Ridge Sioux Reservation in South Dakota and the site of a mass grave resulting from a military confrontation between the Sioux and the U.S. Army in 1890. Approximately two hundred Native Americans under the leadership of the militant AIM seized this site and held it for seventy-three days beginning on February 27, 1973. They looted, defaced, or burned several buildings and homes, destroyed a museum, took eleven elderly hostages, and barricaded themselves against assault from both federal marshals and the Ogala Sioux, who considered the takeover a criminal act. Again the focus of the Indians' grievance was on what they regarded as a trail of broken treaties. An agreement was finally reached with the AIM to end its occupation on May 9, 1973, making it "the longest sustained armed confrontation fought on western soil in American history" (Hoff 1994, 38).

The restraint demonstrated by the Nixon administration in this case, according to Joan Hoff, certainly helped to avoid massive bloodshed. Indeed, Hoff believes that the Nixon administration should be credited for showing great restraint in the face of increased Native American militancy on the part of young red power activists throughout this confrontational period. In fact, this was one area in which the Nixon administration did not further fuel the racial fires that threatened to tear the nation apart. Although the AIM continued its militant activities into the later years of the 1970s—taking an unused Roman Catholic seminary in Wisconsin in 1975 and demanding that it be turned over to the Menominee tribe, for example—other groups, such as the Navajo Tribal Council, resisted such aggressive tactics. At the same time, many Indian leaders advocated abandoning violent protests and confrontations in favor of seeking redress through Congress, the BIA, and the courts. The result, according to Myron Marty, was the 1975 Indian Self-Determination and Education Assistance Act, which gave Native American tribes greater control over their own affairs and over deciding how education funds would be used in public schools.

Racial Tensions Continue

As advances were made for minorities in some areas and major setbacks occurred in others in the political struggle for racial equality, race relations in the United States continued to deteriorate. Fed by growing inner-city ghettos, white flight, and white backlash—as well as by the continued demands of blacks and other minorities for changes in the system—America came to resemble a great cauldron of racial tensions that threatened to boil over and consume the nation. In 1970, for example, Yale President Kingman Brewster Jr. expressed doubt that black revolutionaries could get a "fair trial anywhere in the United States" after a special coroner's jury ruled that the previous year's killing of two Black Panthers in a predawn police raid was justifiable. That same year, a student dormitory at Jackson State College in Mississippi was riddled with police bullets that ended up killing a student and a local high school senior, both black, and George Wallace urged Southern governors to defy federal integration orders. Only two years later, Wallace was to become a paraplegic for life, shot while campaigning for president and against racial integration.

The conflict and the horror continued throughout the decade and throughout the nation. In 1971, Wilmington, North Carolina, became the scene of extensive racial violence beginning in late January with incidents of arson, bombings, and shootings. Attica Correctional Facility in Attica, New York, was also the scene of the bloodiest one-day encounter between Americans since the Indian massacres of the late nineteenth century. Inmates of the overcrowded prison became outraged when they discovered differences in sentences and parole decisions that appeared to have a racial bias. In response, the angry prisoners took over several cellblocks and killed several guards. When the state police moved in a few days later, thirty-nine inmates were killed and more than eighty were wounded in the fifteen minutes it took for the police to retake the prison. Two years later, "zebra" killings terrorized San Francisco for 179 days as black fanatics armed with .32 Baretta handguns and other weapons shot whites at random in the streets.

Civil Rights in the Seventies: Withered

These events demonstrate clearly that racial tensions in the United States continued to run at a fever pitch in the 1970s. From the controversies raging over the heads of children riding school buses to the continued social segregation of the races; from the incidents of violence and homicide to the wasted activism of Native Americans; and from Allan Bakke to white backlash and "benign neglect," the 1970s held little promise for bridging the divide. Indeed, the civil rights movement in the mid- to late-1970s contrasted sharply with what it had been a decade earlier. During the later period, there were few organized protests as civil rights leaders reexamined their strategies in the face of strengthened opposition, and the extension of the Voting Rights Act, which abolished literacy requirements, was the only civil rights law enacted during these years. Frank Robinson became the first black manager of a major league baseball team in 1975, but discrimination was still commonplace throughout the country and at all levels of society. Although the Supreme Court upheld racial quotas in reapportioning legislative districts, Marty argues, there were signs that court actions favoring the cause of African Americans and other minorities were less likely in the future. All in all, Marty argues, the outlook did not look good.

The legacy of the civil rights movement in the 1970s was merely a continuation of the tensions that threatened to tear the nation apart. The seventies were years of neither progress nor regress, although the backlash against minority groups became more visible. No one was quite sure how to deal with it.

From Billie Jean King to Episcopal Priests: The Women's Movement Matures

In the two decades before 1970, the role of women in American society was based on certain universal and seemingly unchangeable assumptions: mother, wife, and homemaker. These were the roles to which every "normal" American woman was assumed to aspire and expected to conform. The feminine ideal, in those "golden" days of the 1950s, was one of effortless domesticity: American women were marrying earlier than ever before, were having more babies than ever before, and were isolated in their new suburban homes as never before. It all seemed part of the American dream. Then sometime during the raucous decade of the 1960s, the dream soured. Betty Friedan wrote a book called *The Feminine Mystique* in which she argued that women were losing their human identities in this suburban world of house, spouse, and children. The book had a huge impact on women across the nation, and a backlash against the mindless stereotypes of the 1950s inevitably followed. Friedan's quip that isolated suburban women seemed endlessly consigned to delivering children, "obstetrically once and by car forever after," as well as her pronouncement that she wanted "something more than [her] husband, [her] children, and [her] home" resonated strongly with the growing number of women who were graduating from college in the 1960s (in Hargreaves 1973, 555). The whole status of women as individuals began increasingly to be called into question, and the New Feminism, or women's lib, was born.

After years of relative inactivity, the women's movement emerged in the 1960s as a by-product of Friedan's consciousness-raising book and the larger civil rights movement. The increase in the number of working women combined with the involvement of many women in the civil rights struggle, argue Findling and Thackeray, led to the awareness that women in American society were faced with many forms of legal, economic, social, and cultural discrimination. By the early 1970s, the women's movement had taken off, and it came to be seen as a dramatic turning point in sex role beliefs as well as in the acceptance of the necessity of women's movement itself. Indeed, one poll taken in the early 1970s showed that in a two-year period the number of college students who believed that women were oppressed doubled. A Gallup poll tracking women's answers to a question about sex discrimination confirms this dramatic turning point: in 1962 two out of three women denied having been treated unequally; in 1970 half said they had been discriminated against; in 1974 two-thirds reported unequal treatment and were in favor of efforts to improve women's status (Skolnick 1991, 105).

There was, quite simply, a sea change in perceptions of women during this period, a new view of women as individuals able to make choices about their lives—working, marrying, child rearing—along with a new tolerance for whatever choices they might make. During this period, for example, college-trained American women found themselves relatively unsuited to life in the suburbs, restricted to the employ of rearing children and caring for home. By 1970, reports Robert Hargreaves, more than four married women out of every ten had outside jobs. Polls taken in the early seventies also showed that women interested in entering such fields as business, medicine, engineering, and law were outnumbered by men in 1970 by a ratio of eight to one, but by only three to one in 1975. The number of women entering law schools between 1969 and 1973 increased fourfold. In addition, the size of the family decreased during the 1970s as women waited longer to marry, delayed having children, and had fewer children. This last was due, in part, to a revolution in the use of contraceptives and the legalization of abortion.

However, in spite of the fact that the proportion of women in the workforce was growing in leaps and bounds, the world of work in the United States was still very much a man's world. According to one federal survey, the average woman employed full time in 1972 was earning only $3 for every $5 paid to a man with a similar job. Women were also highly concentrated in jobs at the low end of the pay scale, and gender discrimination in employment was still widespread. Further, even though these women were college educated, they were still not being educated at the nation's most prestigious institutions of higher learning: it was not until 1970 that American Ivy League schools began to go coeducational.

Organization and Activity in the Women's Movement

Friedan's book raised the consciousness of many women about their status, and as activist white women were shunted aside by the thrust of black power in the civil rights movement, they began to organize on their own behalf. In 1966 the National Organization for Women (NOW) was founded. This mainstream organization lobbied Congress for legislation that would end women's inferior status. Led by Friedan, says Frederic Siegel, the NOW's initial program was in the best American individualist tradition, calling for equal rights, equal opportunity, and an end to discrimination. The appeal of this liberal, equal-rights approach was first made apparent in a surprisingly successful national demonstration that occurred on August 26, 1970: the Women's Strike for Equality. The demonstration was held on August 26 to commemorate the fiftieth anniversary of the passage of the Nineteenth Amendment, and it was the largest demonstration ever held for women's rights. The size of the crowd at Central Park was estimated at about thirty-five thousand, but the action was truly nationwide, involving women and men of all ages, social classes, and occupations. Some scholars, such as Winifred Wandersee (1988), have even gone so far as to say that this event marked the beginnings of the women's movement as a mass movement.

The August 26 demonstration was just the beginning of the advances that the women's movement was going to make during the seventies. Indeed, many of the demands articulated by and pushed for by the NOW and by other mainstream women's lib groups received legislative sanction in the early 1970s. For example, women's rights advocates began to urge schools to give girls the same opportunities in such fields as mathematics and sciences as were open to boys, as well as to prepare them for careers formerly closed to them. An eventual result of these efforts, says Myron Marty, was Title IX of the Educational Amendments of 1972, which also led to greater equality in support for participation by girls in athletics and other school activities. Similarly, Congress enacted legal guarantees of equal pay for equal work, equal access to education, equal employment opportunities, and equal access to credit. In 1978, Congress also passed the Pregnancy Discrimination Act, which barred the disparate treatment of pregnant women for all employment-related purposes.

Central to the NOW's efforts and the efforts of other concerned women during this period, however, was the Equal Rights Amendment (ERA), which would have forbidden any kind of discrimination on the basis of gender. Originally written by the suffragist Alice Paul in 1923, the ERA was finally passed by Congress in 1972 and sent to the states for ratification. However, opposition to the ERA was intense from conservative organizations, and even some working women were opposed to the amendment, state Findling and Thackeray, because they feared that it would annul protective laws in the workplace and the exemption of women from the military draft. A long and bitter struggle ensued for ten years before the amendment fell short by three states of the number needed for ratification, even though polls showed 60 percent of both men and women supported it. However, many states passed their own equal rights legislation, which did remove much of the discriminatory legal features against women.

Women who considered themselves "traditionalists" played a big part in the defeat of the Equal Rights Amendment. Believing that the women's movement had dealt mainly with the concerns of professional women, most of them with college degrees, these traditionalist women found a spokesperson in Marabel Morgan. Her book *The Total Woman* was published in 1975 and urged a woman to scorn the feminists' concerns and to cater to her man's special needs. The traditionalists' most outspoken and influential leader, however, was not Marabel Morgan but Phyllis Schafly, according to Myron Marty. Schafly charged that feminists' criticisms of traditional roles for women were an attack on ways of life that had brought them great fulfillment and respect. She was quite successful in organizing the traditionalist women's fight against the ERA.

Meanwhile, the traditionalists had found a friend in President Richard Nixon, who seemed unable to bring himself to actively support the ERA before its passage by Congress in 1972. Even though the president and his advisers could see the political implications and advantages of women's issues, the administration seemed unable to change its condescending, sexist attitudes and behavior. Indeed, the administration was slow to provide its support even though the President's Task Force on Women's Rights and Responsibilities, along with the Committee on Population and Family Planning and the Citizen's Advisory Committee on the Status of Women (also appointed by Nixon), reinforced most of the demands of the emerging women's movement, particularly on the issues of abortion and the ERA. There simply was not enough male staff support, argues Joan Hoff, within the White House for women's issues to prevail over other domestic concerns. Indeed, the Nixon White House was well known for being a bastion of older, white men, and of course Nixon's circle of insiders were all men. The outsiders were men as well, and the administration had overall a poor record in appointing women to high-level positions in government.

Although the NOW was a central organizing and activist force for the maturing women's movement during this time period, it would certainly be a mistake to see it as the only organization working hard within the movement during the 1970s. In 1971, for example, the National Women's Political Caucus (NWPC) was established as an organization where women from the two major political parties, along with independent feminists, could work to persuade both political parties to give women and their issues more attention in the political arena. The caucus' first move was to hold training sessions across the country for women delegates to the 1972 Democratic Convention. During the convention itself, the NWPC also worked with the NOW to lobby for planks favoring the ERA and the federal funding of child care centers. By 1976, the NWPC had acquired even greater sophistication and influence, state Simon and Danziger (1991); it questioned presidential candidates on their positions on women's issues, monitored candidates' campaign staffs to determine the number of women in decision-making positions, and led a move for a written guarantee at the presidential nominating convention that women would constitute 50 percent of the delegates at the 1980 convention. While this final proposal failed, Jimmy Carter did meet with the women's leaders and agreed to appoint women to high-ranking positions in his administration if he were elected.

The NWPC also created, with the help of several other women's organizations, a Coalition for Women's Appointments, which existed during the Nixon and Ford administrations and became particularly influential after Carter's election. These groups drew up lists of potential women appointees, collecting resumes and submitting them to the presidential transition office. Simon and Danziger argue that the work paid off: more women were appointed under Carter than during any previous administration. In addition to the coalition and the NWPC, the National Women's Education Fund was created in 1973. This group used tax-deductible funds to train women for campaign work and for holding elective or appointive office. The Women's Campaign Fund was also established in 1974 to raise money for federal candidates.

Supreme Court Decisions Push the Movement Along

Although the activism on the part of many women's groups really pushed this phase of the women's movement toward maturity in the 1970s, the Supreme Court must be given credit for aiding the feminist cause with several important decisions during the decade. In 1971, for example, the Court struck down an Idaho law that preferred the use of men over women as estate administrators. It also let stand a Fifth Circuit Court of Appeals ruling that the bona fide occupational qualification exception allowed only for business necessity and not for convenience exceptions. Thus Pan Am's refusal to hire male attendants because of alleged "customer preference" was judged to be illegal (Simon and Danziger 1991, 59). *Drewery's Limited v. Barnes* in 1972 further provided that an employer must set the same retirement age for women as for men, and that same year the Court ruled that sex classifications were "suspect" and therefore required "compelling justification." Then in 1973, the Court handed down a decision that the U.S. military had to provide the same benefits to women that it offered to men.

In a case settled out of court—also in 1973—government attorneys filed a sex discrimination suit against AT&T, one of the nation's largest corporations. While not admitting guilt, AT&T agreed to reimburse millions in back pay to women and minority workers in its employ. *Cleveland Board of Education v. LaFleur* came next, in 1974. In that case, the Court ruled that the school board's policy of automatically dismissing pregnant schoolteachers in their fourth month violated the due process clause of the Fourteenth Amendment. Then in 1975, the Court held that the Social Security program's assumption of traditional roles (husbands as the sole salaried wage earners) constituted gender-based discrimination and was entirely irrational.

A few months later, in *Taylor v. Louisiana,* the Supreme Court held that the Sixth Amendment required that a jury be selected from a jury pool representing a cross-section of the community. Further, it ruled that when women were systematically excluded from jury panels, the representative cross-section requirement was not fulfilled. Although it was not the Supreme Court but a federal court of appeals, yet another important decision was handed down in favor of women in 1977: for the first time, sexual harassment was found to constitute sex discrimination (prohibited by Title VII), setting the stage for the Supreme Court to later endorse the viability of legal action for sexual harassment claims in the 1980s.

The Abortion Issue Gives Birth to a New War

Obviously, the 1970s were years of active judicial advances on behalf of women. The most important (and certainly the most controversial) Supreme Court decision of the decade, however, was clearly *Roe v. Wade.* In that case, the Supreme Court declared on January 22, 1973, that many state laws that prohibited or severely limited abortions were unconstitutional, affirming a woman's right to control her body and her privacy. Following the Court's decision, the number of abortions performed increased dramatically: in 1977, for example, doctors performed 1.3 million legal abortions. In fact, Myron Marty reports that every ten live births were matched by three abortions.

Once again, the NOW was central in bringing about this groundbreaking and controversial decision. In fact, the first formal call for the repeal of restrictive abortion laws can be traced to the Bill of Rights for Women, adopted by the NOW at its first annual convention in 1967. The last section demanded "[the] right of women to control their own reproductive lives by removing from the penal code laws limiting access to contraceptive information and devices and by repealing laws governing abortion" (O'Connor 1996, 30). This resolution marked the beginning of the formal and informal link between the women's rights movement and the movement to achieve abortion rights. In fact, soon after the NOW's call for repeal, other rights-oriented organizations followed suit, including the National Abortion Rights Action League (NARAL). By 1971, the pressure from these women's rights groups, abortion rights groups, and professional medical and legal associations had led fourteen states to revise their abortion laws to allow abortions in some circumstances. Four additional states had completely repealed their restrictive abortion statutes. However, according to Karen O'Connor (1996), change in the states was a slow and piecemeal process.

Thus, women's rights advocates increasingly came to believe that the courts represented their best chance to change restrictive abortion laws. A court strategy became the goal, according to O'Connor, because a single positive judicial decision from a federal court could be much more effective than years of efforts in many states, years that would require lots of money and organization. Thus, women's rights activists took a lesson from the earlier experience of African Americans, who had discovered that litigation could be an extremely effective method for winning constitutional rights. So the test cases of *Roe v. Wade* and *Doe v. Bolton* (which was decided shortly after *Roe*) were put into action, and the Supreme Court decision lived up to all expectations: more than simply finding the Georgia and Texas laws unconstitutional, the seven-justice majority in *Roe* effectively invalidated the abortion laws of all but four states.

Feminists regarded the decision as a legitimization of a woman's repro-

ductive rights, including the right to choose whether to terminate an unwanted pregnancy. On the other side of the issue, groups such as the national
Right-to-Life organization, the Catholic Church, and many fundamentalist
Protestant denominations saw the decision as allowing and legalizing the
murder of children. Since the decision in 1973, they have organized to wage
an intense battle to get the decision overturned and to end the practice of
abortion in the United States, giving rise to the "pro-life" movement. Indeed,
the Supreme Court's decision in 1973 functioned as a catalyst rather than as
the last word on abortion, spurring the creation of new interest groups and increased activity by existing groups. The pro-life movement was quickly successful, beginning in the 1970s and continuing into the eighties and the
nineties.

Shortly after the *Roe* decision, for example, several pro-life organizations
began to lobby Congress to pass a Human Life Amendment, which would
negate *Roe* through passage of a constitutional amendment banning abortion. Then Senator Jesse Helms was successful in amending the Foreign Assistance Act to ban the use of federal funds for abortion services or research. In
1974, the Hyde Amendment to the Health, Education, and Welfare appropriations bill cleared Congress, barring the use of federal funds for abortions except where the life of the mother would be endangered if the fetus were
brought to term. In confirmation of the Hyde Amendment, the Supreme
Court ruled in 1977 that nothing in the Constitution required that states use
Medicaid money to fund elective abortions, nor did any federal law, thus dealing a blow to those opposing the amendment. That same year, the Senate
voted to bar the funding of elective abortions except in cases of rape, incest, or
medical necessity. The result, according to Karen O'Connor, was a steep decline in the number of publicly funded abortions.

In response, those who believed that abortion decisions should be the
prerogative of women in consultation with their physicians began to organize
and reactivate what would later be called the "pro-choice" movement. As the
two sides squared off beginning in the 1970s—pro-life versus pro-choice—
the middle ground disappeared. The 1976 presidential campaign, for example, became a battleground that had abortion as the major issue in the contest
between Gerald Ford and Jimmy Carter. Indeed, the well-organized anti-
abortion movement made abortion the focus of the campaign with the candidacy of Ellen McCormack of the Right-to-Life Party. Her bid in particular
drew attention to the anti-abortion cause and elevated the importance of the

issue in the election. Nothing was resolved in that election, however, although Jimmy Carter's policies of the late 1970s further energized the pro-life movement for the coming decade. Thus, abortion continued to play a central role in the women's movement of the eighties and nineties, becoming a thorny problem that still resists adequate resolution.

Other Advances of Women in the Seventies

It was not just the organized groups, legislation, and Supreme Court rulings that advanced the goals of women in the feminist movement during the 1970s. Indeed, many social breakthroughs also occurred as the movement matured and as all levels of society began to recognize the changing status and role of women in America. In 1970, for example, U.S. women balked at a new midi-skirt length decreed by fashion arbiters. Unsold garments were returned to their manufacturers, and women wore their skirts as long or short as they liked. Then in 1972, *Ms. Magazine* began publication with former *Look* editor Patricia Carbine as publisher and feminist Gloria Steinem as editor. The magazine sold three hundred thousand copies of its preview issue in eight days and had two hundred fifty thousand subscribers by the end of its first year of publication. Why? Because *Ms.* dealt with issues of sexuality, employment, discrimination, and other feminist issues, whereas traditional women's magazines such as *Ladies Home Journal* and *Good Housekeeping* continued to focus on domestic interests, celebrities, and romantic fantasies. (Use of the term "Ms." in place of "Miss" and "Mrs." was controversial for a number of years, and only gradually did it gain acceptance. The *New York Times* only began to use it in 1986.)

Other publications also began to fulfill the need for materials that would sympathize with the movement's struggle to improve women's working conditions and to help women better understand themselves. In 1973, for example, a women's health collective—a discussion group of eleven women, itself a sign of the times—published *Our Bodies, Ourselves,* encouraging women to understand and control their own bodies. By 1976 it had sold eight hundred fifty thousand copies. Later, in 1978, both *Self* magazine and *Working Woman* magazine joined *Ms.* in providing relevant publications to the burgeoning ranks of professional women engaged in breaking out of discriminatory gender stereotypes.

And women were busy breaking out of those confining stereotypes. Indeed, four Episcopal bishops went so far as to defy church law in 1974 by ordaining eleven women to the priesthood, and only a few months later the Episcopal Church itself broke with long-standing tradition in formally approving the ordination of women. In the realm of sports, Billie Jean King defeated Bobby Riggs in the much-publicized tennis "Battle of the Sexes" in 1973. In the political world, meanwhile, women were making strides all over the globe. Argentina's Isabel Martinez de Peron became the hemisphere's first woman chief of state in 1974, and only four years later, conservative leader Margaret Thatcher became Britain's first woman prime minister at age fifty-three (by the largest majority any party had received since 1966). Even at home, women were increasingly earning political offices, as Jane Byrne was elected the first woman mayor of Chicago and Ella Grasso was elected governor of Connecticut in 1975, making her the first to be elected for governor without succeeding her husband.

In other highly publicized actions that had immediate and direct effects on only a few women but had symbolic effects for many, the military academies of West Point, Annapolis, and Colorado Springs began to admit women to their programs in 1975. In that same year, Myron Marty reports, Harvard University changed its practice of admitting men and women in a five-to-two ratio and instituted equal admissions instead.

The Role of Radicals in the 1970s Women's Movement and the Backlash of the Eighties

All of these changes in the social, political, and economic world could not occur without a reaction. Indeed, the 1970s was a time of tremendous accomplishment for the women's movement, dramatically changing the lives of women and getting issues that had previously been ignored on the public policy agenda. However, the 1970s was also a time that witnessed the beginnings of a backlash against such advances and against the movement itself. It was not just the activities of mainstream groups such as the NOW that were pushing the issues important to women during this time. Indeed,Winifred Wandersee (1988) argues that in the 1970s the women's rights movement was strongly influenced by radical feminist organizations that emerged out of the New Left (such as the Women's Liberation Front, the Redstockings, and the October Seventeenth Movement), and they challenged the traditional family structure and other social and political institutions in America that they saw as male dominated.

The radical feminist groups used demonstrations and "speakouts" to bring attention to issues such as abortion and rape; they worked to establish women's centers, communes, and collectives; and they advocated the development of women's studies programs in colleges and universities. Some of them even advocated an alliance with the male-dominated Left in order to bring about a socialist revolution, while others attacked the institution of marriage and even the practice of sex, claiming both were methods men employed to dominate and subjugate women. In fact, one group—the Feminists—went so far as to picket the New York Marriage License Bureau to protest the institution of marriage. The extreme rhetoric and abrasive tactics of this more radical arm of the women's movement soon created a backlash similar to the one over the civil rights movement, producing a lessening of sympathy for women's issues. Adding to the impact of the more radical elements of the movement in creating a backlash, according to Winifred Wandersee, was the simple fact that most Americans were reluctant to accept the implications of the feminist challenge, no matter what form it took.

So a backlash was born, and the women's movement contributed to the conservative political climate that emerged by the late 1970s and continued into the 1980s. It did so primarily by offering a focus that allowed the right wing to mobilize forces of opposition. Two issues in particular—abortion and the ERA—led to the highly effective organization of conservatives, both men and women. The late 1970s and early 1980s, for example, witnessed the rise of conservative, Christian-based political organizations that espoused traditional family values according to Findling and Thackeray. Indeed, the massive success of Jerry Falwell's Moral Majority, which was founded in 1979, attests to the strength and organization of such groups. In less than a year, Falwell's new political action group had registered millions of new voters, taking advantage of the political climate that was to sweep Ronald Reagan into the presidency in 1980.

The Legacy of Social Movements in the Seventies: Backlash

In earlier times, despite rising resentments and growing restlessness, dominant groups in the United States had kept others in their place and had managed to ensure their own "domestic tranquility." By the early 1960s, however, the civil rights movement had assumed a new intensity. Court decisions and legislation enabled African Americans to claim rights long denied them, but they were not alone in getting "out of their place," according to Myron Marty. Women, Native Americans, Hispanics, Asian Americans, senior citizens, students, homosexuals, persons with disabilities, and members of other groups all became engaged in activities designed to ensure their rights.

However, although activists for changes in many different aspects of American society increased in number in the late 1960s, they still represented only a tiny slice of the population. While many more mainstream Americans generally supported the goals of these activists, the methods employed by the protesters soon began to concern the majority. In a short time that concern turned to anger and alienation, and ultimately, a backlash against those agitating for change was born. By the early 1970s, opposition to the protesters became more widespread and noisier. Middle-class Americans, Nixon's great "silent majority," saw themselves as having worked hard for what they got, as having played by the rules. They were loyal, trustworthy, taxpaying citizens. What did they have to show for their patriotism, hard work, monogamous lifestyle, and religious commitments? Perhaps a small house with a large mortgage. Perhaps a low-paying job with unrewarding duties and little job security. What they felt they had plenty of was worries about the future.

Their own place in society was in jeopardy—not because of economic vulnerability, but because their values were being threatened by those who wanted to change the social order. As Myron Marty described it in his 1997 book, "Everything seemed to be coming apart, collapsing, disintegrating, right before their eyes . . . the way of life they cherished every day, right at home, was under assault. So they protested, too, against the protesters" (96). Everything seemed too big and too complex to those representing Middle America: gasoline shortages, inflation, and declining real wages caused distress, and racial problems defied solution. The changing roles of women upset traditional ways, and environmental problems reminded people that they could not take the future for granted. The nation was in a bad mood, was pulling itself apart, and the backlash intensified.

So the backlash against the War on Poverty, the antiwar protests, and the civil rights movement that started to pick up steam in the late 1960s became full blown as the 1970s progressed. According to Marty, George Wallace's successes in attracting disaffected citizens forced Richard Nixon into a reac-

tionary mode, and the forces of backlash gained momentum. Nixon's resignation in disgrace six years later blunted the power of the forces he had drawn
together in his presidency, and the election of Jimmy Carter and his cautious
but ineffective presidency meant that the backlash had merely been slowed.
The election of Ronald Reagan in 1980, however, again gave the backlash a
platform and set the stage for the dominance of political power by those
whose styled themselves as conservative. This intensifying backlash and the
rise to power of those at its head, then, was the legacy of social movements in
the seventies.

The Seventies' Cultural Earthquake

An Age of Loss, an Age of Birth, an Age of Change

THE 1970S BEGAN with violence, protests, and disorder as many groups in American culture fought for change or resisted it. Thus coming out of the smoky haze of the 1960s, the seventies began like a pounding hangover. It was a fevered, rancorous, tumultuous time for the nation, and there was a feeling of impending doom overhanging Americans, as if the apocalypse was about to descend. This sense of negativity was the result, at least in part, of the self-doubt that racked the nation—doubt about the country's capacity to solve its problems or even to survive with its institutions and social structures reasonably intact. While the 1970s began with revolt, however, the decade did not end that way. By the mid-seventies, the war in Vietnam had ended. The War on Poverty had faded away. The Nixon presidency had collapsed in the national wound of Watergate. The civil rights revolution had lost its momentum. The 1960s were finally over.

Accordingly, America had to come to terms with the cultural changes wrought by the 1960s, and this required a period of adjustment, of transition, to a new era. The rest of the 1970s were about this transition. It was about the conflicting forces of those who still resisted the changes and those who embraced them and wanted more. Demands for change constantly tested the traditions and practices of families, schools, churches, and organizations of all kinds. So the controversy and the divisions in American society continued to simmer throughout the decade.

As these cultural transitions occurred, they resulted in a gradual displacement of the "modern" standards and behaviors that had prevailed at midcentury. The modern behaviors were replaced by new ones reflecting conditions that Myron Marty calls "postmodern." In modern times, the emphasis had been on progress achieved through rational, coherent, single-minded processes. Commitment, predictability, and stability contributed to the progress that was sought and valued, and organizational structures tended to be centralized and hierarchical, with clearly drawn boundaries. In addition, government was seen as a positive force for change. But by the middle of the 1970s, the United States of the 1950s had been permanently transformed, and postmodern conditions began to dominate. Marty argues that postmodern conditions were expressed through decentralization in economic structures and fragmentation in social structures. They were characterized by skepticism over government's ability to act constructively for change and by short-term rather than long-term commitments. Quite simply, swift changes in ways of doing things became common in the late seventies. Consumer-driven decision making in business, government, entertainment, and other aspects of life dominated.

The American Family: Love, Sex, Marriage, and Divorce

Changes in family patterns and activities were prominent during the 1970s, and they reflected a gradual shift in cultural values. In fact, sociologist Arlene Skolnick has written that by the middle of the 1970s, "American family life had been shaken by a series of social changes as broad and traumatic as any that had occurred in the past. . . . Standing about in the ruins of structures that had, little more than a decade before, seemed stable and change-less—lifelong marriage, sexual morality, parental authority, the 'traditional' family—Americans groped for an explanation of what had shattered them all" (1991, 127).

The cultural earthquake that shook these structures so profoundly commenced with two important trends that had begun in the late 1960s—rising divorce rates and declining birthrates—and accelerated during the 1970s. Between 1960 and 1967 the divorce rate increased from 2.2 per 1,000 to 2.7, but by 1974, it stood at 4.6 per 1,000. Rates continued to increase until the mid-1980s. Meanwhile, the birthrate per 1,000 declined annually from 23.7 in 1960 to 14.9 in 1974. This was not so much because fewer women were having babies, but rather because women were having fewer children—a consequence of marrying later and waiting longer to start a family. Indeed, the median age at the time of marriage rose for both men and women, and the size of the average household declined from 3.1 to 2.8 persons during the decade. As more women pursued careers outside of the home, the old relationships within families changed in other ways as well. For example, although women were having fewer children, many more of those children spent time in the care of persons outside their immediate family, says Myron Marty, usually with a relative or sitter coming to their homes. Indeed, as early as 1975 the "typical nuclear family," consisting of a working father, a homemaker mother, and two children, represented only 7 percent of the population.

Another trend that accelerated in later years was the increase in single-parent families. In 1970, 87.1 percent of households with children included both a father and a mother, but by 1980, that number had dropped to 71.9 percent. In fact, the number of single women heading families increased by 50 percent in the 1970s, to eight million. The statistics were even more extreme for black families, with 64.3 percent of black households with children having two parents in 1970 and only 48.1 percent in 1980. These important movements in the numbers depicting family life in the 1970s reflected a real change in values in America during these years: reverence for marriage and parenting diminished, argues Myron Marty, as desires for other forms of personal happiness and fulfillment gained prominence.

One big factor in explaining these changes in family values during the decade was the coming of age of the seventy-five million Americans born between 1946 and 1964: the baby boomers. By 1975, nearly two-thirds of that seventy-five million were making their presence felt as adults. Some older ones went to Vietnam, some went to college to avoid the draft and to join campus protests, some went to college to earn degrees and to prepare for careers, and some drifted into the counterculture. Many simply got jobs, married, and established families of their own, expecting their lives to be much like their parents' had been. But the baby boomers as a whole were big players in the emergence of a "singles' culture" that gave rise to bars, clubs, and apartment houses catering to unmarried people. Women, who were making their own strides toward greater independence during the 1970s, found great pleasure and satisfaction in this singles' culture. For both men and women however, according to Myron Marty, it offered companionship and fun, free of obligations. By 1974, 32 percent of Americans believed marriage to be obsolete, and the number of men and women in all age groups who never married increased during the decade. In addition, reports Marty, the number of persons living alone increased by 60 percent in the 1970s; by the end of the decade nearly one-fourth of American households consisted of one person.

Indeed, these years saw significant changes in the way men and women related to each other and developed relationships. Women felt increasingly free to accept roles that had belonged exclusively to men before: they would ask men out on dates, provide the transportation, and pay all or part of the expenses of the evening. As conventional rituals were discarded, sexual relationships developed at younger ages and earlier in acquaintanceships. Anyone professing the old belief that the purpose of sexual intercourse was to produce babies was regarded as quaint: the new belief was that sexual relations existed for pleasure and fulfillment rather than simply as a passage into "normal" society through marriage, giving birth, and raising children. Indeed, the early 1970s were full of immensely popular books on sex: Alex Comfort's *The Joy of Sex,* David Reuben's *Everything You Wanted to Know about Sex but Were Afraid to Ask, The Sensuous Woman* by "J," and Masters and Johnson's *Human Sexual Inadequacy.* Meanwhile, the number of unmarried men and women living together increased by 50 percent between 1970 and 1980. Thus, freer relations between the sexes inside and outside of marriage gave rise to what has been called the "sexual revolution." The consequences of that revolution were clear to all: the new and looser sexual mores governing American culture in the 1970s produced pregnancies outside of marriage in record numbers, as well as staggering increases in the number of reported sexually transmitted diseases.

Even in relationships between men and women that did not involve sex, things were more open and relaxed. Coed residence halls at colleges were common by the early 1970s, for example, and many institutions of higher learning began to accept women as well as men for the first time. Myron Marty reports that among younger teenagers, interactions at school led to the loose formation of groups for "hanging out" at shopping centers or in the family rooms of middle-class homes. Indeed, the shopping mall was a phenomenon whose impact on American culture and commerce was profound. By 1971, there were more than thirteen thousand shopping centers in the

United States. In the next fifteen years their number more than doubled! They quickly became magnets for groups of America's teens (particularly in the suburbs), who often replaced dating and "going steady" with the less formal rituals of "hanging out" in large coeducational groups. Meanwhile, the impact of the mall on the inner cities, according to Theodore White (1973), was equally profound but had a different effect: the shopping centers of the suburbs that were so attractive to the teens began to destroy the central city by draining off its commercial vitality.

The loosening of sexual restrictions during the early seventies extended as well to the gay and lesbian communities in America. As homosexuals began to define themselves more by their distinctive lifestyles rather than simply by their sexual practices, Myron Marty argues, homosexuality gained more prominence and gay men and lesbians became more open in their relationships. In fact, a series of riots in the summer of 1969 sparked by a police raid on a gay bar and dance club in Greenwich Village gave birth to the modern gay and lesbian movement. Thus, gay men and lesbians began to abandon their silence and to fight openly for an end to discriminatory practices during the seventies. Medical judgments concerning the nature of homosexuality also began to change. In 1973, for example, the American Psychiatric Association removed its categorization of homosexuality as a mental disorder. Marty claims that in response to these transformations, the public's perception of homosexuality also changed: although antipathy toward homosexuals in some segments of the population remained strong, attitudes toward individual gays and lesbians became more tolerant.

America's Youth, the Clash of Generations, and the Counterculture

As the United States emerged from the 1960s, a large segment of its youth was in a state bordering on rebellion. Across the country, campus after campus was disrupted by rioting, strikes, and violent protests that were directed against the war in Vietnam but more generally against all forms of authoritarian control in American society. The protesters rejected the old conventions, they meant to break down the barriers of age and race, and they frightened the vast majority of the older generations. With young people— the hope for the future of the nation—everyday screaming their hatred for "Amerika" or making statements of renunciation and rejection, it was difficult to feel hopeful. Nearly every form of established authority was a target for challenge by disillusioned youth and minorities—from the general laws, to the church, to their very own homes—and an alarmingly high proportion of young men and women reported that they felt subject to illegitimate authority. Even as the alienated continued their relentless and total rejection of the existing social and political order, however, they found themselves facing off with the growing fortitude of those who still clung to traditional values.

So America was a nation divided and polarized, with the possibilities for discussion and reconciliation seemingly remote. Indeed in 1970, Walter Hickel—then Nixon's secretary of the interior—wrote a famous letter to the president that was leaked to the press and shared with the nation. Hickel wrote that a large number of American youth believed that they had no way to communicate with the government outside of violent confrontation. In 1970 the U.S. government also published *The United States President's Commission on Campus Unrest,* which detailed the elements of "youth culture." The commission indicated in this report that in its commitment to liberty and equality, the new youth culture was very much in the mainstream of American tradition. However, what that culture doubted was that America had managed to live up to its national ideals. Over time, the commission concluded, these doubts grew, and the youth culture became increasingly imbued with a sense of alienation and of opposition to the larger society.

According to Robert Hargreaves (1973), it was the opinion of President Nixon's Scranton Commission that the unrest that plagued the nation was rooted in the rise of this new youth culture, which had found its identity in the rejection of the work ethic, the materialism, and the conventional norms of older America. "Indeed," said the commission's report, "it rejected all institutional disciplines externally imposed upon the individual, and this set it at odds with much in American society." Thus, although the Vietnam War was certainly partly responsible for this extraordinary movement, it was not the sole birth mother of youth radicalism. Hargreaves ponts out that similar turmoil occurred in other countries such as France and Japan where the war was hardly an issue at all, and the rebellion in the United States was already well under way before the betrayals of Vietnam made that conflict a focal point for protest.

So what was the cause of this new youth culture and the accompanying rebellion? An obvious starting point was the sheer size of the younger generation of the seventies, with half the total population of the United States at that time under twenty-five years old, again a result of the biggest and most prolonged baby boom in American history. They had no memories of the two great events that molded the attitudes of their parents—the Great Depression and World War II. They were the first generation to grow up with television, which exposed them from an early age to the outside world. As a generation, Robert Hargreaves reports, they were far better educated than their parents and far more affluent than their parents at the same age. Five times as many of them went to college as in the 1930s, and more than twice as many young people were living alone and away from their families than had at the beginning of the 1960s.

But by the mid-1970s, many of the factors that had so fired up this youth generation in the 1960s and in the first year or so of seventies had all but disappeared. By 1973, those young people who were graduating from college had come to political awareness at a time when America was racked by war, riots, and political assassinations, with the draft and antiwar demonstrations a part of their personal experience. But the freshmen that were just beginning college had been shaped by very different forces. For starters, eighteen-year-olds had won the vote in 1971 when the Twenty-Sixth Amendment to the U.S. Constitution, lowering the voting age to eighteen, went into effect. In addition, Robert Hargreaves argues, the draft had ended, the American combat role in Vietnam was over, and events on campuses across the nation had cooled quite a bit. Indeed, by 1974, American college students were not protesting on campus but were instead taking part in the latest fad: streaking! Thus, the 1970s witnessed the cooling of the passions of the counterculture: the revolt of the 1960s had ended by the early seventies. But the decade was also left to struggle with its legacies.

Illicit Drug Use: A Legacy of the Counterculture

Hippies, rebellion, and the counterculture were completely alien to the daily lives of most Americans. Yet those who knew nothing about the counterculture, as well as those who empathized with it and those who despised it, were unquestionably affected by it. Of course, the counterculture had a profound effect on both the symbolic and the superficial, including the wardrobes and the hairstyles of young and old, as well as on music and entertainment. Although these were superficial changes, according to Myron Marty, they were widespread and durable. The counterculture also had deeper and more profound effects, however, in other ways, particularly in its embrace and even encouragement of drug use. In the early 1970s, for example, polls showed that as many as 60 percent of college students had used marijuana, and the numbers were shooting up rapidly: figures reported by the National Institutes of Health estimated in October 1969 that five million Americans had used or experimented with marijuana; just five months later the estimate was raised to eight million; and by June 1970, the figure had reached twenty million.

Of course, the counterculture alone cannot be held responsible for this increase in drug use. Evidence suggests that the majority of soldiers in the army, particularly those in Vietnam, also indulged in extensive drug use. In June 1970, for example, the army reported that in the previous year drug use by troops had doubled. By August 1970, new estimates indicated that three out of ten soldiers had at least sampled marijuana and hard drugs such as heroin. Myron Marty reports that another survey revealed that the number might be as high as six out of ten. Of course, when those soldiers returned home—if they did return home—they brought their dependencies with them. Meanwhile, more and more Americans were consuming more and more alcohol. Between 1960 and 1975, in fact, the annual per capita consumption of alcoholic beverages increased by one-third. The increase came in part from the fact that teenagers began drinking at earlier ages and in larger quantities. Further, with the liberation of women from old constraints, according to Myron Marty, their drinking levels approached that of men. One of the most important side effects in this increase in drinking was an increase in the number of automobile accidents in which drunk drivers were involved.

Thus, the 1970s were years that struggled with the impacts and effects of a culture that accepted heavy drinking and drug use. This truth was dramatized to the nation in 1975 when Karen Ann Quinlan went into a coma after drinking alcohol mixed with small doses of Librium and Valium. The pretty twenty-one year old from New Jersey was kept alive for more than eight years, even after her respirator was turned off in 1976 following a court battle. She was fed by a nasal tube and given antibiotics to ward off infections, despite the fact that there was no hope of recovery, and her much-publicized case continued to raise arguments about the right to die and concerns about America's obsession with controlled substances. Similarly, the extent of the drug culture was a hot topic for discussion in 1974, when *High Times* magazine began publication with advertisements for JOB rolling papers. "Yippie" Tom Forcade had started the magazine with $20,000 dollars allegedly derived from drug smuggling, and the publication's stories referred to marijuana as a "medical wonder drug" and ridiculed the Drug Enforcement Administration. Forcade, however, came to an ignominious end when he shot himself to death in November 1978 following the fatal crash of his best friend's plane on a smuggling mission (Trager 1992).

There were other incidents that raised concern over the increasing use of drugs, particularly marijuana, by America's youth. In 1975, for example, Mexican authorities began spraying illegal marijuana fields with the herbicide paraquat in a $35-million U.S.-funded program to wipe out the narcotic plant. However, harvesters marketed the weed even after it had been sprayed, and the Centers for Disease Control in Atlanta were forced to issue a warning that cannabis tainted with paraquat could cause irreversible lung damage. Although no case of paraquat poisoning was ever confirmed, demonstrations by pot smokers in Washington finally forced the government to cut off support for the program in October 1979. That same year, the state of New York had to modify the severe penalties (mandatory life sentence for anyone convicted of selling any amount of heroin, cocaine, morphine, or other "hard" drug) of a law pushed through by former Governor Nelson Rockefeller in 1973. It was necessary to modify the law because hundreds of persons were serving longer terms in New York for selling or possessing small amounts of drugs than for rape or robbery. The law had also not helped to control the drug traffic, and state courts were backlogged with cases of people standing trial rather than working out plea bargains.

A Political Backlash

A large segment of the electorate was clearly upset at what was "going on" among the nation's young people. The hippie movement, the drug culture, the "new" sexual morality, the antidraft and anti-Vietnam movements, the Black Panthers, and the general and random rebelliousness of college students were inevitably to become matters of political controversy. A Harris poll found most Americans to be shocked and dismayed by the disorder and unable to comprehend the demands of many of the protesters. The poll revealed that 68 percent of the public regarded campus demonstrations as unjustified and 89 percent supported calling in police or the National Guard to restore order. The "liberals" were quickly charged with responsibility for this breakdown in the discipline of society. Many Americans believed that it was the liberals who had created the climate of permissiveness that had led to such out-rages! It was the conservative Right that gained politically, making such men as Ronald Reagan, then governor of California, and Vice President Spiro Agnew seem politically invulnerable.

Indeed, the collective wisdom of this time instructed that the country was turning to the Right. The American people were more conservative in 1968 than they were in 1964, and they were even more conservative than that in 1972: many became President Nixon's "silent majority." It was said by the press and poets alike that the Kennedy and Johnson administrations were pre-occupied on the domestic front with the needs of the poor and of the blacks. In the process, they forgot about the problems of the white middle- and work-ing-class majority. Now that majority was demanding attention. In addition, according to common knowledge, the erosion of the traditional foundations of American society—the dollar, respect for authority, laws, and morality—frightened mainstream Americans. If the oratory of social justice was the mantra of American leadership in the 1960s, the 1970s produced a rhetoric that was dramatically altered in tone. It began in 1970, with the Nixon ad-ministration making "law and order" the keynote. Now the president's main target was inflation, followed closely by crime and pornography, instead of racism and poverty.

Crime and Politics

As a candidate for president in 1968, Richard Nixon capitalized on these fears by making crime in the streets an issue. His campaign theme of law and order seemed to be a transparent effort to take advantage of the backlash against the protest movement, as well as of concerns generated by the riots of African Americans in Los Angeles, Detroit, and other cities. And it worked, fitting well with his Southern Strategy of wooing whites. Sensationalized re-ports of violent crimes did fill the airwaves and the newspapers, undoubtedly creating an exaggerated sense of vulnerability for people already concerned about instability and its threat to their daily lives. Increases in crime were a le-gitimate concern: between 1967 and 1974, crime grew rapidly, and it contin-ued to rise or remained steady in most categories throughout the rest of the decade. However, this was the result, in part, of a bulge in the population pro-file of young men between the ages of seventeen and twenty-four, the years when some youths are most susceptible to committing crimes of violence and property.

Nonetheless, the average American was deeply frightened by the threat of crime, and most felt vulnerable even in their own neighborhoods. The installation of burglar alarms became commonplace, for example. The routine screening of airline passengers to prevent hijacking, begun in 1973, was a reminder of a relatively new kind of crime that Americans now needed to be concerned about. Indeed, Americans were horrified in 1972 when seventeen persons, among them eleven members of the Israeli Olympic team, were shot to death by Arab (PLO) terrorists at the Munich Olympics. Crime was also much closer to home, however. Local reports of violent crime alone were enough to make ordinary Americans worry about their security, and high visibility crimes made them aware that even the rich and famous were vulnerable.

One of the best examples of this came early in the decade when a jury found ex-convict Charles M. Manson and his hippie cult family—whom Manson had allegedly brainwashed with drugs, sex, and religion—guilty of all seven Tate-LaBianca murders. It was only a few years later that a twenty-six-year-old female member of the Charles Manson "family" made an unsuccessful assassination attempt against President Ford. This was one of two such attempts against the president's life; the other was made in the same month by a forty-five-year-old former FBI informant (also a woman). Similarly, extensive press coverage accompanied the kidnapping in 1974 of publishing heiress Patricia Hearst, age nineteen, by San Francisco black militants calling themselves the Symbionese Liberation Army. First the kidnappers demanded $2 million in ransom; then they demanded $230 million in free food for the poor of California. The nation was horrified. Then shock set in when Hearst was recorded by an automatic camera at a San Francisco bank robbery in April: she was holding a submachine gun for the robbers. When FBI agents at San Francisco apprehended Patricia Hearst in 1975 along with the remnants of the Symbionese Liberation Army, she was held on bank robbery charges.

That same year, Teamster boss Jimmy Hoffa disappeared. It was widely believed that he had been murdered by underworld figures. Then in 1976, New York's .44-caliber killer claimed his first victim early in the morning of July 29. A man who eventually proved to be David Berkowitz of Yonkers had approached an Oldsmobile that was double-parked in front of a Bronx apartment house and opened fire. This tragedy was only the start of a twelve-month spree in which Berkowitz terrorized the city, killing five women and one man and leaving seven wounded. He was not arrested until August 1977, when the psychotic postal worker claimed that he had acted on orders from the dog of his neighbor Sam Carr, who did not know him. In the meantime, however, the "summer of Sam" had left Americans panicky and fearful about such horrific and senseless violence.

Such fear certainly may have contributed to changes in the American approach toward the death penalty. In 1972, the Supreme Court had ruled that the death penalty as usually enforced constituted cruel and unusual punishment and was therefore unconstitutional. Fewer than five years later, however, the Court reversed itself, ruling in a seven-to-two decision that capital punishment did not constitute cruel and unusual punishment. In those five years, Congress and most states had drafted new death penalty laws for murderers, and the Court upheld such laws in Georgia, Florida, and Texas. Indeed, only a few months later convicted murderer Gary Gilmore went before a firing squad at his own request in Utah, becoming the first convict to die after what had amounted to a ten-year moratorium on capital punishment in America. His execution was followed by one hundred fifty more in the next fifteen years.

Television

Over the last fifty years, according to Findling and Thackeray (1996), television has moved from the status of a toy with a flickering image to a powerful and influential communications medium that commands an important place in the lives of most Americans. The decade of the 1970s was the second decade of television's dominance of home life, and in some ways it witnessed the high point of television's preeminence in American culture. Despite the ban on tobacco advertising in 1971, revenues from television commercials reached all-time highs. With the increase in advertising fees, the practice of a program having just one sponsor (which originated with radio) came to an end. Meanwhile, Myron Marty reports that the average number of hours of viewing per home per day had increased from just over five hours in 1960 to almost six hours in 1970, nearly 18 percent. By 1978, 98 percent of U.S. households had television sets (the majority with color television and with two or more sets), up from 9 percent in 1950 and 83.2 percent in 1968. When *TV Guide* celebrated its twenty-fifth anniversary in 1978, it had long had a larger circulation than any other weekly magazine.

The success of network television led to new departures in television pro-gramming during the decade, with an emphasis on political and social rele-vancy. In 1971, for example, producer Norman Lear introduced a show intended to deal with racial tensions in an unconventional and controversial but appealing way. So the star of *All in the Family* was a lovable bigot named Archie Bunker who tried his best to head his embattled family. According to Myron Marty, Archie became the mirror against which many Americans ex-amined their own vocabularies and conduct on racial matters. *The Mary Tyler Moore Show,* about an unmarried career woman (1970), and *M*A*S*H,* a so-cially relevant comedy set in the Korean War, also filled the bill in directing television's fare toward more realistic political and social awareness.

As urban markets grew, television aimed its programming at younger, more commercially lucrative markets as well. Not one of the top ten programs in the Nielsen ratings of 1968–69 remained there after five years. By then, tel-evision programs had also acquired an ethnic mix more representative of the American population, including *Sanford and Son*—which was ranked third in the 1975 Nielsen ratings and which featured scenes from rough-and-tumble aspects of African-American life—and *The Jeffersons.* These programs and oth-ers in the top ten reflected greater permissiveness in language, plot, and de-pictions of sex, as well as the importance of being relevant to American life. Other new programs, such as *Saturday Night Live,* a mix of slapstick and satire, showed the same characteristics. Myron Marty claims that NBC aimed this program, which premiered in 1975, specifically at baby boomers.

Indeed, later in the decade, as Hollywood films began to be more sexually explicit, television responded with such shows as *Dallas, Love Boat,* and *Char-lie's Angels;* this last was ostensibly a detective show but was clearly designed to reveal the physical attributes of its three attractive lead actresses. The some-times controversial subject matters of shows such as these caused the Federal Communications Commission (FCC) to declare the first hour of the evening as "family viewing hour" in 1975. In 1976, however, the courts declared the FCC decision to be a violation of the networks' First Amendment rights. Even so, according to Findling and Thackeray, the networks moved their more ex-plicit shows to later prime-time slots. Meanwhile, Time Incorporated launched a new magazine, *People,* in 1974. This breezy publication focused on the personalities and lives of celebrities. According to Myron Marty, "Its pho-tographs and short features were intended to appeal to readers conditioned by television to accept superficiality and ephemera as the daily fare of 'celebrity journalism' " (1997, 167). By then, the circulation of the weekly *National Enquirer*—which for a half-century had been the best source of stories on crime, gore, miraculous and bizarre occurrences, gossip, and sex—had reached four million.

The Roots Miniseries

In 1977, a serial of a different nature attracted the largest audience in the history of television: Alex Haley's *Roots*. Running on consecutive evenings for a total of twelve hours, this dramatic depiction of the harsh life experienced by Haley's slave ancestors gripped the emotions of as many as 130 million viewers. Myron Marty argues that among black Americans, it inspired a new sense of pride, while many whites were compelled to face a legacy of guilt for the cruelty and exploitation inflicted on slaves by their forebears. The program also stirred viewers to explore their own family's roots; in the months following the miniseries' airing, the National Archives showed a 40 percent increase in visitors. In addition, the number of black genealogists using the archives' resources tripled.

Television and Sports

When ABC's Roone Arledge decided in 1970 to broadcast National Football League games on Monday nights, he produced another profound change in America's relationship with television. The team of announcers on ABC's broadcast included Howard Cosell, a tough-talking New York lawyer who had gained fame principally through his interviews with Muhammed Ali. Cosell's role on Monday nights was to be the man Americans loved to hate, an irritant charged with creating controversy. He succeeded in this role, and the viewership of Monday night football games increased dramatically. As other networks then jumped into the game and imitated Arledge's innovations, according to Myron Marty, sports programs claimed increasing shares of television time. By the mid-1970s, television and sports were so intertwined that television held a firm grip on the scheduling of sporting events. Athletes, coaches, team owners, and team sponsors all tried to use the medium to propel themselves to fame and fortune.

Television News and Current Events

Since its inception, television has also been an important influence in the world of news and current events. In its earliest days, television producers filled up unsold airtime with live broadcasts of news events. By the 1960s, due to the advent of more portable cameras and satellite transmission, television began to witness historical events and bring them live to America's viewers. Network television news departments covered the aftermath of the assassination of President John F. Kennedy during that decade, as well as the events of the civil rights movement and much of the tragedy of the Vietnam War. This coverage had a profound impact on the way the nation viewed these events, says Findling and Thackeray, shaping American opinions and responses. Indeed, noted newscaster Walter Cronkite's on-air declaration that the war in Vietnam was a terrible mistake had a significant effect on public opinion about the war. Vietnam was truly television's first war, and sitting in their living rooms, Americans could feel the horror and the violence reach out and touch them in their comfortable homes. Of course the impact of those emotions was enormous. Similarly, revelations during the televised Watergate hearings in 1973 about what President Richard Nixon and his chief aides knew about that scandal helped to create the public attitudes that brought on Nixon's resignation the following year.

On a more day-to-day level, the suppertime newscasts of the three major networks had become the "social cement" that bound together audiences from city to farm, creating the first genuinely national audience. By the early 1970s, statistics demonstrated that the majority of Americans were relying mainly on television newscasts for their impressions of what was happening in the world. In that sense, says Robert Hargreaves, the regular news programs of the three main networks had become the most important source of news in America. What was most frightening about this was the news that Americans were not getting. Because of the limited time in the half-hour format of the major news programs—with at least five minutes of the thirty spent on commercials—these television news programs provided but snippets, the headlines, of the pressing events of the day. Richard Salant, president of CBS News, once set up in type the complete spoken text of his nightly program and found that it would fit into less than a half-page of the *New York Times*.

Television and Political Campaigns

It was inevitable that television, which had become the most powerful instrument of communication ever devised, would also become a key factor in how political candidates were elected and how public officials governed. This had been especially true in presidential politics since 1952, when Nixon used television to deliver his famous "Checkers" speech. That speech ultimately kept him on the ticket as vice president and probably saved his political career. So it is no surprise that Nixon was well schooled and well prepared on how to use television to control his image and his message in the 1970s. In fact, Nixon's campaign strategy was formulated by a team of media experts, who changed the way all future campaigns would be run when they introduced the staged question-and-answer sessions with TV-studio audiences that appeared to viewers as spontaneous. However, these programs were actually very tightly controlled, with only those partial to Nixon in the audience, call-in questions rewritten by Nixon staffers, and Nixon reading his answers from cue cards. Commenting on this concept that he helped to create, Roger Ailes later said, "This is it. This is the way they'll be elected forevermore. The next guys up will have to be performers" (St. Clair 1996, 139).

Television and Technology

As television remote controls became popular during the seventies, channel hopping was encouraged, especially as cable channels grew in number and reach during these years. By May 1978, for example, subscribers were seeing cable broadcasts in an estimated twelve million homes. Meanwhile, Sony had introduced a video-recording system known as Betamax in 1975, but it could only be purchased in a package containing a videocassette recorder (VCR) and color TV that cost as much as $2,295. In a very short time, however, JVC's Video Home System (VHS) had displaced Betamax because of its longer recording time and lower cost. VCRs quickly overcame consumers' misgivings about such new technology, according to Myron Marty, and television viewing was revolutionized. With VCRs attached to their TVs, viewers could arrange to watch what they wanted when they wanted for the first time. They could also fast-forward through commercials, and VCRs could be used to watch rented cassettes. Indeed, within a decade, consumers were spending almost $2 billion on rentals. By the end of the 1980s, about two-thirds of American homes with TVs owned at least one VCR.

Television found yet another way to claim time in the daily lives of Americans when video games, introduced by Atari in 1975, became a national craze. They were initially played through a computerized control box that converted the television screen into fields for a variety of games. By 1976, video-game sales had reached $250 million. Video-game arcades also became popular in shopping centers, restaurants, airports, and other public places.

Movies

The dominance of television did not bring about the demise of the motion picture industry as some had predicted years earlier. Going to the movies remained a popular social activity for many Americans: people were still willing to pay more to see movies on a big screen. Indeed, box-office revenues broke the record set the previous year in 1975, even though Americans had to pay higher and higher admission prices at their local theaters. Blockbuster films brought in much of the industry's revenue in these years, says Myron Marty. Steven Spielberg's *Jaws* was the big moneymaker in 1975, with violence and terror wrought by a huge man-eating shark. In 1977, *Star Wars* became the next blockbuster, with its special effects and romantic take on fighting a "just" war. In fact, it was with the incredible success of *Star Wars* that a new phenomenon was discovered. To the shock of movie-company executives, they found an attendance pattern for the movie that they had never seen before: many viewers, especially teenagers, were not just coming back to see the movie twice—the usual pattern for a blockbuster film—they were coming back three and four times. Some were even watching it twenty or thirty times! The older generation was mystified, not understanding why anyone would see a movie three times if he or she could get the message the first time around. For the new generation, the medium was the message.

That medium was carrying all of the messages of cultural transition in the seventies. Indeed, film producers learned how to push the depiction of sex and violence to the limit during the decade. The loosening of sexual mores and the sexual revolution during the late 1960s and early 1970s prompted profound changes not only in television, but also in film with such movies as *Saturday Night Fever.* While four-letter words became a staple of Hollywood films, the degree of violence shown in many of those films also increased dramatically, with popular movies such as *Deliverance* and *Apocalypse Now* adding their own versions of blood and gore to the frightening teeth-gnashing in *Jaws.*

In conjunction with the sex and violence, Myron Marty argues that three themes were evident in the most significant movies of the early seventies, and these themes mirrored the condition of the society that found them attractive. All three were variations on alienation and loneliness. *M*A*S*H,* produced in 1971, mocked the standard war pictures and revealed American disillusionment with the war in Vietnam. *A Clockwork Orange,* also produced in 1971, portrayed violence and extreme versions of the practice of behavior modification advocated by some psychologists. *The Godfather,* produced in 1972, and *The Godfather II* (1974) revealed an extremely pessimistic side of American life, portraying a patriarchal and closely knit family dominated by a tough, protective godfather as a refuge from society's pervasive ills.

This last foreshadowed a new theme that was to emerge in American culture and, thus, in American films and entertainment toward the end of the decade. The rise of nostalgic longing for simpler times brought about by the extreme cultural turmoil that most Americans experienced—from the changing role of women to the apparent decline of the family—gave birth to a new genre of popular entertainment. Films such as *The Buddy Holly Story* and *American Graffiti,* which evoked a prettified, innocent 1950s, became enormously popular, as did television comedies such as *Happy Days.* Similarly, *The Waltons,* set in the 1930s, became one the most popular TV series of the 1970s. It portrayed a family with boundless love and understanding. Meanwhile, *Grease* became the longest-running show in Broadway history and *Vanities,* another show glorifying the 1950s, became the longest-running play in off-Broadway history.

Popular Music: From Rock to Disco

As rock and roll evolved in the later 1960s, the many groups of performers that sprang up, several of which attracted huge followings, played a central role in the cultural transitions of the early 1970s. The number of records and tapes sold to American listeners exploded during this era. In 1950, record sales totaled $189 million. Five years later, they had reached $277 million. By 1971, sales of records and tapes amounted to $1.7 billion in the United States alone, and in just two more years, sales topped $2 billion. That was only one part of the story: in 1973, record and tapes sales reached $555 million in Japan, $454 million in West Germany, and $441 million in the Soviet Union. Of course, all of these sales made a number of the rock and roll superstars— leaders of protests against the "establishment"—big moneymakers. *Forbes* magazine estimated that in 1973 at least fifty superstars earned between two million and six million dollars annually.

Both the stars and the superstars paid a high price for the money they made and the adulation they received from their groupies and fans. Heavy performance and recording schedules and frenetic lifestyles took their toll on the performers. More than that, though, the rockers often lived lives that were saturated with sex, drugs, and alcohol. The seemingly outrageous lifestyles of these stars were attractive to their fans, but often they ruined the performers themselves. Indeed, the 1970s witnessed the deaths of many of the era's central musical figures. Janis Joplin, whose intense performances were laced with obscenities, died of an overdose of heroin in 1970. Jimi Hendrix, known as the most extreme acid-rock guitarist of the times, had also been the victim of an overdose of sleeping pills just a month before. Jim Morrison, whose performances were filled with raw power and sexuality, died of a heart attack in 1971, clearly a victim of the excesses of his lifestyle. Joplin, Hendrix, and Morrison were all only twenty-seven years old when they died. Elvis Presley, the "king of rock and roll," died later in 1977 at the age of forty-two. It is commonly accepted that Presley's addiction to barbiturates had a hand in his early death.

Rock music gained wider acceptance as the seventies progressed, not by moving closer to mainstream America, but by drawing mainstream America closer to it. Indeed, Myron Marty argues that some performers were able to gain critical acceptance of their distinctive sounds. The lyrics of Bob Dylan, set to folk melodies, for example, were ambiguous enough to express the protests of almost anyone. The performances of the group he took on tour with him, The Band, easily reflected the outlook of his own baby-boom generation. Some consider Dylan's style as marking the beginning of the use of the term "rock" instead of "rock and roll." Other performers also helped to extend the influence of rock music. Simon and Garfunkel and the Beatles, for example, were two groups that had caught on quickly with young people and then later attracted older listeners. Indeed, the big names in rock music in the mid-1970s were softer ("pop-rock") and more mainstream, such as Elton John, Billy Joel, Stevie Wonder, and Bruce Springsteen.

The flip side of that, however, were the rock groups that appealed to truly distinctive audiences. Some groups, such as the Rolling Stones, drew fans with a blues-based, hard rock style. As experimentation with drugs moved through the counterculture and began to become more popular with young people in general, acid-rock groups such as Jefferson Airplane and the Grateful Dead gained wide popularity. Also gaining fans during those years were groups modeled on Led Zeppelin, whose loud, blues-based music combined with sexy stage shows was called heavy metal. Punk rockers, most notably the Sex Pistols, took things in yet another direction, says Marty, emphasizing rebellion and featuring such things as screaming obscenities and hair that had been dyed orange.

In the later years of the decade, disco—which blended pop, rock, and various other styles accompanied by repetitive rhythms and dance beats—became another musical phenomenon. Initially it was regarded as dance music by black singers, but it captured widespread attention with the hit movie *Saturday Night Fever*. This 1978 movie starring John Travolta resulted in discotheques (like the infamous Studio 54 in New York) enjoying a resurgence unequaled since the early 1960s in major U.S. and European cities. It also resulted in extreme popularity for the movie's sound track by the Bee Gees, which sold thirty million copies worldwide. The discotheques attracted dancing revelers of all ages, and the "scene" at many of them was laden with dancing, sex, and plenty of drugs. Disco garb, including skin-tight Lycra jeans and dresses slit thigh-high, appeared everywhere, and the disco beat filled the air waves while disco record sales zoomed upward. Indeed, highly formula-conforming disco records by Van McCoy ("The Hustle"), the Bee Gees ("Jive Talkin' "), and others dominated popular music until 1979. Disco's popularity soon faded, but for a time it was all the rage.

Health and Fitness

There were several worrisome trends in American lifestyles that gained momentum during the 1970s. First was the tendency toward eating more and more meals outside of the home. According to estimates in 1973, one meal in three was eaten outside of the home, and the vast majority of those were consumed at fast-food restaurants, the number of which doubled between 1967 and 1974. Indeed, McDonald's had fewer than one thousand restaurants in 1967 and more than three thousand in 1974. And new ones were opening at the rate of one every day. In 1972, in fact, McDonald's passed the U.S. Army as the biggest dispenser of meals. By then it had served twelve billion burgers. The fact that its menu items were loaded with fat and calories—almost 1,100 in a meal consisting of a Big Mac, a chocolate shake, and a small order of fries—did not keep customers away. This, even though the National Center for Health Statistics reported that Americans on average weighted fourteen pounds more in 1978 than they had fifteen years earlier.

Even the foods consumed at home were questionable in terms of their nutritional content, particularly after accounting for the fat and additives that they were often loaded with. For example, by 1970 the huge number of frankfurters consumed by Americans had an average fat content of 33 percent, up from 19 percent in 1941. Some of those franks were more than half fat! In contrast, Kaboom! breakfast food, introduced by General Mills in 1970, turned out to be 43.8 percent sugar. Artificial flavorings and sweeteners and heavy doses of salt and sugar were in fact common in most of the foods available to American consumers during this period, and food colorings and chemical preservatives were ubiquitous.

Meanwhile, advertising for foods was laden with ambiguities. Foods were called "natural" without any attention paid to what that meant. Restaurants served "shakes" containing no dairy products. Producers of imitation chocolate bars synthesized from various agricultural products and made tasty with artificial flavor mixed with bulking agents could describe their concoctions as "all natural." All in all, says Myron Marty, it was not until 1973 that the Food and Drug Administration began to require standardized nutrition information on food labels and the listing of such things as calories and grams of protein, fat, and carbohydrates per serving. This move was in line with a growing movement among some Americans toward eating "health food," and they spread the gospel of organic gardening and hailed the virtues of oats, dates, sunflower seeds, prunes, and raisins. Nonetheless, many Americans still did not know enough to take advantage of the important information that was newly available on the packages of the foods they consumed.

The seventies was the time, however, when Americans were becoming more informed about another great threat to the national health—cigarette smoking—although it did little to curb American's love affair with tobacco. In

1971, for example, U.S. cigarette sales reach $547.2 billion, despite a new ban on radio and television advertising. Then in 1972, a new surgeon general's report on smoking warned that nonsmokers exposed to cigarette smoke could suffer health hazards. In 1976, the first low-tar cigarettes—Merit—were introduced by Philip Morris with a $40 million advertising budget: in no time at all, they had captured 1.5 percent of the market.

It was not until later in the decade that one particular advocate against cigarette smoking starting grabbing headlines: Health, Education, and Welfare Secretary Joseph Califano. A onetime heavy smoker who had quit at the urging of his children, Califano told the press in 1978 that cigarette smoking was slow motion suicide and announced a new government campaign to discourage children and teenagers from smoking. The campaign was also aimed at helping the fifty-three million U.S. smokers quit the habit. However, the American Tobacco Institute called the Califano plan an intrusion on civil liberties, and the secretary also refused to challenge the $80 million in Department of Agriculture programs that were then supporting tobacco prices. To further muddy the picture, President Carter later undermined Califano's announcement by pledging government support of efforts to make cigarettes "even safer than they are" on a visit to North Carolina a few months later (Trager 1992).

Several diseases also provided a threat to national health during the decade. In 1975, for example, Lyme disease was identified in Lyme, Connecticut. Transmitted primarily by the bite of a tick found on white-tailed deer, the bacterial infection of Lyme disease often led to serious neurological, cardiac, and arthritic complications. It spread quickly throughout most of the Northeast and Middle Atlantic states, Wisconsin, Minnesota, and the West Coast. Then in 1976 a "swine flu" epidemic threatened the United States. On the advice of medical authorities, President Ford mounted a $135-million inoculation program. Forty-eight million Americans received influenza shots, but the warning ultimately turned out to be a false alarm. Only 6 cases of swine flue were recorded, but 535 of those inoculated developed the rare paralytic affliction Guillain-Barré syndrome. The result was that hundreds of the victims brought suit against the government. That same year, Legionnaires' disease killed twenty-nine members of the American Legion who had gathered at Philadelphia's seventy-two-year-old Belevue Stratford Hotel for the legion's annual meeting. The disease eventually proved to be a rare form of pneumonia.

One of the biggest fads or trends marking the mid- and late-1970s was a new American obsession with running. It would hardly be accurate to say that a fitness craze swept the country, for many Americans continued to lead sedentary lives. However, running and jogging claimed the interest and time of millions of Americans. For example, the first New York Marathon was held on September 23, 1970, and it attracted 126 starters who ran around Central Park four times. In short order, however, the event began to grow and grow until it was attracting more than 25,000 runners. Indeed, in 1978 Jim Fixx's *The Complete Book of Running* became popular nonfiction, capitalizing on the new U.S. passion for jogging and finding 620,000 buyers. That same year, Americans bought thirteen million pairs of running shoes and forty-two million pairs of "look-alike" jogger-type sneakers. As those running-obsessed Americans became insatiable consumers of running gear of any kind, they caused the rapid growth of several new companies. Nike, for example, was founded in 1972, and according to Myron Marty, it soon gained a dominant place in many sports. Perrier water, which was introduced to U.S. markets in 1976, was another to benefit. Although consumers preferred cheaper brands such as Canada Dry in blind taste tests, Perrier sales reached $177 million in a decade as fitness-minded Americans consumed it in outrageous quantities.

Bicycling also reached new levels of popularity in the early 1970s, when for the first time since 1897, Americans purchased more bicycles annually than automobiles. Sixty percent of them were purchased by adults! Other nonteam sports, such as golf and tennis, held their appeal as well. In 1975, for example, U.S. tennis racket sales peaked at 9.2 million units, although they fell to 5 million by 1978. Among the young, skateboarding gained wide popularity. Sometimes skateboards were used for stunts and sometimes just for fun, but before long the craze had become competitive, with cash prizes awarded in regional events.

America's Love Affair with Sports

Spectator sports, however, consumed far more of the ordinary American's time than did the sports in which citizens actually participated. Indeed, as television carried more and more games into spectators' homes, more and more Americans became spectators. Regular season games drew substantial audiences, but the playoff games hooked many more audiences. In particular, the NCAA basketball tournaments that today boast extraordinary numbers of viewers gained enormous popularity in the 1960s and 1970s. The astonishing success of the UCLA teams coached by John Wooden was particularly intriguing to viewers in these years, according to Myron Marty: after winning the championship in 1964 and 1965, they missed one year, but then, for seven consecutive years they were the big winners. The broadcast of the 1972 Munich Olympics also attracted large numbers of viewers as U.S. swimmer Mark Spitz won a record seven gold medals.

Other long-standing records were broken during this era, gripping sports fans across the nation. Hank Aaron, for example, broke Babe Ruth's career home run record in April 1974 by hitting his 715th home run off a pitch by Al Downing of the Los Angeles Dodgers. Of course, the fact that some questioned whether he could have done it if he had not played about twenty-five additional games as a result of the lengthened major league baseball season only heightened fans' interest in the record and in the sport. Equally controversial was the hype surrounding the decision of the American League in 1973 to install a gimmick advocated by the unconventional owner of the Oakland Athletics, Charles Finley: the designated hitter. The DH, as it became known, permitted teams to field a tenth player who would bat in place of the pitcher. The National League refused to use the DH, generating lots of controversy and creating odd situations when teams from the two leagues met annually in the World Series and All-Star games. Baseball's Pete Rose of the Philadelphia Phillies again drew attention to the sport in 1979 when he became the all-time leader in National League singles.

Probably the most controversial figure among sports fans was heavyweight boxing champion Muhammed Ali, who loved the spotlight and was always ready to do what needed to be done to attract it. The controversy began in the late 1960s, when Ali refused to be inducted into the military (after his request for conscientious objector status was denied). He was stripped of his title, arrested, and sentenced to five years in prison with a fine of $10,000. In 1970, Joe Frazier regained the world heavyweight boxing title by knocking out Jimmy Ellis in the fifth round, and then Frazier defeated Ali to retain his heavyweight title the next year. It was not until 1974 that Ali regained the world heavyweight boxing crown by knocking out George Foreman; he then held it until February 1978. The fans loved it—both those who loved Muhammed Ali and those who loved to hate him!

Even chess became a focus of attention in the United States and the world in the early 1970s when Bobby Fischer became the first American to win the world chess title. He defeated the Soviet grandmaster Boris Spassky 12.5 games to 8.5 at Reykjavik, Iceland, winning a record purse of $250,000. The event drew unprecedented attention around the world to the game of chess. A different kind of attention, however, was generated at the 1976 Super Bowl, according to Myron Marty, when television cameras panning the sidelines focused on the Dallas Cowboys cheerleaders. Dressed in tight-fitting, low-cut, skimpy outfits, they drew admiration from many male viewers and complaints from those who considered it another instance of sexual exploitation for commercial purposes. For good or bad, though, almost everything done in professional sports at that time was designed to have consumer appeal.

Religion

The United States during the seventies was, at least on the surface, surprisingly more religious than for the major part of the nation's history. At the time of the Civil War, only 16 percent of Americans adhered to an organized religion, while during the early 1970s, two out of every three officially belonged to one of the four major religious groups—Protestants, Catholics, Jews, and the Eastern Orthodox. At the same time, however, one cannot say that the decade of the seventies was exactly ruled by religious fervor in the United States. In fact, a nationwide survey taken in 1971 revealed that 75 percent of the general public felt religion as a whole was losing its influence on American life, and the majority of Protestant ministers, Roman Catholic priests, and Jewish rabbis agreed. Many of these religious leaders admitted to having considered leaving the religious life, and they often complained that it was difficult to define a role for themselves that the public would embrace. In fact, the American people did want someone to guide them, but they did not want authority figures. So while belief in America was not dead, argues Robert Hargreaves, it was beginning to take on more and more noninstitutional and nonsecular forms. This latter fact was probably best illustrated by the incredible popularity of such hits as *Jesus Christ Superstar* and *Godspell,* which attracted overflow crowds at churches, theaters, and outdoor rallies.

Several factors led the way for changes in religious commitment in the 1970s. One factor that surely had a profound effect was the change in the age distribution of the American population that has already been discussed. The disproportionately youthful population apparently felt less need for religious affiliations or perhaps believed that such affiliations could not serve their needs. The changes in family structure about which we have already spoken, along with increased demands on family time, also must have had some effect on involvement in religious activities. Some individuals undoubtedly also "dropped-out" of the formal religious institutions as they protested against authoritarian structures and against the position taken by their churches and denominations on social issues. Indeed, there were sure signs during the seventies that many individuals were "dropping out" or otherwise changing the degree and type of their religious commitments and activities, according to Myron Marty. Total attendance in churches and synagogues declined, reaching the point where only four in ten claimed to be regular churchgoers during the early 1970s. Financial contributions also declined, and, measured in constant dollars, money spent on church construction decreased in five years by more than one-third from the $1 billion spent on it in 1970. Yet another concern was the sharp decline in the numbers of persons studying in seminaries to be pastors and priests.

Evangelism

Since all the other aspects of the American way of life were in flux, it is not surprising that religious beliefs and practices also began to change during this period. The stresses brought on by rapid cultural change usually find expression in spiritual yearning and experimentation, and the 1970s were no exception as transitions in American culture gave birth to new movements within religious life. As many abandoned their traditional religious approaches, they searched for alternatives that could fulfill their spiritual needs. Some who sought an alternative to traditional forms of religious practice found it in the Jesus Movement that sprang up in California in the late 1960s and early 1970s. The first ones in the movement were known as "Jesus freaks," young persons claiming to be "born again." Their lives had lost meaning and purpose, they said, and finding it neither in drugs nor in the counterculture, they responded to calls to focus everything on Jesus. The apparent innocence, simplicity, and spirit of community that those in the early Jesus Movement demonstrated, according to Myron Marty, helped the movement to spread rapidly. In 1971, the Religious News Writers Association called it the news event of the year in religion.

While this Jesus Movement faded away rather quickly, a new one just as quickly followed it, retaining the earlier movement's emphasis on new birth through Jesus. These "born-again" Christians sought to convert others to beliefs in personal salvation, and they represented a part of the upsurge of evangelicalism that occurred in the 1970s. Between 1963 and 1978, the percentage of Americans claiming to have been "born again" and to have personally experienced salvation rose from 24 percent to 40 percent. By the end of the 1970s, more than fifty million Americans claimed to be evangelicals. Indeed, *Newsweek* called 1976 "the year of the evangelicals."

Televangelism played a large role in raising money and in promoting evangelical political and spiritual causes. Evangelist Oral Roberts showed that it was possible to build an expansive television ministry by combining evangelical preaching with faith healing. Jimmy Swaggert likewise reached huge audiences, as did Jim and Tammy Bakker's PTL (Praise The Lord), which became a multimillion-dollar religious empire.

In 1979, televangelist Jerry Falwell used his *Old Time Gospel Hour,* which aired on more than three hundred U.S. television stations and sixty-four foreign stations, to launch an explicit political movement: the Moral Majority. Joining forces with other well-funded conservative organizations, Falwell's new political action group registered millions of new voters by November 1980 in an effort to block the Equal Rights Amendment, to impede reform of the criminal code, to disrupt the White House Conference on the Family, and to fight abortion liberalization. His success gave him reason to say, "We have enough votes to run the country. And when the people say, 'We've had enough,' we are going to take over" (Marty 1997, 233).

Communes, Cults, and Jonestown

The most radical members of the early Jesus Movement formed highly disciplined "families" and rejected everything they regarded as "establishment." They typically lived communally, shared everything, and required members to renounce their biological families. Distraught parents, believing their offspring to be under the influence of mind control, sometimes tried to retrieve them with the aid of "deprogrammers." The Jesus Movement, however, was only the tip of the iceberg. In fact, one of the more dramatic developments of the 1970s was the rise of a number of religious groups that were out of the ordinary. Some observers designated these groups as "alternative religions," but the label that caught the public imagination was the term "cults." Hare Krishna followers, for example, handed out literature, tried to sell books, and begged for contributions in airports. The Unification Church of the Reverend

Sun Myung Moon was another aggressive recruiter of new members, often known as the "moonies," in the 1970s. The rise in influence and popularity of cults during the decade was a great source of concern for many Americans, as they became convinced that young people were being manipulated by cult leaders to do things they would not otherwise do. The conviction of the Charles Manson "family" of the murder of actress Sharon Tate and some of her companions in the early years of the decade served only to dramatize and heighten these concerns.

However, the power of cult leaders to control their members and the fears that many Americans had about them were horribly and resoundingly confirmed by another incident that occurred toward the end of the decade, in November 1978. In a scene of "the most sickening religious mayhem since 1535" (Trager 1992, 1067), nearly one thousand members of the People's Temple, a California-based religious cult, died in a mass suicide-murder at the cult's commune in Jonestown, Guyana. U.S. Congressman Leo Ryan of California had arrived at the remote settlement on November 17 to investigate complaints from his constituents about the treatment of relatives in the commune that was established by former San Francisco clergyman Jim Jones. Accompanied by seventeen staff members and several newsmen, Ryan met with Jones, who denied any mistreatment but kept most commune members away from Ryan. Nonetheless, some twenty members of the People's Temple told Congressman Ryan that they wanted to leave, and they accompanied him to Port Kaituma airport on November 18.

However, as the group began to board two small planes, cult member Larry Layton pulled a handgun and fired, wounding two people before fleeing. Three other men then arrived, wounded Ryan and four others, and then shot each in the head. After a planeload of survivors managed to take off for Georgetown, cult leader Jones ordered nine hundred eleven of his followers to drink Kool-Aid laced with cyanide. Those who refused were shot or forcibly injected with cyanide. In the end, Jones was found shot in the head, although it was unclear whether he shot himself or was murdered. In all, only thirty-two escaped the disaster (Trager 1992).

Technology

So much of American life was in flux during the decade of the seventies, but the rapid changes that came in technology were, more often than not, a source of pride and security for many. Indeed, the 1970s saw continued advances in agricultural productivity, with the average U.S. farm worker producing enough food and fiber for forty-seven people, up from forty the decade before. In 1970, Boeing 747 jumbo jets went into transatlantic service for Pan Am, and the Concorde supersonic jet exceeded twice the speed of sound for the first time on November 4 of that same year. However, not all of the technological breakthroughs of the seventies were glamorous and exotic. An example of a simpler, more widely used technological development was the soft contact lens, which received FDA approval on March 18, 1971. Although the lenses cost $300 (almost $1,000 in 1990 dollars) and were intended to last only one year, they were much more comfortable than the hard lenses introduced in 1939.

Similarly, 1972 unveiled the Polaroid SX-70, which produced a color print that developed outside of the camera while the photographer watched. At the other end of the decade, Americans found that they could purchase the pleasure of hearing high-fidelity sound in any location without disturbing their neighbors. This came about in 1979 with the arrival of Sony's Walkman cassette player, a $200 pocket stereo with two pairs of miniature earphones.

Space Exploration

Perhaps the greatest technological feats of the seventies, giving rise to great American pride and a sense of confidence, were the ventures of America into space. The most famous event occurred not in the seventies, but on July 20, 1969. On that date, hundreds of millions of Americans had watched and listened to Neil Armstrong and Edwin Aldrin first land on the moon in *Apollo 11*'s lunar module and then take the first steps and conduct the first experiments on the surface. One of the six remaining missions, *Apollo 13*, survived a near-disaster without a moon landing, but the other five were successful, the last occurring in December 1972. In that same year, the unmanned U.S. spacecraft *Pioneer 10* lifted off from Cape Kennedy on a 639-day, 620-million-mile journey past the planet Jupiter.

A year later, the United States had launched *Skylab I* while *Pioneer 10* passed Jupiter. Then 1975 witnessed the first U.S.-Soviet linkup in space on July 18, as an American *Apollo* spacecraft and a Soviet *Soyuz* spacecraft united and the astronauts and cosmonauts exchanged visits 140 miles above the earth.

In the same year that *Apollo* had its last successful mission (1972), the National Aeronautics and Space Administration (NASA) proposed to begin a space shuttle program to provide the means for further scientific exploration and possible future colonization and commercial activities. On January 5 of that year, President Nixon signed a bill that authorized the $5.5 billion, six-year program to develop the shuttle, a craft that lifted off as a rocket and returned to earth as an airplane. In 1977 America had the thrill of seeing those plans come to fruition when the first space shuttle was tested successfully.

Breakthroughs in Medical Technology

Equally positive were several medical breakthroughs in the United States and abroad that gave hope to many people. Several technological developments during these years vastly improved physicians' abilities to diagnose diseases and injuries. In fact, three such diagnostic tools were developed almost simultaneously during the early 1970s. The computed axial tomography (CAT) scanner, which had been developed in England with money from sales of Beatles records in 1972, began to be marketed in the United States in 1973. By 1974, the device—which assembles thousands of X-ray images into a single, remarkably detailed picture of the body's interior—gained wide use not only for diagnosing brain damage but also for whole-body scanning. Similarly, Nuclear Magnetic Resonance (NMR), used to measure the absorption of radio waves in a magnetic field, enabled physicians to distinguish healthy tissue from diseased tissue. Ultrasound, marketed in 1974, made use of ultrasonic waves to visualize such things as the development of a fetus. Each year, according to Myron Marty, increasing numbers of persons benefited from CAT scans, NMRs, and ultrasound.

Ultrasound gave some joyous news to Lesley Brown in 1978, when she found that she was pregnant with the world's first test-tube baby. The baby, named Louise Brown, was born on July 25 at London's Oldham Hospital. It was at the same hospital that consultant gynecologist Patric Steptoe and physiologist Robert Edwards had fertilized an egg from Lesley Brown's womb with sperm from her husband, and then reimplanted the fertilized egg in the mother's womb. The successful pregnancy of Lesley Brown and the birth of Louise gave hope to millions of couples with fertility problems and signaled another birth: that of a revolution in fertility treatment. Other such conceptions and births followed as use of the procedure spread.

The Birth of the Information Age?

The 1970s also witnessed the beginning of a revolution that was to transform the United States and, in fact, the whole globe. While word processors with cathode-ray tube displays and speedy printers began to replace typewriters in 1974, Microsoft was being founded in Seattle by computer whiz Bill Gates, nineteen years old, and his friend Paul Gardner, twenty-two. Gates, who wrote his first computer program at the age of thirteen and scored a perfect eight hundred on his math SAT, had dropped out of Harvard to start the business that was to become the world's biggest seller of computer software and to make Gates a billionaire before he was thirty. Only a year later, in 1976, Apple Computer was founded in a California garage. Founders Stephen Wozniak and Steven Jobs were college dropouts who raised $1,500 and spent six months designing the crude prototype for Apple I, the first personal computer (Trager 1992).

At the same time, word processors made by Wang Laboratories began to revolutionize offices with work stations that shared central computers, and fax machines began to gain ground as second-generation technology cut transmission time from six minutes per page to three. Then in 1977, Wozniak and Jobs introduced the Apple II personal computer. Although it required users to employ their TV sets as screens and to store data on audiocassettes, it was a substantial advance over Apple I. Even more important, it retailed at only $1,298, making it an affordable luxury for many Americans, and it caught on quickly in homes and in schools. This set in motion the development of personal computers by IBM, and it caused the rapid expansion of software-producing Microsoft. In less than two decades, personal computers would go from being affordable luxuries to near necessities for many Americans as the information age was born.

That information age was not limited to business machines and personal computers. Other technological changes, such as the Universal Product Code (UPC), also came into use during the seventies, revolutionizing retail and other industries. In 1973, a committee that had been formed in 1970 by U.S. grocers and manufacturers to improve the productivity of their workers issued a recommendation for a UPC for all supermarket items. The package code was designed to permit electronic scanners at checkout counters to "read" the price of each item and trigger a computer that would record the price automatically, thus eliminating checker error and facilitating inventory control. At first, retailers balked at installing the costly equipment required by the UPC, while consumers complained about the elimination of individually marked prices. However, when it became clear that the benefits to retailers would offset the costs, the UPC became widely employed. More than one-fourth of the nation's supermarkets were using electronic scanners by the end of 1975, and their use spread to all kinds of merchandise and to a variety of operations requiring packaging and sorting. Indeed, by the late 1990s, about 90 percent of all U.S. retail chains employed scanners, and more than one million of them were in operation worldwide.

Conclusion

The 1970s was a decade that witnessed great transitions in American culture: there were violent protests and dramatic changes in sexual mores. The decade began with the revolt of the 1960s still playing out and still wreaking havoc on American society. By 1974, however, the revolt of the 1960s had ended. Those troubled times came to a close, but other troubles remained as America entered into a period of readjustment. By the eighties, as that adjustment was completed, the changes that had been wrought brought their prices: teenage pregnancy among the poor, heavy drug use among the young, and the dark shadow of Acquired Immunodeficiency Syndrome (AIDS) hovering over sexual liberation.

But the costs and losses were not limited to the eighties. The seventies had its many losses too, from the icons of an earlier and seemingly simpler time, such as Charlie Chaplin and John Wayne, to the icons of the explosive and rebellious youth culture, such as Janis Joplin and Jimi Hendrix. The nation felt the fear of the "summer of Sam" as well as the pain of the mayhem at Jonestown. It fretted over Karen Quinlan's coma and the Three Mile Island accident. The nation also faced more common and widespread losses as it confronted dramatic upheavals in family life and the role of women. There was widespread fear that institutions, the government, the family, and even individual personalities were completely breaking down. In fact, "narcissism" became a loaded word that expressed the sense of chaos and fragmentation that Americans felt. A favorite quotation of the time was from Yeats's "The Second Coming": "Things fall apart; the centre cannot hold." Faced with rapid shifts in almost every aspect of life, Americans lost their customary belief in a better tomorrow, and they began to embrace "tradition" and to turn to an idealized past for solace. As they did so, a conservative backlash was born.

Thus, life in the seventies was a life full of changes, transitions, and losses. But there were also births: of the automatic teller machine in 1973, and of the first test tube baby in 1978. America's first space shuttle flight brought pride and a sense of wonder to an embattled nation, as did Mark Spitz's record seven gold medals. Amidst the controversies and conflict there was also a special celebration that reminded the American people of their common—and uncommon—heritage and the promise that it held: the two hundredth anniversary of the Declaration of Independence. Indeed, the celebration of the Bicentennial inspired a variety of different events, including fireworks, parades, parties, races, games, and historical reenactments. Some celebrations featured the distinctive styles of various ethnic groups, pointing out the important contributions made by immigrants throughout two centuries of American history. Some celebrated with exhibitions of arts and crafts, and the most American of foods—sweet corn, watermelon, and hot dogs—were on the menu everywhere. Across the nation, bells in churches, schools, and firehouses pealed out in joyous celebration, and television and radio helped to draw everyone into the big party.

Of course, celebrations on the Fourth of July were only part of the observance of the Bicentennial. The American Revolution Bicentennial Administration (ARBA) distributed the $51 million that Congress had appropriated to finance projects and programs throughout the year. Indeed, the ARBA's master calendar of observances listed 27,146 active projects and events in 11,639 cities and towns. People from around the world, including Britain's Queen Elizabeth II, traveled to America to help the nation celebrate. Also as a part of the Bicentennial, according to Myron Marty, people joined forces to restore historic buildings and sites, to plant trees, to build parks, and to compile pictorial and oral histories.

In fact, few occasions have drawn ordinary Americans into common celebration as fully as did the marking of the Bicentennial, and this great occasion gave the nation the gift of a moment of healing in a decade fraught with betrayal, loss, and instability. Many believed that the experience of the Bicentennial demonstrated that America had indeed been healed from the wounds of the previous years. They agreed with *Time* magazine when it observed in July 1976 that "after thirteen consecutive years of assassinations, race riots, youth rebellion, Vietnam, political scandal, presidential collapse, energy crisis, and recession, the nation's mood seems optimistic again" (July 5, 1976, 8). Indeed, Myron Marty claims that the celebration of the Bicentennial of the Declaration of Independence in 1976 brought moments of accord in a decade of discord.

7

Limits and the Legacy
of the Seventies

"GRAND EXPECTATIONS" perhaps best sums up the feeling of Americans during the three decades or so after the end of World War II. During this period, Americans developed ever-greater expectations about the capacity of the United States to create a better world abroad and a happier society at home. High expectations, rooted in vibrant economic growth, swelled as never before in the 1950s and peaked in the 1960s, as faith in the wealth of the United States and in the capacity of the federal government to promote progress aroused unprecedented rights-consciousness on the home front. In addition, America's political leaders stimulated enormous expectations about the nation's ability to direct world affairs. Indeed, by every conventional measure the postwar world born in 1945 was a great success: more goods were produced and sold than ever before; more people were working; and the standard of living had never been higher. According to James Patterson (1996), more than ever before—or since—Americans came to believe that they could shape the international scene in their own image as well as fashion a more classless and equal society at home.

Thus, standing on the verge of the decade that was the 1960s, Americans believed themselves to be at the threshold of a new golden age. Their nation stood at the apex of power in the world. Never was a nation more confident in its power, more certain of its destiny, than the United States at this time. "Proud in its strength, admired for its benevolence, envied for its wealth, America regarded itself more than ever as 'the last best hope of mankind.' The nation seemed intent on saving the world by its example and by its very exertions," observed Robert Hargreaves in 1973 (3–6). Indeed, John Kennedy had declared in his inaugural address: "We shall pay any price, bear any burden, meet any hardship, support any friend, oppose any foe." The future, as far as it could be foreseen, offered endless expectations of the same.

This wonderful time in the history of the United States has often been called the "Pax Americana." In those golden postwar years, says David Calleo (1982), American power, imagination, and energy seemed limitless, inducing much of the rest of the world into a pattern of American design. Of course, this euphoric faith in a limitless and powerful America could not and did not last—it slammed up instead against the reality of the 1970s. By the time of the early 1970s, the suspicion was already growing that the golden era was ending, and there was a pervasive sense that something was deeply and terribly wrong. According to Richard Barnet in his 1980 book, that new mood "[was] no conventional pessimism, but rather a loss of faith rooted in a sense of betrayal." He explains it thus: "We worked hard. We educated our children. We believed in the future. We followed the rules of success. And, somehow, it [had] turned out wrong" (1980, 15). Instead of the boundless horizons they had been promised, Americans discovered that limits were popping up everywhere. New words began to enter their vocabularies during the seventies: "limits," "lowered expectations," "lifeboat ethics," and "zero-sum economics."

Quite simply, the history of the 1970s was a history of a rapid succession of shocks to America that ushered in a politics of austerity. Suddenly the word on every lip was "scarcity." The world monetary system designed at Bretton Woods toward the end of World War II collapsed, taking with it America's unique role as world banker. U.S. forces withdrew in defeat from Vietnam. It seemed that from nowhere, faraway people—whose traditional role was to be conquered, bought, or ignored—had acquired the power to produce panic in the industrial world. The Arab oil producers raised the price of oil fivefold, and America's affluent society found itself with cold houses and endless lines at gas pumps. Indeed, the great symbol of this new world without options was the energy crisis. As Barnet describes it: "Burn gasoline and cities choke in fumes. Burn coal, and the delicate ecological balance of the earth is jeopardized. Take the nuclear route, and you court catastrophe" (1980, 16). The energy crisis was thus one of the first lessons in limits of the seventies; it taught Americans how it feels to be powerless even as it forced them to come to terms with environmental limits. It dramatized more effectively than any other experience that America's strong, industrial society was dependent on world resource systems and, even more important, that control was shifting away from it.

To understand scarcity, says Richard Barnet (1980), one must understand that the crucial resource is energy, for it is the key to all others. If energy were unlimited, it could be used to produce limitless quantities of drinkable water from the sea, to synthesize food for billions of people, or to excavate the rich mineral deposits at the very depths of the earth or in outer space. Energy is the resource for gaining access to all the other resources, according to Barnet. So the energy crisis indeed became the symbol of new limits, as Americans—ironically—discovered how far those limits could extend. Soon, cheap food had gone the way of cheap energy. Across the world a billion people were on the edge of starvation, and in the United States, supermarket prices jumped 60 percent in five years. Water was a growing problem everywhere, with droughts in the West and floods in the East. Unemployment was growing; for the first time in the postwar period, it became a serious problem. Inflation grew even as unemployment did, creating the worst of all worlds: stagflation.

Economic downtimes taught Americans another lesson about limits. In the 1960s, for example, the gross national product had increased at an average rate of 4 percent or more. By the end of the 1970s the increases had declined to 2.9 percent per year. As if to symbolize this crisis in production in the United States, for example, more cars were recalled for defects in 1977 than were made! Between 1970 and 1973, purchasing power—adjusted for inflation—grew by 7 percent. In the remainder of the seventies, however, there was no growth at all. Further, the inflation rate by the end of the 1970s had risen to 12.5 percent. Quite simply, Americans had always prided themselves on having the highest standard of living in the world, but in the 1970s, it dropped all the way from the first to the tenth. According to Myron Marty, Americans were surprised to find that in fighting the war in Vietnam, continuing the cold war, and waging war on poverty, the United States had simply taken on too much.

This, too, gave birth to a new realization. Until the late 1960s, Americans generally perceived the United States to be the most powerful and most glorious nation in the world. Similarly, Americans believed that their chief executive, the president, had the power to do just about whatever he wanted, and that he would use that power only to do good—for the nation and for the world. However, a changing world situation in the early 1970s brought down the house of cards. Vietnam, the first war that America could not win, clearly demonstrated that the United States was no longer the hegemonic power in the world, that it was a multipolar world. Indeed, the Nixon Doctrine of the early seventies was a clear and pragmatic acceptance of this change and of the limits of American power. There were now several seats of power emerging to challenge U.S. hegemony, and this quickly led to American détente with the Soviet Union and rapprochement with China. In short order, says John Robert Greene (1992), it had become painfully clear that American power in the world was limited and that the shine of American glory was tarnished.

Perhaps this fact was best exemplified by the advent of Soviet nuclear parity with the United States in the early seventies. After six years of frenzied bomb crafting, the Soviets were suddenly in a position to meet Americans head-on in a nuclear confrontation. The United States would now have to face this fact, a clear challenge to its previously unlimited superiority in the world, and the awareness of this new limitation was exceedingly frightening to Americans. To most people, the actual use of even one of these ferocious weapons was unthinkable, but nuclear technology had reached the stage in the 1970s where both America and the Soviet Union could absorb the most violent attack that could be launched. This was true even under ideal conditions of surprise; either country would still survive to strike back with sufficient force to inflict "unacceptable" damage on the enemy. At that time in American history, says Robert Hargreaves, unacceptable damage was calculated as a quarter of the population killed and half of industry destroyed. This was necessary to be sure that the deterrent would actually deter. For the first time in human history, says Robert Hargreaves, man had invented and prepared a weapons system that was too terrible to use. In fact, the two cold war enemies had piled up enough such horrible weapons by the decade of the seventies that they could destroy each other many times over.

Thus, while the United States remained a superpower, a giant among nations, the ideals of Pax Americana were no longer credible. Instead of spreading peace across the globe and a better and more democratic way of living, suddenly America was spreading fear of unwinnable wars and of nuclear Armageddon. Instead of being the embodiment of power, strength, and leadership in the world, the United States seemed weak, unable even to control the spread of Communism in the tiny and unimportant countries of Indochina. So the internationalism of the older generation of Americans that had led to the notion of Pax Americana was, in the words of historian Arthur Schlesinger, noble but flawed: its flaw was its overcommitment of resources and rhetoric (in Hargreaves 1973, 3–6). America, like other nations of the world, came to understand that there are limits to its enormous power. The seventies were about this fact, and about the slow and agonizingly painful withdrawal from that earlier overcommitment.

Although in the realm of foreign policy Richard Nixon was able to see clearly the truth of the limitation of American power in the world (the Nixon Doctrine), he did not see the other new limits that came along with these changes. He, in fact, refused to accept the limits that were now imposed on the president's power. He did not see that Americans were questioning their presidents, particularly after the betrayals of the Johnson administration. With Johnson, the American presidency was changed—the press and the public were not willing to trust him blindly when he could not articulate a clear justification for the American presence in Vietnam. According to John Robert Greene (1992), he became a prisoner in the White House to the antiwar protesters, and his standing in the polls plummeted. Nixon took over Johnson's job, determined to restore the power of the presidency, to restore the glory of the American presidency, and to stop the erosion of presidential power. Nixon went way too far in pursuing these goals, however, not understanding the limits now present. The true irony of it is that in refusing to accept new limits on the power of the president, Nixon and the actions of his administration damaged the institution of the presidency even further. Indeed, Nixon and Watergate limited the power of future American presidents in the extreme. Though Richard Nixon strove to make the American presidency imperial, instead he made it imperiled. Gerald Ford's power and influence, as an example, were more limited than any other president's.

The Legacies of the Seventies

This, then, is the great legacy of the 1970s: the lesson of limits—limits on economic growth, on resources, and on the ability of the earth to continue to absorb environmental degradation. It was about the limits of American power in the world and the limits of the American system to respond to new and complex situations. It was about America coming to terms with these limits. Jimmy Carter understood about these limits from the day he took office. Writing of his inaugural address in his memoirs, he states: "I then broached a concept that was to prove painfully prescient and politically unpopular: limits. We simply could not afford everything people might want. Americans were not accustomed to limits—on natural resources or on the power of our country to influence others or to control international events." After citing the passage from his address dealing with limits, he goes on to write, "At the time, it was not possible even for me to imagine the limits we would have to face. In some ways, dealing with limits would become the subliminal theme of the next four years and affect the outcome of the 1980 election" (Carter 1982, 21).

Some of the events of the seventies left other legacies for the nation—beyond the limits we have already spoken of—that cannot be ignored, however. Two events of the seventies, in particular, profoundly shaped that decade as well as the rest of the decades of the century: Vietnam and Watergate. As well, the massive social changes wrought during the seventies that were discussed in great detail in chapter 6 also provided an important legacy all their own.

Vietnam

Clearly, the legacy of Vietnam was not restricted to the sense of limitation that it engendered, nor even to the economic havoc that the war wreaked on the American economy, although these are two important results of the conflict in Southeast Asia. Another important legacy of America's unhappy experience in Vietnam was that from then onward, America's foreign policy choices were curtailed. Because Americans feared that the same tragedy could occur again elsewhere, the American government found that it had fewer choices of action on the world scene. Thus on the one hand, there has been a greater reluctance by Americans to commit conventional forces to action in various trouble spots around the world, even when the situation seemingly called out for such intervention. A good example of such a situation was Congress's refusal to release military aid for Angola in late 1975.

On the other hand, there have been occasions when the president, wanting to "make America stand tall again" (Findling and Thackeray 1996, 177) after the defeat in Vietnam, has ordered a large-scale military operation against a hapless foe in order to score an easy win. This occurred in 1983 when President Reagan sent a large contingent of troops to the Caribbean island of Grenada, ostensibly to protect American medical students studying there, but in reality to topple an unfriendly leftist government. It also occurred in 1989 when the Bush administration sent several thousand troops into Panama in

order to bring Manuel Noriega—the country's leader and a former CIA operative—to justice for alleged drug trafficking.

The resistance of the Veteran's Administration and the American government to take responsibility for and to acknowledge the use of the defoliant
Agent Orange during the Vietnam War produced yet another lesson from that
conflict. In late 1979, a class action lawsuit was brought against five chemical
manufacturers of Agent Orange. The suit was eventually settled out of court
for $180 million while the American government continued to deny culpabil-
ity (even as evidence to the contrary mounted). Thus, America's faith in its
government and its whole political system was challenged in yet another way
by the events in Vietnam.

Added to this is the legacy of the more than 2,200 servicemen who were
missing in action in the Vietnam conflict. After the war, uncertainty persisted
over whether all of the Americans held as prisoners of war (POWs) had been
released. In addition, whether those missing in action (MIA) or held as prisoners of war were alive or dead could not be determined. Although North
Vietnam returned about eight hundred POWs in compliance with the terms
of the 1973 Paris Peace Agreement, a number of veteran's groups and politicians continued to maintain that there were still hundreds, perhaps thousands,
of Americans in North Vietnam prison camps. This emotionally charged issue
proved so politically intense, according to Findling and Thackeray, that it
blocked serious negotiations concerning the normalization of relations with
Vietnam for many years. Unfortunately, it has also blocked some of those
most damaged by the wounds of the war from really healing. Indeed, questions about the MIA-POW issue still persist, making the issue one that continues to haunt America long after the end of the war, particularly for the
families of servicemen still unaccounted for.

Yet another legacy of the Vietnam War was the profound difficulties that
Vietnam veterans experienced in readjusting psychologically to "normal" life
after returning home to the United States. Although this has been a concern
after each of the wars in which Americans fought, it was a particular issue following the Vietnam War—a war that America wanted to forget. After Vietnam, the soldiers returned home not in victory but in defeat, and not to
appreciative parades but to a public that had grown bitter and cynical about
the war. The public transferred that bitterness to the veterans, calling them
"baby-killers" and "drug addicts." Quite simply, the nation did not want to be
reminded of its disastrous defeat in Vietnam. Thus bitter and frustrated sol-

diers, many with drug dependencies, came home to a bitter America that was at best indifferent and at worse, say Findling and Thackeray, overtly hostile. Many veterans developed a condition called "post-traumatic stress disorder," characterized by feelings of deep depression often alternating with uncontrollable rage, intolerable flashbacks, and severe insomnia. For a large number of veterans this meant the inability to hold a job, alienation from family and friends, homelessness, and in many cases, suicide. In fact, some figures suggest that more Vietnam veterans have committed suicide since the war than died in it.

The trauma of the Vietnam War was, of course, not limited to those who fought in the war and the troubles they faced as they came home. For the war was in many ways also fought at home, and much of its trauma grew out of the great conflicts over American foreign policy that it represented. The nation became more highly divided than at any time since the Civil War. America was committing troops and resources to a war that a significant number of Americans regarded as immoral and unjust. The failure of those in top positions of authority to consult with those experts who were opposed to the Vietnam War, says Arthur Neal (1998), resulted in a serious crisis of authority in the social realm. Instead of welcoming those with contrary points of view, those who believed the war was unwinnable, the top decision makers stereotyped them as unpatriotic, disloyal, and soft on Communism. Only those who were considered "team players" were allowed to participate in the decision-making process. Thus, the harsh exclusion of dissent, as well as the use of deception and misrepresentation in continuing the Vietnam War, made major contributions to a profound loss of confidence in political authority in American society.

Watergate

Of course, the ultimate crisis of that authority in the seventies came with Watergate. As Richard Nixon attempted to establish an all-powerful, unquestioned executive in American government, he changed forever the relationship between the American people and their president. The chief executive could no longer be seen as a benevolent father, selflessly watching out for his children and guiding the ship of state through stormy seas. Instead, anyone who wanted to be president was automatically suspect, someone to be watched carefully and restrained from taking advantage. At the same time,

Americans' trust in their government suffered: cynicism rose, political participation fell, and the ideal of politics as public service seemed to be dead. In reality, the very notion of democracy—of belief in participatory government—was threatened.

It was not just the relationship between the president and the people that suffered debilitating changes. The same legacy sparked an institutional hostility and conflict between the president and Congress that is still a major factor in American politics today. Again, the presidency was seen as an institution that needed to be restrained, and the legislative branch of government assigned itself as the enforcer, taking on the role with great zeal. As the conflict between the branches heightened in the aftermath of Watergate, gridlock has often been the result, once again damaging the democratic process.

In addition, the presidents that came to power after Watergate have often found themselves boxed in by the scandal's legacy. In fact, Bob Woodward argues that the biggest legacy of Watergate was the independent counsel law that created prosecutors with unlimited time and leeway to dig into allegations against high government officials, particularly presidents. The last decades of the century saw each American president struggling to deal with this ugly legacy of Watergate, from Reagan's Iran-Contra affair and Bush's "passportgate," to the Monica Lewinski scandal in Clinton's administration. As Woodward describes it, Watergate created a "presidency in twilight," making those who took on the job isolated and bitter (1999, 10).

Similarly, Watergate spawned a new relationship between the executive branch of government and the press. Never again was a president to enjoy unquestioned respect and acceptance from the press. Instead, these two important institutions in American government are now and forever locked in a macabre dance; the media works to dig up—or manufacture, if necessary—the latest executive wrongdoing while the politician strives to manipulate the press's unwanted attentions to his or her best advantage. Again, the awful result has been a disgusted and lethargic public, cynical about the role of both institutions in American politics.

Yet some believe that the forced resignation of Richard Nixon confirmed the integrity of the political process. Indeed, all of the major branches of government played a key role in his removal from office. As Arthur Neal wrote in 1998, "There were men of integrity who chose to resign rather than carry out Nixon's orders, which were improperly given. Even the Nixon supporters within his own party came to feel betrayed and decided that nothing short of

Nixon's resignation was acceptable. The abuse of power became an insult to the men and women of integrity who had devoted their lives to public service" (1998, 174). Thus it could be argued that the primary legacy of Watergate was the confirmation of the importance of constitutional authority. The American system is one of governing by laws rather than by the whims and actions of individual men and women. Nixon's resignation confirmed that under a constitutional government, even the most powerful man in American politics can be forcefully removed from office.

Unfortunately for the nation, that does not seem to be the lesson and the legacy of Watergate that most Americans remember.

Limitations, Social Changes, and the Legacy of Nostalgia

As we know from the discussions in chapters 5 and 6, the seventies were a decade of social earthquakes. By the early 1970s, for example, sexual mores had been transformed: abortion became legal; homosexuals came out of the closet and marched in the streets; unwed girls and women began to keep their babies; and unwed middle-class couples openly moved in together. During these same years, there were equally dramatic departures in family life: skyrocketing divorce rates, a surge of women into the workplace, and rising rates of single motherhood. Women had gained the freedom both to have children and to pursue careers, but society and its institutions had not adapted to a world where women were in the workplace to stay. Meanwhile, says Arlene Skolnick (1991), men had felt the ground shift under their own definitions of male roles as women challenged traditional notions of gender. Quite simply, the solid American family of Mom, Dad, and kids was seemingly no more, and those most committed to the traditional order watched as their deeply held values and assumptions were swept away.

By the end of the 1970s, the decade of revolt and liberation had spawned an inevitable backlash, and public discourse about social mores and, in particular, about the family came to be dominated by nostalgia and laments about narcissism and moral decay. As Arlene Skolnick describes it, after social upheaval, Watergate, Vietnam, energy crises, inflation, and economic stagnation, nostalgia settled "like a haze on American political and cultural life" (1991, 9). A profound sense of cultural despair set in as the country's economic and foreign problems worsened. Notions about the decline of the American family became entangled with notions about the decline of the

American character, which in turn became entangled with notions of the decline of the economy and of the American empire. Underneath it all was a profound collective yearning for enduring emotional bonds and a fear that the social fabric had become dangerously frayed.

Instead of looking forward to a new and exciting future, Americans hungered for the stability, order, and tradition of a lost golden age. According to Arleme Skolnick, the election of 1980 marked a turning of the cultural as well as the political tides: a "new politics of old values" swept Ronald Reagan into the presidency. The "liberated" America of the 1970s had become a land of sexual fear, television evangelists, and antidrug and antipornography crusades. Thus the legacy of the social earthquake was the backlash and the coming to power of a conservative president who promised to restore all that had been lost since "the proud decades": American might abroad and the traditional family at home (1991,4–5). While Americans daydreamed about Norman Rockwell families, the conditions facing their own families worsened. In sum, the 1970s ushered in a period of critical change in American life, redefining cultural assumptions and transforming the terms of political debate.

Limits, Losses, Betrayals—and a Legacy of Hope?

As *Time* magazine noted in the summer of 1979: "Nobody is apt to look back on the seventies as the good old days" (1979, 24). This statement conveys a sense of the widespread pessimism about the state of American affairs that marked public discourse at the end of the seventies. Many of the events that occurred during the seventies were national traumas for the American people, creating natural responses of fear and a sense of vulnerability. The central hopes and aspirations of personal lives were temporarily put on hold during these difficult times and were instead replaced by the darkest of anxieties, according to Arthur Neal. Those anxieties were heightened by a perception of the future as cramped, as limited.

In fact, the seventies seemed particularly bleak because in many ways they were. Peter Clecack described it thus in his 1983 book about the decades of the sixties and the seventies:

Americans were chastened by a steady accumulation of unpleasant social facts, from the costly military defeat in Southeast Asia and the subsequent erosion of United States global power and prestige to energy shortages and impending scarcities of other renewable resources. The mounting list of major and minor social problems seemed endless. Old problems persisted, and new ones took shape: apocalypse, the nuclear arms buildup suggested, had been wrenched from divine control and made possible by human arrangement. Selfishness, narcissism, and incivility appeared to be on the rise. Respect for authority and participation in public spheres appeared to be in decline. (36–37)

By the end of the decade, Christopher Lasch's *The Culture of Narcissism* was laying out the malaise that seemingly plagued America: "Hardly more than a quarter-century after Henry Luce proclaimed 'the American century,' American confidence has fallen to a low ebb. Those who recently dreamed of world power now despair of governing the city of New York. Defeat in Vietnam, economic stagnation, and the impending exhaustion of natural resources have produced a mood of pessimism in higher circles, which spreads through the rest of society as people lose faith in their leaders" (xiii).

The seventies were about limits, losses, and betrayals. Watergate was perhaps the greatest betrayal of the 1970s, but there were plenty of others. From the revelations of the Pentagon Papers to the secret bombing of Cambodia; from My Lai to Watergate; from Ford's pardon to Three Mile Island; and from the tragedy at Jonestown to the tragedy at Kent State—all of these events made Americans feel great loss. All of these events helped Americans to feel as though their world was coming to an end, to feel an impending sense of doom. Polls in the late seventies found uneasiness, pessimism, and apprehension among Americans. Disillusion and cynicism, helplessness and apprehension were the words that Americans used to describe the national impact of the decade. As one New York sales clerk summarized it, "Things seem to be out of our control" (Sheils et al. 1979, 157).

However, the betrayals and the losses of the seventies must be juxtaposed with the moments of healing that came during the decade. And there was healing, with Gerald Ford's wholesome presence in the White House, with a new and strong movement to protect the environment, with the first successful test flight of America's space shuttle, and with the celebrations of the nation's Bicentennial. The slow transition from American hegemony to a more plural world was not, in itself, a defeat for America, for this was exactly what American policy in some ways aimed at, says David Calleo. Instead, the real test of victory or defeat lay in the ability of Americans to accept the new world order, to accept their limitations.

Seemingly, the experiences of the seventies showed that the people of the United States had great trouble fitting within the mutual constraints of an integrated world system, of accepting its diminishing relative economic, political, and military superiority. But at the end of the decade, Americans were again striking a note of hope. As they looked toward the eighties, Americans told reporters for *Newsweek,* for example, that they were scared but optimistic. They continued to demonstrate that good old American faith that problems can be solved, that most people want to do the right thing, and that, somehow, the country would come through.

Did the nation rise to the challenge? Only the stories of the last two decades of the century can tell us the answer.

Sources and Selected Readings

Index

Sources and Selected Readings

Abrahamsen, David. 1978. *Nixon versus Nixon: An Emotional Tragedy.* New York: New American Library.

Anderson, Jack, and James Boyd. 1983. *Fiasco.* New York: Times Books.

Arieff, Irwin. 1980. "Carter and Congress: Strangers to the End." *Congressional Quarterly Almanac,* 96th Congress, 2d session, 3–5.

Art, Robert. 1973. "Bureaucratic Politics and American Foreign Policy: A Critique." *Policy Sciences* 4:482–83.

Barnet, Richard. 1980. *The Lean Years: Politics in the Age of Scarcity.* New York: Simon and Schuster.

Barnett, Doak. 1971. *A New U.S. Policy toward China.* Washington, D.C.: Brookings Institution.

Broder, David. 1980. "Is It a New Era?" *Washington Post,* Nov. 19, sec. 1a.

Brown, Seyom. 1979. *The Crisis of Power: An Interpretation of United States Foreign Policy during the Kissinger Years.* New York: Columbia Univ. Press.

Calleo, David. 1982. *The Imperious Economy.* Cambridge: Harvard Univ. Press.

Carney, Francis, and H. Frank Way Jr., eds. 1971. *Politics 1972.* Belmont, Calif.: Wadsworth Publishing Company.

Carter, Jimmy. 1982. *Keeping Faith: Memoirs of a President.* New York: Bantam.

Clecack, Peter. 1983. *America's Quest for the Ideal Self: Dissent and Fulfillment in the 60s and 70s.* New York: Oxford Univ. Press.

Congressional Quarterly Almanac. 1973. "Major Congressional Action: Foreign Policy." 93d Congress, 1st Session. Vol. 29:792.

Congressional Quarterly Almanac. 1973. "Leadership, Vetoes, Membership Changes, Rules Action." 93d Congress, 1st Session. Vol. 29:27–62.

Congressional Quarterly Almanac. 1977. "Major Congressional Action: Economic Policy." 95th Congress, 1st Session. Vol. 33:95–96.

Drew, Elizabeth. 1981. *Portrait of an Election.* New York: Simon and Schuster.

Eastland, Terry. 1996. *Ending Affirmative Action: The Case for Colorblind Justice*. New York: Basic Books, Harper Collins Publishers.

Ebinger, Charles, Wayne Berman, Richard Kessler, and Eugenie Maechling. 1982. *The Critical Link: Energy and National Security in the 1980s*. Cambridge, Mass.: Ballinger Publishing Company.

Evans, Rowland, Jr., and Robert D. Novak. 1971. *Nixon in the White House: The Frustration of Power*. New York: Random House.

Findling, John, and Frank Thackeray, eds. 1996. *Events That Changed America in the Twentieth Century*. Westport, Conn.: Greenwood Press.

Firestone, Bernard, and Alexej Ugrinsky, eds. 1993. *Gerald R. Ford and the Politics of Post-Watergate America*. Vol. 1. Westport, Conn.: Greenwood Press.

Ford, Gerald. 1979. *A Time to Heal: The Autobiography of Gerald R. Ford*. New York: Harper and Row.

Gaddis, John Lewis. 1983. "The Rise, Fall, and Future of Détente." *Foreign Affairs* 16 (winter): 35–73.

Genovese, Michael. 1990. *The Nixon Presidency: Power and Politics in Turbulent Times*. New York: Greenwood Press.

Greene, John Robert. 1992. *The Limits of Power: The Nixon and Ford Administrations*. Bloomington, Ind.: Indiana Univ. Press.

———. 1995. *The Presidency of Gerald R. Ford*. Lawrence, Kans.: Univ. Press of Kansas.

Haas, Garland. 1992. *Jimmy Carter and the Politics of Frustration*. Jefferson, N.C.: McFarland and Company.

Hargreaves, Robert. 1973. *Superpower: A Portrait of America in the 1970's*. New York: St. Martin's Press.

Hargrove, Erwin. 1974. *The Power of the Modern Presidency*. New York: Knopf.

———. 1988a. *Jimmy Carter as President*. Baton Rouge: Louisiana State Univ. Press.

———. 1988b. "The Politics of Public Goods." In *Leadership in the Modern Presidency*, edited by Fred Greenstein, 228–59. Cambridge: Harvard Univ. Press.

Hersh, Seymour. 1981. "1971 Tape Links Nixon to Plan to Use Thugs." *New York Times*, Sept. 24, sec. 1.

Hoff, Joan. 1994. *Nixon Reconsidered*. New York: Basic Books.

Hoff-Wilson, Joan. 1988. "The Corporate Presidency." In *Leadership in the Modern Presidency*, edited by Fred Greenstein, 164–98. Cambridge: Harvard Univ. Press.

Hyland, William. 1987. *Mortal Rivals: Superpower Relations from Nixon to Reagan*. New York: Random House.

Johnson, Richard. 1974. *Managing the White House: An Intimate Study of the Presidency*. New York: Harper and Row.

Jones, Charles. 1988. *The Trusteeship Presidency*. Baton Rouge: Louisiana State Univ. Press.

Jordan, Hamilton. 1982. *Crisis: The Last Years of the Carter Presidency*. New York: Putnam.

Kaufman, Burton. 1993. *The Presidency of James Earl Carter, Jr.* Lawrence, Kans.: Univ. Press of Kansas.

Kissinger, Henry. 1987. "Special Introduction to *A Time to Heal*." In *A Time to Heal*, by Gerald R. Ford, 2. Norwalk, Conn.: Easton Press.

Lasch, Christopher. 1978. *The Culture of Narcissism: American Life in and Age of Diminishing Expectations*. New York: Warner Books.

Lenczowski, George. 1990. *American Presidents and the Middle East*. Durham, N.C.: Duke Univ. Press.

Leonard, Thomas, Cynthia Crippen, and Marc Aronson. 1988. *Day by Day: The Seventies*. New York: Facts on File Publications.

Marty, Myron. 1997. *Daily Life in the United States, 1960–1990: Decades of Discord*. Westport, Conn.: Greenwood Press.

Mathews, Tom. 1980. "A Foreign Policy in Disarray." *Newsweek*, May 12, 42–53.

Morris, Roger. 1977. *Uncertain Greatness: Henry Kissinger and American Foreign Policy*. New York: Harper and Row.

Neal, Arthur. 1998. *National Trauma and Collective Memory*. Armonk, N.Y.: M. E. Sharpe.

Nelson, Keith. 1995. *The Making of Détente: Soviet-American Relations in the Shadow of Vietnam*. Baltimore: Johns Hopkins Univ. Press.

Nessen, Ron. 1978. *It Sure Looks Different from the Inside*. Chicago: Playboy Press.

Nixon, Richard. 1970. "US Foreign Policy for the 1970's: A New Strategy for Peace." In *The Department of State Bulletin*, vol. 62.

———. 1978. *RN: The Memoirs of Richard Nixon*. New York: Simon and Schuster.

O'Connor, Karen. 1996. *No Neutral Ground? Abortion Politics in an Age of Absolutes*. Boulder, Colo.: Westview Press.

Patterson, James. 1996. *Grand Expectations*. New York: Oxford Univ. Press.

Pfluger, Friedbert. 1989. "Human Rights Unbounded: Carter's Human Rights Policy Reassessed." *Presidential Studies Quarterly* 99 (fall): 705–16.

Porter, Roger. 1988a. "Ford's Presidency: Brief but Well Run." *New York Times*, May 15, sec. 1.

———. 1988b. "A Healing Presidency." In *Leadership in the Modern Presidency*, edited by Fred Greenstein, 199–227. Cambridge: Harvard Univ. Press.

Reeves, Richard. 1975. *A Ford, Not a Lincoln*. New York: Harcourt Brace Jovanovich.

Rosati, Jerel. 1993. "Jimmy Carter, a Man before His Time? The Emergence and Collapse of the First Post-Cold War Presidency." *Presidential Studies Quarterly* 23 (summer): 459–76.

Schell, Johnathan. 1976. *The Time of Illusion*. New York: Knopf.

Sheils, Merrill, Lea Donosky, Pamela Abramson, and Henry Hubbard. 1979. "I'm Scared, but I'm Optimistic." *Newsweek*, November 19, 157–75.

Siegel, Frederick. 1984. *Troubled Journey: From Pearl Harbor to Ronald Reagan*. New York: Hill and Wang.

Simon, Rita, and Gloria Danziger. 1991. *Women's Movements in America*. New York: Praeger Publishers.

Skolnick, Arlene. 1991. *Embattled Paradise: The American Family in an Age of Uncertainty*. New York: Harper Collins.

Sloan, John. 1993. "Groping toward a Macrotheme: Economic Policymaking in the Ford Presidency." In *Gerald R. Ford and the Politics of Post-Watergate America*, vol. 1, edited by Bernard Firestone and Alexej Ugrinsky, 277–91. Westport, Conn.: Greenwood Press.

Smith, Gaddis. 1986. *Morality, Reason, and Power*. New York: Hill and Wang.

St. Clair, James. 1996. "Interpretive Essay on Television." In *Events That Changed America in the Twentieth Century*, edited by John Findling and Frank Thackeray, 131–45. Westport, Conn.: Greenwood Press.

Strong, Robert. 1991. "Jimmy Carter and the Panama Canal Treaties." *Presidential Studies Quarterly* 21 (spring): 269–86.

Switzer, Jaqueline, and Gary Bryner. 1998. *Environmental Politics*. New York: St. Martin's Press.

Szulc, Tad. 1978. *The Illusion of Peace*. New York: Viking.

Thompson, Kenneth W. 1988. *The Ford Presidency*. Lanham, Md.: Univ. Press of America.

Time. 1974. "The Pardon That Brought No Peace." Sept. 16, 10–23.

Time. 1976. "The Big 200th Bash. July 5, 8–34.

Time. 1977. "Carter Spins the World." Aug. 8, 8–23.

Trager, James. 1992. *The People's Chronology*. New York: Henry Holt and Company.

Vance, Cyrus. 1990. "Carter's Foreign Policy: The Source of the Problem." In *The Carter Presidency*, edited by Kenneth Thompson, 135–44. New York: Univ. Press of America.

Vig, Norman, and Michael Kraft. 1990. *Environmental Policy in the 1990s: Toward a New Agenda*. Washington, D.C.: CQ Press.

Wandersee, Winifred. 1988. *On the Move: American Women in the 1970s*. Boston: Twayne Publishers.

Watt, Kenneth. 1974. *The Titanic Effect: Planning for the Unthinkable*.New York: E. P. Dutton and Company.

White, Theodore. 1969. *The Making of the President—1968*. New York: Antheneum Publishers.

———. 1973. *The Making of the President—1972*. New York: Atheneum Publishers.

Whitney, Simon. 1982. *Inflation since 1945: Facts and Theories.* New York: Praeger Publishers.

Woodward, Bob. 1999. "Hammered." *Washington Post Magazine,* June 20, 9–23.

Zimmerman, Warren. 1986. "Making Moscow Pay the Price for Rights Abuses." *New York Times,* Aug. 1, sec. 1.

Index